AF600615

THINKING RADICAL DEMOCRACY

The Return to Politics in Post-war France

Thinking Radical Democracy

The Return to Politics in Post-war France

EDITED BY MARTIN BREAUGH,
CHRISTOPHER HOLMAN,
RACHEL MAGNUSSON, PAUL MAZZOCCHI,
AND DEVIN PENNER

UNIVERSITY OF TORONTO PRESS
Toronto Buffalo London

Toronto Buffalo London
www.utppublishing.com

ISBN 978-1-4426-5004-6

Library and Archives Canada Cataloguing in Publication

Thinking radical democracy : the return to politics in post-war France / edited by Martin Breaugh, Christopher Holman, Rachel Magnusson, Paul Mazzocchi, and Devin Penner.

Includes bibliographical references.
ISBN 978-1-4426-5004-6 (bound)

1. Political science – France – Philosophy – History – 20th century. 2. Democracy – France – Philosophy – History – 20th century. 3. France – Politics and government – Philosophy – History – 20th century. I. Breaugh, Martin, 1973–, author, editor II. Holman, Christopher, 1979–, author, editor III. Magnusson, Rachel, 1980–, author, editor IV. Mazzocchi, Paul, 1979–, author, editor V. Penner, Devin, 1980–, author, editor

JA84.F8T45 2015 320.0944'09045 C2014-907821-8

University of Toronto Press acknowledges the financial assistance to its publishing program of the Canada Council for the Arts and the Ontario Arts Council, an agency of the Government of Ontario.

University of Toronto Press acknowledges the financial support of the Government of Canada through the Canada Book Fund for its publishing activities.

This book has been published with the help of a grant from the Federation for the Humanities and Social Sciences, through the Awards to Scholarly Publications Program, using funds provided by the Social Sciences and Humanities Research Council of Canada.

Contents

Acknowledgments

The idea for this book first began percolating in spring 2009, during a York University graduate seminar entitled "The Return of Political Philosophy in Contemporary French Thought," taught by Martin Breaugh. Since then a number of people have helped in transforming the project from an idea to its published form. Asher Horowitz and Steve Newman offered kind support and sage advice during the formative stages of the project. Daniel Quinlan was instrumental in guiding us through the publication process, and Wayne Herrington coordinated the production of the book. We benefited from the behind-the-scenes work of many other staff at the University of Toronto Press, and also from the meticulous copy-editing of Barry Norris. The reviewers assigned by the University of Toronto Press offered critical insights that helped to improve individual chapters, as well as the overall vision for the book. Many of the ideas for the book, and for individual chapters, were presented during the monthly "Workshop in Political Theory" held in York University's Political Science Department – thanks to the many people who attended these gatherings and engaged in spirited discussions and debates about all things "political theory." This book has been published with the help of a grant from the Federation for the Humanities and Social Sciences, through the Awards to Scholarly Publications Program, using funds provided by the Social Sciences and Humanities Research Council of Canada.

THINKING RADICAL DEMOCRACY

The Return to Politics in Post-war France

Introduction: Radical Democracy and Twentieth-Century French Thought

CHRISTOPHER HOLMAN, MARTIN BREAUGH, RACHEL MAGNUSSON, PAUL MAZZOCCHI, AND DEVIN PENNER

Many of the most interesting political situations of our time do not fit the mould of our most common political categories. Consider a few of the political situations that have shaped our present here in North America. There are, first of all, a number of situations that have been officially coined as "movements" – the Occupy movement, the Maple Spring in Quebec, Idle No More, and so on. But there are also any number of widespread and varied organized resistances to, say, the construction of oil and gas pipelines, particularly Keystone XL and Enbridge; the exploitation and injustices faced by refugees, migrant labourers, and immigrants; the problem of food insecurity, particularly through the slow food and local food initiatives; our "outdated" education system, through efforts as diverse as charter schools, forest schools, free schools, and African-centred schools; and thousands of more localized disputes over resource development, land-use planning, access to child care, colonialism, waste disposal, industrial relations, obesity, cancer, racism, and so on. Although many of these situations seem obviously political in one way or another, especially taken together, it is not at all evident how so. Moreover, even less clear is how these political situations relate to democracy: are these movements, initiatives, and disputes simply examples of "debates" within a democratic system? Are some of them challenges to a democratic system? Or are some instances of democracy itself?

On the one hand, this failure of political situations to line up with our political categories might speak to the need to rethink our political and democratic theories. On the other hand, it also might suggest that political situations inevitably defy neat categorization. The inspiration for this volume stems from this second possibility: what if this defiance of categorization – and the indeterminacy, difference, or division it entails

– is part of what characterizes the political, and maybe even democracy itself? And if it does, how should we make sense of this? How must we rethink politics and democracy? To explore these questions, this volume turns to a collection of political thinkers who, we argue, are a part of a radical democratic tradition of political theory that emerged in France in the latter part of the twentieth century. Indeed, we argue that what distinguishes this tradition is a particular preoccupation with indeterminacy, difference, or division.

The Deliberative versus Agonistic Debate in Contemporary Democratic Theory

A key debate in contemporary democratic theory is that between the advocates of, respectively, deliberative and agonistic models of democracy. The initial motivation for the rise of theories of deliberative democracy was recognition of the need to transcend mere voluntarism in the political sphere. Voluntaristic models of democracy are characterized above all by the desire to give immediate expression to the will of the people. The problem, however, is that this expression does not take account of the quality of thought entering into the people's will – for instance, the citizenry's level of political education. According to the voluntaristic model, whatever the collected citizenry desires – no matter what that desire is or how it came to be – is a legitimate policy objective that political action should aim to achieve. Against this simple voluntarism, deliberative democrats argue that democratic decisions are legitimate only to the extent that they have been formed under circumstances that allow for the adequate education of each participant and the exchange of knowledge among participants.[1] The central concern for deliberative democracy thus becomes outlining or defining those institutional forms that are capable of functioning as spaces for the type of conversational interaction that allows for the rational and reflective articulation of informed policy positions.

Although most agonistic democrats agree with the deliberative assumption that political decisions must be grounded in self-conscious and reflective judgment, they criticize deliberative democrats along several lines. Most importantly, they reject deliberative democracy's seeming reduction of democratic practice to a formal organization of merely technical exercises. Democracy cannot be reduced to a procedure, for example, as it is not possible to introduce democracy into a society simply by inserting a deliberative technique grounded in principles of rational discussion and comprehension. Such a reliance on procedures and rationality covers up a fundamental value of the democratic imaginary: the freedom of people to choose for themselves the direction of their activity without regard to any external principle that would structure their behaviour in advance. From the standpoint of democracy, there are, for instance, no transcendental or metaphysical ideals capable of orienting and directing the human community. This is the problem that deliberative democrats seem to obscure through their emphasis on political techniques designed to achieve "correct" or "proper" judgments. In a sense, the specific form of the deliberative method is conceived as a foundational guarantee of rational decision-making. This can be seen in, for example, the work of the most eminent of deliberative democratic thinkers, Jürgen Habermas.

Habermas is explicitly concerned with justifying the democratic project against philosophical relativism, but without falling back on an original or first philosophy. Ultimately, however, Habermas adopts just such a foundational ground. The foundational moment in his thought lies in his elevation of the ideals of communicative rationality, which are oriented towards mutual understanding and grounded in concrete procedural mechanisms, to a universal fact that organizes democratic practice. To support this position, Habermas is forced to appeal to an admittedly quasi-transcendental structure of language. As he writes, for example, "[t]he utopian perspective of reconciliation and freedom is ingrained in the conditions for the communicative sociation of individuals; it is built into the linguistic mechanism of the reproduction of the species."[2]

In short, the defence of Habermas's theory of communicative action depends upon the potential for constructing a public sphere in which language is homogeneous and universal, in which all are capable of comprehending one another to the extent that all share the same linguistic potential and all participate in identical modes and orders. What is reproduced is the liberal ideal of perfect human rationality; it is thus not surprising that many theorists of deliberative democracy end up advocating fundamentally liberal institutions, including variations of representative democratic practice. If it is assumed that individuals can be reduced to a positive content that can be objectively comprehended and organized – if I am capable of telling you who I am and what I want, and you are capable of understanding this – the ground is cleared for a model of political representation that tries to embody perfectly the will of citizens. Deliberative democracy thus becomes a refined version of representative democracy.[3] The difference is that the representative is no longer responsible for giving a direct, embodied expression to the will of the represented; rather, the representative participates in a deliberative activity that is structured in such a way that one can rationally conclude that a given represented citizen would have come to the same policy conclusion had he or she also participated in the deliberative process.[4] Here, even though citizens do not directly participate, the idea is that there is good reason to believe that any rational citizen would reproduce the decisions of a deliberative assembly so long as the deliberative process was properly organized – that is, so long as the deliberative technique was correct. Representation thus undertakes a deliberative shift: it does not look towards the immediate representation of a popular will, such as in voluntaristic models, but rather to the creation of an informed will through the application of specific deliberative techniques. What is represented is what the people would will *if* they had the opportunity to deliberate meaningfully on political issues themselves.

From a democratic perspective, the problem with such deliberative accounts of decision-making is that they seem to suffer a double lack. First, they lack democratic inclusivity, or concern for the creative participation of citizens in making the political decisions that affect their lives. Second, since such accounts implicitly assume that it is possible to grasp or outline the objective contours of citizens' interests, they ignore the unpredictable and irrational parts of human will. The second problem actually implies the first: it is illegitimate to restrict participation on the grounds of inclusive representation because it is ultimately impossible to thematize human interest, which is always multiple and changing, and consequently eludes systematic capture.

In the end, what deliberative democracy seems to mask in its attempt to homogenize human interest through an objective conception of rationality is what agonistic democrats take to be the ontological condition of human difference. For most deliberative democratic theories, there is at best a minimal recognition of this difference. It is true, for instance, that people are initially taken to have unique interests, values, goals, and so on. Indeed, it is the function of deliberative processes to provide institutional mechanisms that allow for the mutual recognition and exchange of these unique interests, since the human will is open to alteration. If the latter were not the case, voluntaristic modes of democratic practice would be acceptable. However – and even though deliberative democrats reject the idea of a predetermined universal moral will – there is nevertheless assumed to be a potential universal political will insofar as people are seen as capable of moving towards agreement founded on mutual understanding. This means that each person's original uniqueness is gradually stamped out through a fixation on deliberative interactions aiming at universality, which are designed to revise particular opinions by judging the quality of their correspondence to general moral principles. If the people do not immediately think identically, in other words, they might well do so given the proper institutional conditions. Consequently, social division is viewed as a contingent fact to be overcome, and precisely because it can be overcome, there is no need for an expansive and directly democratic practice. Democracy, on the contrary, is achieved when a minimal number of representative citizens are given access to institutions governed by deliberative techniques.

While deliberative democracy sees division and difference as obstacles to be overcome, agonistic democracy, by contrast, asserts that there is no political arrangement capable of eliminating human difference. According to this view, deliberative democrats are correct in theorizing a human will open to discursive practice, to processes of learning and self-alteration. They are incorrect, though, in thinking that such discursive practice should be oriented towards the formulation of ethical principles that can be rationally evaluated according to objective and universal standards of competency or rightness. This is impossible to the extent that human beings can never be rendered identical, both because they are different from one another, perpetually socialized in unique ways, but also because they themselves are contingent beings, perpetually open to time, perpetually changing the nature of themselves through their actions and interactions. The recognition of this fact of human difference leads agonistic democrats to affirm the necessary place of conflict and contestation in political engagement, and the impossibility of reconciling this conflict and contestation in a finally found and eternal political form. But it also means extending democratic space so as to incorporate as many unique wills and interests – as much difference – as possible. The critique of reconciliatory projects thus has been made by a variety of contemporary political theorists, including William Connolly, Bonnie Honig, Chantal Mouffe, Andrew Schaap, James Tully, and others.[5]

The purpose of this book, however, is not to engage with the specific contributions of these authors to the agonistic-deliberative democracy debate, which by this point are well known.[6] Rather, the chapters introduce to readers a political tradition of thought that contributes greatly to this theoretical debate that organizes much contemporary democratic thought. In particular, it introduces readers to a radical democratic tradition of political theory that emerged in France in the latter part of the twentieth century, and that attempted to contribute to the positive theorization of forms of democratic practice that are able simultaneously to affirm principles of freedom and equality and those of social division and difference. The thinkers identified with this tradition are shown to anticipate the contemporary agonistic-deliberative debate through their juxtaposition, in unique and multiple ways, of democracy and division.

The Eclipse of Political Philosophy in Post-war France

The subtitle of this book is "The Return to Politics in Post-war France." A full appreciation of the democratic contributions of the thinkers collected in this volume requires, first of all, an understanding of just how their work constituted a return to the tradition of political thought. In the immediate post-war years, it is possible to speak of an eclipse of political philosophy in France.[7] Specifically, from 1950 onward, a certain type of social scientific research dominated the academic scene in France. Within the field of political science, it is possible to identify three poles that monopolized intellectual production: Marxism, functionalism, and post-structuralism. Each of these poles contributed in its own way to covering up the potential for politics. To be more precise, each at least partially denied the possibility for conscious and reflective civic intervention aiming at the reinstitution of the social sphere; that is to say, each one at least partially denied the capacity for the self-articulation of the political community in time. To get some sense of why this was the case, we should briefly look at each tradition.

In post-war France the potential for the deployment of a critical or heterodox Marxist analysis was largely closed off the by the political and ideological dominance of the Parti communiste français (PCF). Most leftist theory and practice was carried out in an intellectual context dominated by an orthodox Marxist framework that affirmed an objective philosophy of history. History was thought of as a rational totality governed by observable laws or principles that could be organized into a stable system of knowledge if the proper scientific techniques were used. Those capable of applying such techniques were intellectual specialists drawn from the elite of the revolutionary party, and therefore this "scientific" Marxism tended towards a bureaucratic hierarchy between the knowing few and the unknowing many, who needed to be led in the "right" direction. This interpretation of Marxism was nothing particularly new – it went back to the mechanical materialism of the nineteenth century and Engels's dialectics of nature. It was reproduced only in the context of twentieth-century French thought, including in the structuralist analysis of the most important and influential Marxist theorist of this period, Louis Althusser, who is best known for appropriating the concept of "epistemological break" and applying it to the development of Marxist thought.[8] In the words of Cornelius Castoriadis, "[t]he idea of an 'epistemological break,' conceived as the passage from a 'prescientific' philosophical state to an essentially guaranteed and already attained 'scientificness,' is an aberration that dates back to the vulgar materialism of the 19th century (and to Friedrich Engels)."[9] As Castoriadis suggests, this concept implies a movement from the pre-scientific world of ideological thought, unencumbered by the "true" essence of material reality, to a new historical and scientific world of thought capable of mapping the laws and structures of reality with precision. In Marx's case, his early works are said to be pre-scientific, but his later works – those after 1857 – are seen to be permeated fully by his two great scientific innovations: dialectical materialism in the sphere of philosophy, and historical materialism in the sphere of history.[10] For our purposes, we do not need to undertake a detailed elaboration of Althusser's understanding of the scientific content of Marxism, but simply to note the degree to which it participates in a philosophical tradition that closes off the potential for free human creation by subordinating politics to more fundamental structural laws. Even though Althusser speaks of the "relative autonomy" of politics, he ultimately denies such autonomy by suggesting that politics is determined by the economy in the "last instance."[11] It is this problematic conception of politics that led two of Althusser's early collaborators, Étienne Balibar and Jacques Rancière, ultimately to turn away from Marxism in favour of the more open-ended, radically democratic approach that is the subject of this volume.[12]

The denial of politics found in structuralist Marxism's scientific mapping of the human world is repeated in the tradition of functionalism, especially as it is handed down from American sociology in general and the work of Talcott Parsons in particular. The structural brand of functionalism – which notably has indigenous French roots in the thought of such key figures as Auguste Comte and Émile Durkheim – attempted to apply certain biological principles of organization and relation to the study of human societies, presuming human societies could be analysed in organic terms like any other biological entity. The central concern thus became to explain the perceived identity and coherence of society in terms of the complex functional relationships among the various elements of the system, with each element assumed to be looking towards the preservation and stabilization of the whole. The most common criticisms of such models have to do with their inability to theorize social conflict and freedom. Given the functional nature of the elements, how, for example, does one explain the emergence of stratification, division, and discontinuity in society? What, furthermore, is the role of agency if social roles are heavily structured, if not absolutely determined, by the needs and values of the system?

In the French context, functionalism's most outstanding representative, Michel Crozier, attempted to address some of these criticisms. Crozier is best known for his study of bureaucracy, which for him formed part of a more comprehensive functional theory of human organization, itself "the essential element of a sociology of action valid for a global study of society."[13] Crozier, though, claimed to want to develop a functionalist method that did not once and for all hypostatize organizational reality, but that sought to account for systematic change through the investigation of the potential for agency within the organizational structure. Ultimately, however, he concluded that all action and change is highly mediated by the institutional context that structures human norms. Human values are not directly modifiable, but subject to change through the modification of institutions, which then act back upon values.[14] The potential and desirability for subjective change is thus highly limited, a fact that is revealed in Crozier's reaction to the most important political event in France in the 1960s, the May 1968 movement. Although, in the face of the protests, Crozier admitted to the need for adjustment in the political and educational systems, he maintained that this adjustment had to proceed "rationally and meaningfully."[15] What this meant was that the students and workers must not attempt simply to impose their desires, but adapt to the shifting realities of the fundamental structure. They must not attempt to change themselves, but "adjust to change."[16] Indeed, in Crozier's estimation the gravest threat was "the obsessive regression of most forces of renewal among the young, and especially in the intellectual world, toward the impossible dream of total change."[17] In the final instance, then, this episode would seem to have revealed starkly the incapacity of Crozier's structural functionalism to theorize a rational form of political intervention capable of critically interrogating the fundamental structure of institutional reality.

The apolitical tendencies of so-called post-structuralism are of a different quality than those of structuralist Marxism and functionalism. They can be gleaned by looking briefly at the thought of its best-known representative, Michel Foucault, whose work represents a highly original contribution to the understanding of knowledge, power, and subjectivity. Foucault rejects all forms of essentialist thinking, maintaining that there exists no primary human content that one can isolate as existing before the exercise of power upon it. Power is theorized as positive, as that which constructs the self by immersing it in a series of discourses. Such discursive construction is exclusive – that is, it excludes all content that is considered external to self-identity: it simultaneously posits both oneness and otherness, both self and "not-self," or "other-to-self." Hence, there is no so-called normal self without psychosis, perversion, abnormality, criminality, and so on. Because defining "normality" requires defining "abnormality," discursive construction necessitates marginalization. As Foucault's critics ask, though, how is political resistance to the exclusionary construction of selves possible when no fundamentally emancipatory content exists that grounds expelled identities? In Gad Horowitz's words, "[i]f power and resistance are always everywhere, how could we realistically hope for any change *more* radical than the alteration of the balance between them?"[18] It seems as though a critical Foucaultian practice cannot aim at a radical political transformation, but just a more inclusive set of socially legitimate forms of being. In place of politics, we thus get a form of the cultivation of the self – transgressive action looking perpetually to reinvent and reorient "normal" modes of being.

Indeed, in a revealing interview, Foucault himself was posed this problem. He was asked: "Does a mode of thought which introduces discontinuity and the constraints of system into the history of the mind not remove all basis for a progressive political intervention? Does it not lead to the following dilemma: either the acceptance of the system or the appeal to an unconditioned event, to an irruption of exterior violence which alone is capable of upsetting the system?"[19] In the face of this question, Foucault in fact conceded that he believed that a progressive politics was incapable of transcending the specific rules governing a discursive practice. In other words, politics is always severely bounded, with political potential demarcated in some meaningful sense by the historical laws operating in any particular sphere. Speaking of individual people, he writes:

> They have doubtless had difficulty enough in recognizing that their history, their economy, their social practices, the language they speak, their ancestral mythology, even the fables told them in childhood, obey rules which are not given to their consciousness; they hardly wish to be dispossessed, in

> addition, of this discourse in which they wish to be able to say immediately, directly, what they think, believe or imagine; they prefer to deny that discourse is a complex and differentiated practice subject to analyzable rules and transformations, rather than be deprived of this tender, consoling certainty, of being able to change, if not the world, if not life, at least their "meaning," by the sole freshness of a word which comes only from them, and remains forever close to its source.[20]

In short, despite working from greatly different assumptions regarding the nature of human reality and being, Foucault and Crozier inhabit the same position with respect to politics, affirming that individuals must not fall into the trap of presuming that they are capable of acting too freely.

Sources of Return

It is within the context of the theoretical domination of these three intellectual currents that we must appreciate the significance of the return to the tradition of political philosophy in France in the latter third of the twentieth century. Although it is impossible to identify definitively the factors that caused a renewed appreciation of political things – that is, a renewed appreciation of citizens' capacity to assert creatively their autonomy and agency in the political realm – we can nevertheless identify a few trends that contributed to breaking the apolitical hegemony of structural Marxism, functionalism, and post-structuralism. First, there is the "new political anthropology" of Pierre Clastres, a theorist best known for his 1974 volume, *Society Against the State*.[21] Through his ethnographical studies, Clastres attempts to reveal the unique political philosophy of certain so-called primitive societies of the Amazon basin. Against traditional Eurocentric anthropology, which suggests that non-state societies are non-political societies and should be defined according to this negative characteristic, Clastres demonstrates the highly sophisticated political modalities and relations that can be found in such communities. Specifically, he shows that these societies are explicitly political because they aim to integrate all individual members into an autonomous social totality that self-articulates its own specificity. He furthermore shows how this self-articulation is oriented towards the prevention of the emergence of a division in society between rulers and ruled. Power here is not a command-obedience relation, but rather the active attempt to repel the institution of the state form: "The example of primitive societies teaches us that division is not inherent in the social being, that in other words, the State is not eternal, that it has, here and there, a date of birth."[22] What Clastres and the indigenous people of South America are able to show us, then, is that politics cannot be reduced to a specific form of institutional practice, but has to do with the larger issue of a society's or social group's inscription of its unique sense of being into space and time.

In addition to the work of Clastres, another trend contributing to the break with apolitical thought is the critical reappraisal of the totalitarian experience, especially as manifested in the Soviet Union. Particularly relevant here is the pioneering early work undertaken by Claude Lefort, a student of Maurice Merleau-Ponty, and Cornelius Castoriadis in the journal *Socialisme ou Barbarie*. In the pages of this journal, Lefort and Castoriadis undertake a radical critique of Soviet bureaucracy as a new form of domination, obscured furthermore by the apologetics of the PCF and various Marxist academics. Their analyses demonstrate that the type of domination that existed in the Soviet Union was not so much economic as it was specifically political, and therefore suggested that the Soviet Union represented a new type of social formation that did not obey the economic laws of traditional Marxist theory. Like the case of primitive "societies against the State," the implication is once again that a specifically political intervention is capable of producing unique social relations that, in this instance, reflected the generation of a new bureaucratic form of society. Although such critiques of bureaucratic domination became more common through the 1960s – also apparent, for instance, in the unconventional Marxism of Guy Debord and the Situationist International – they were further strengthened following the 1973 publication of Alexandr Solzhenitsyn's *Gulag Archipelago*, as well as Lefort's seminal book on Solzhenitsyn, *Un homme en trop*.[23] In the wake of such works, it was difficult to ignore the political form of totalitarian domination in the Soviet Union.

What the insights of Clastres, Lefort, and Castoriadis all point towards is recognition of the need to consider politics as an autonomous realm of human existence that cannot be reduced to other spheres of being and doing, such as the religious or the economic. Politics, on the contrary, must be considered as a central and independent human realm. A final trend in the break with apolitical thought, then, was a renewed interest in those figures in the history of political thought who were seen as confirming investigations into primitive and totalitarian societies insofar as they had also theorized the singularity of the political. In particular we see a return to the ideas of two early modern thinkers, Niccolò Machiavelli and Étienne de La Boétie. With Machiavelli, for example, we see an appreciation of the specificity of a political form of virtuous practice that cannot be assimilated to fixed and universal moral laws. Rejecting ethical rules that would restrict and determine in advance the potential range of political action, Machiavelli commanded that politics be an activity that is always concretely situated in the realities of the here and now. Similarly, La Boétie created a concept of "voluntary servitude" that is also put to the test of political history and the politics of his time. He did not theorize rulership and subjugation in terms of any sort of natural pathos of distance, but rather as purely customary relations, with domination eventually a result of habituation to contingent and artificial hierarchies. In short, like Machiavelli and La Boétie, the thinkers of the return to political philosophy in France recognized the need for an engagement in a constant back and forth between ideas and history, undertaken to put theoretical concepts to the test of empirical reality.

Further intellectual support for the idea of the autonomy of the political came from more contemporary thinkers. As we have seen, though, for various reasons these thinkers had to come from outside France. Although there was some original political philosophy in post-war France produced by figures such as Julien Freund and Raymond Aron, it was largely marginalized within the academy. As Mark Lilla points out, for example, "Aron was almost entirely without influence among his fellow individuals in the post-war decades."[24] A couple of extremely important theoretical supports were found, however, in the work of two German émigrés living in the United States: Hannah Arendt and Leo Strauss. Although both would make significant contributions to the theorization of the autonomy of the political, there nevertheless would be enormous differences between the two – most importantly for our purposes, with respect to the question of democracy. These differences are in some sense reflected in what could be described as the double form of the return of the political in France: on the one hand, we can identify an historical liberal return;[25] on the other, we can identify a radical democratic return. It is the latter, of course, that is the subject of this book.

The Historical Liberal Tradition

The return of the study of political things in France required, first of all, a new engagement with the tradition of liberal thought, particularly as expressed in the work of the great French liberals of the nineteenth century, including Alexis de Tocqueville, Benjamin Constant, and François Guizot. This return to liberalism, though, was historical in orientation, which is to say that it distinguished itself from two major trends in contemporary liberal thought: analytical liberalism and neoliberalism. Represented in this case by figures such as Pierre Manent and Marcel Gauchet, historical liberalism comprehends that forms of thought are perpetually evolving, forever intertwined with their historical contexts of emergence. There cannot be a return, in other words, to an ideologically pure theory grounded in absolutely valid or axiomatic truths of human behaviour and organization, such as are assumed by various representatives of the liberal tradition from John Locke to John Rawls. Indeed, with respect to Rawls and analytic political philosophy – although it might just as well apply to the deliberative democratic tradition – Manent writes: "What goes by the name of political philosophy or theory today is rather angelology. In an otherworldly space – perhaps separated from this earth by a 'veil of ignorance' – beings who are no longer, or not yet, truly human deliberate over the conditions under which they would consent to land on our lowly planet and don our 'too solid flesh.' They hesitate a lot, as well they might, and their abstract reasonings are complex and multifarious, if so hypothetical that they carry little weight."[26]

The neoliberal tradition similarly lacks a historical sensibility. This can be seen especially when it is contrasted with nineteenth-century French liberalism, which explicitly emphasized the role and importance of the political, and consequently rejected the idea that politics should disappear in order to give way to the regulative power of market forces. In this regard Manent is extremely critical of the specific form of European development, which he sees as being structured to replace the authority of the nation-state with a form of bureaucratic governance oriented towards ensuring the autonomy of market forces.[27] What Manent and the political/historical liberals affirm instead is the nation-state's essential role in wealth redistribution, as well as the possibility of democratically deciding the means and ends of a political community.

In the end, however, the identification of democracy with the formal structure of the political nation-state places severe limits on the democratic potential of this tradition. On this point the attempt of historical liberals such as Manent to reduce democracy to a minimal institutional expression makes their view perfectly consistent with liberalism more generally. James Ingram aptly makes this point in an article that traces the distinctions to be made between the traditions of twentieth-century

French liberal and radical democratic thought by comparing the diverging trajectories of two theorists heavily influenced by Lefort: Marcel Gauchet and Miguel Abensour. Ingram reminds us of the need to remember the historical non-correspondence between the concepts of liberalism and democracy, the former referring to a mode of limiting rule for the sake of the preservation of abstract right, the latter to an active form of rule: "On one side, (left) liberals emphasize principles, laws and institutions that would produce just outcomes, understood in terms of rights and entitlements. On the other, radical democrats emphasize the politics that would lead to a more just society, understood in terms of power and participation."[28] Indeed, several contemporary democratic theorists, such as Sheldon Wolin and Chantal Mouffe, have attempted to call attention to the differing theoretical and practical concerns of liberalism and democracy. In Mouffe's words, "[o]n one side we have the liberal tradition constituted by the rule of law, the defence of human rights and the respect of individual liberty; on the other the democratic tradition whose main ideas are those of equality, identity between governing and governed and popular sovereignty."[29] The liberal tradition attempts to place limits on the expression of social conflict for the sake of the general stability of the social unit. Even with the historical liberals, a particular mode of institutionalization is used to close the space for political expression, replacing it with the affirmation of a comprehensive system of negative rights and liberties. Just as in the case of deliberative democracy, the unwillingness to fully affirm social division necessitates the limitation of democratic potential.

This movement can be seen, for example, by briefly looking at the case of Gauchet, one of the most accomplished of the French historical liberals. Early in his career Gauchet became heavily influenced by Clastres and Lefort, notably adopting Lefort's understanding of the political as the mode by which society attempts to self-articulate the specificity of its being. In a democratic society, though, the place of the political cannot be occupied by anyone or anything if the divisions within the social body are to be given expression. Gauchet attempts to give a refined account of this idea in his best-known text, *The Disenchantment of the World*. Here he defines a democratic regime as one that is perpetually open to interrogation and that refuses the possibility of a communal self-identity that would homogenize the social field and move beyond political contestation among groups. Rather, there is a perpetual competition among social groups that recognize they are incapable of eliminating one another and imposing their own social ideals on the society. Conflict grounded in social difference becomes institutionalized: "Anything in the collective arena can become the object of regulated conflict."[30]

We soon learn, however, that the extent of this conflict is highly circumscribed, as Gauchet goes on to claim that this conflict will allow only for "disagreement on everything other than the principles of confrontation."[31] And what exactly are these principles of confrontation? In the final instance, they seem to imply a typically liberal mode of institutionalization whose parameters have long since been set, the basic structural rules of organization necessary to uphold democratic openness having been known for many years: "Two centuries of historical change have not added a single basic principle, a single fundamental rule, to those we have known since the 18th century. The most contemporary political projects – council communism and self-management – only take the possibilities contained in the premises, namely the rights of the individual, to their ultimate conclusions."[32] Just as Rawls, for example, claims to support pluralism while restricting access to public discussions to those who hold a reasonable comprehensive doctrine – who "share a reasonable public conception of justice"[33] – so Gauchet maintains that debate does not legitimately extend to questions of the fundamental structure of the liberal regime. In a sense the institutional form capable of guaranteeing democratic life has been found, and for this reason we must attempt to block in advance all movements for radical political creation: "Modern democracy will thus develop in an atmosphere of unpredictability and surprise, not invention."[34]

Gauchet does not identify democratic practice with the continual interrogation of all dimensions of the social sphere, but rather with adherence to the basic principles of liberal democratic institutionalization. Just as in the case of deliberative democratic theory, here too the homogenization of fundamental interest is used as grounds to collapse the concept of democracy into its representative form. Moreover, the legitimacy of this move is explicitly affirmed by Manent, who argues that the distinction between direct and representative modes of democratic practice is irrelevant to the contemporary democratic experience. According to him, we have learned through Tocqueville that democracy is not a form of regime per se, but a social state characterized by an equality of conditions. Under such equality, each individual participates in sovereignty through his or her participation in the expression of public opinion, which is given a voice through the political representative, and thus the right to vote is all that matters. As Manent puts it, "one should not attach too much importance to the representative form by which the will of the people is expressed ... The traditional distinction between direct democracy and representative democracy, between ancient democracy and modern democracy, in fact shows itself utterly irrelevant to America."[35]

Although the historical liberal tradition is concerned with the rehabilitation of the political experience, it seems that it ultimately finds itself in the same democratic impasse as the deliberative tradition. Democracy is not fully affirmed for three interrelated reasons: 1) social difference is limited by the positing of an underlying notion of legitimate being/doing; 2) a certain form of political institutionalization is seen as a guarantor of legitimate political outcomes; and 3) this form of political institutionalization is reduced to various principles of liberal representation. It is against this threefold pacification of democracy and social difference that the second tradition of the return of political philosophy in France, the radical democratic tradition, positions itself.

The Radical Democratic Tradition

What does it mean to speak of a democratic theory as radical? On the one hand we can approach the term from an etymological perspective. As Marx famously reminded us, "[t]o be radical is to grasp matters at the root."[36] To return to the root of democracy is to return to its initial formulation in the theory and practice of the ancient Athenians. The term originates from the Greek concept of *dēmokratía*, a fusion of *dêmos and kratos*, or people and rule. Democracy refers us to the idea of the active self-rule of the people, who assume responsibility for governing themselves. As pointed out by ancient writers such as Thucydides and Herodotus, democratic practice is closely tied to the concept of isonomy, which refers to a unique sense of political equality. Isonomy is equality in a double sense: it communicates both the equal status of all citizens before the law, but also the equal ability of all citizens to participate in the formation of the law.[37] The latter sense of equality is the necessary ground for any view that sees all citizens as active participants in political deliberation, and it is also not surprisingly the aspect of equality that has been increasingly lost in contemporary democratic discourse.

What we lose sight of when we, like Manent, for example, proclaim the meaninglessness of the distinction between participatory and representative modes of democratic practice, is this second moment of isonomic equality. In contemporary representative democracies, the people are not responsible for *creating* law, but rather for *electing* those elite citizens whom they believe would do the most competent job of creating law. As was recognized in ancient Greece, though, classically pointed out by Aristotle,[38] such electoral selection is a fundamentally aristocratic – and *not* democratic –mode of filling political office. Although the principle of delegation is not itself non-democratic, the idea of attaching delegation exclusively to election is non-democratic because it requires assuming that the task of governing is an expert one to be entrusted only to a minority of elite citizens. To affirm the democratic principle fully is to reject all such specific titles to govern and to posit the equal right and ability of all to participate in the formulation of the political direction of communities. As Jacques Rancière reminds us, there is no specific political knowledge that experts could have that the people could not – the people are perfectly capable of giving law to themselves. Hence the question many of the theorists in this volume ask: what does it mean to think about the actual self-legislation of the people in the context of contemporary societies?

In contemporary democratic thought, however, the term "radical democracy" also has another aspect to its meaning. Democracy is radical to the extent that it is incapable of being reduced to any sort of metaphysical or ontological ground capable of firmly fixing the form of being of the social or the mode of being of the political. Against any stable foundations, democracy is the explicit and permanent self-institution of the social sphere. It is grounded in the perpetual self-activity of the people, who are the only ones capable of giving meaning to their life in common. Nothing beyond or before this act of self-institution is capable of defining the boundaries of political action, as democracy is above all a practice marked by indeterminacy. The ultimate ends of life in society are the object of a never-ending debate between always unique or non-identical individuals, who are incapable of referring their values or norms to an ultimate foundation that would validate or confirm once and for all the organization of society. The impossibility of such validation or confirmation is what leads Castoriadis to characterize democracy as the tragic political regime, for "once one exits from a sacred world, from the imaginary signification of a transcendent foundation for the law and of an extrasocial norm for social norms, the crucial problem of self-limitation thereby arises. Democracy is quite evidently a regime that knows no external norms; it has to posit its own norms, and it has to posit them without being able to lean on another norm for support."[39] It is thus up to the people not only to act for themselves, but also to limit themselves.

The fact of democratic indeterminacy is a consequence of the fundamentally divided nature of the social sphere – the fact that society is always a plurality. Division is an inevitable element of the political, which forms a space for the negotiation of the intersection of the wills of individuals and groups with distinct desires, needs, interests, values, and so on. The indeterminacy resulting from the fact of social division has always troubled the Western tradition of political thought, which in many respects can be considered in terms of philosophy's attempt to mask or neutralize the division at the heart of the political for the sake of the guarantee of social stability. To the extent that political philosophy has actively attempted to overcome that conflict which structures political interaction – and which manifests itself, for example, in dialogue or debate over the normative values to be recognized by the community – it often takes on an anti-political form.[40] This is not to say, however, that the nature of the political has been misunderstood. From Plato to Rawls, the outstanding representatives of Western political thought have clearly recognized that division is the essence of the sphere of politics: divisions continually re-emerge between different parts of society – between those who claim different titles to govern, between those with opposing visions for the community, between those who are members of society and those who are not. But with few exceptions – Machiavelli, in particular – the tradition's canonical thinkers have seen the indeterminacy resulting from these divisions as something to be overcome, not as a condition to be affirmed. The realization of democracy, though, depends upon precisely this affirmation.

It is with this context in mind that this volume attempts to introduce to readers certain of the most outstanding theorists of the return to political philosophy in post-war France, theorists who have consciously rejected the anti-political project, who have attempted to view division and difference not as inevitably destructive of the stability of the political order, but as constitutive of any sort of positive democratic project. It is to these later thinkers – among them Hannah Arendt, Maurice Merleau-Ponty, Pierre Clastres, Claude Lefort, Cornelius Castoriadis, Guy Debord, Jacques Rancière, Étienne Balibar, and Miguel Abensour – that this volume is dedicated. Many of these thinkers are familiar to North American audiences, but most are not recognized as offering any unique insights on politics that the Western canon has not already touched upon. Thus, this collection attempts to deepen understanding of these thinkers by highlighting what we see as their unique contributions to political theory: their shared attempts to think of division, of the indeterminacy of politics, as something productive, creative, and fundamentally democratic. Indeed, common to the thinkers we have selected is an appreciation not only of the possibilities inherent in the indeterminacy of politics, but also of the fact that democracy itself exists only to the extent that division is expressed and affirmed. In fact, it is the threefold exploration of politics, division, and democracy that distinguishes the work of these political thinkers from that of other French philosophers who could be seen to be in the tradition of radical social thought, such as Michel Foucault, Gilles Deleuze, and Alain Badiou. Ultimately, the central theme that we develop throughout the book is how politics, particularly democracy, should embrace and welcome division.

To develop this theme, we map out, first, what the selected thinkers mean by politics; second, how they understand division and its relation to politics and democracy; and, finally, what kinds of possibilities might be opened up by their particular interpretations of politics, division, and democracy. We also pose the following more general questions with respect to the thinkers we present: how might their interpretations of politics challenge the Western canon of political thought, and yet also reinvigorate certain of its themes? To what extent do their interpretations of politics demand that we rethink democracy? What critiques do their interpretations offer the dominant liberal and deliberative democratic discourses? Are their particular interpretations of politics necessarily at odds with other radical theories, such as Marxism or various forms of post-structuralism? And, lastly, can they help us better tackle the political questions and issues that demand our attention today?

Outline of the Work

The volume is organized in three parts, each roughly representing a phase in the development of radical French political thought in the twentieth century. Part I discusses three important forbearers whose insights about the nature of politics, the subject, and the state set the stage for the return to political philosophy in France. Although situated outside of the late-twentieth-century French context identified earlier, Hannah Arendt made an immeasurable contribution to the possibility of thinking about the autonomy of the political and the potential for the institution of political modes and orders that look to affirm human plurality and agency; it would be impossible to speak of a radically democratic return of the political in France without her intervention. In fact, because of the uniqueness of her reception in this particular intellectual context, one could even speak of a "French Arendt."[41] In Chapter 1, Christopher Holman offers a reinterpretation of Arendt's political philosophy against attempts to marginalize her work for its supposed elitism. Building on the agonistic resuscitation of Arendt's work, Holman attempts to show that her affirmation of radical democracy is grounded in a specific ontology of human uniqueness that simultaneously posits both human difference and human equality. Ultimately, the Arendtian good-in-itself that is political creation can be realized only when actors bind themselves together into a political "we" to initiate common projects. Such a constitution, however, depends not upon a homogeneity of human beings, but on an affirmation of radical human otherness. It is precisely the conflictual interaction of human significations that serves as the stimulus to political creation. Politics and democracy are thus seen as being impossible without a specific type of non-antagonistic social division.

Despite serving as a formative influence on Lefort, the political influence of Maurice Merleau-Ponty likewise has been marginalized, as much of the focus on his work has been limited to his philosophy. In Chapter 2, Paul Mazzocchi attempts to draw out the connection between the political import of Merleau-Ponty's ontology of the flesh via his political engagements with Machiavelli and Marx. In attempting to transcend dualistic thinking, Merleau-Ponty's ontology of the flesh posits the world of being as a realm of non-identical identity, in which self and others intertwine in malleable and non-objectifying constellations that inform the indeterminacy of differentiated, but not irreconcilable, modes of being-in-the-world. This develops via the insights and shortfalls of Marx and Machiavelli: on the one hand, Merleau-Ponty adopts something tantamount to Machiavelli's politics of division, but against the potentially objectifying and ahistorical social relations that permeate Machiavelli's *The Prince*; on the other hand, Merleau-Ponty maintains a devotion to the emancipatory and egalitarian impetus of Marx, but rejects the theory of the proletariat as the absolute/universal subject. Ultimately, Mazzocchi suggests that the political contours of the ontology of the flesh emerge in its conception of intersubjectivity and alterity.

Pierre Clastres exerted a subterranean but decisive influence on many of the thinkers of the return of politics in post-war France. The perspectives opened by Clastres' work are found notably in the affirmation of the centrality of the political, the importance of differentiating politics and the state, and the assertion of a type of power that is non-coercive. In Chapter 3, Miguel Abensour[42] eloquently demonstrates how the articulation of a "counter-Hobbes" is a central aspect of Clastres' seminal contribution to a renewed intelligence of the political. As Abensour shows, Clastres challenges the traditional conflation of "politics" and "state" via anthropological evidence from primitive societies: these are not just societies *without* the state but also societies *against* the state. In claiming that primitive societies have their own political logic and their own form of political institutions, Clastres argues that Hobbes was right that war is crucial to explaining primitive society, but wrong in the conclusions drawn from it. War is not what prevents primitive societies from being actual societies, but rather the means through which primitive societies institute themselves politically, acting to establish an "indivisible *we*" that excludes Others. This political interpretation of primitive societies is what Abensour calls the "Copernican revolution of Pierre Clastres": by undermining the idea that only societies *with* a state have politics, Clastres' "new political anthropology" clears the ground for a new approach to politics, one centred on division and conflict rather than on procedures and consensus.

Part II moves to three important figures in post-war France, a period of political turmoil that culminated in the spontaneous student uprising of May 1968. Claude Lefort and Cornelius Castoriadis were identified earlier as being, alongside Clastres, lynchpins of the return to political philosophy in France. Lefort's and Castoriadis's influence emerged through their prominent role in *Socialisme ou Barbarie*, an organization and journal that was born in 1948 and dissolved in 1965. Over this period, these two thinkers developed stinging critiques of the bureaucratic, repressive, and inegalitarian nature of the Soviet Union, as well as an associated critique of Marxism in general. Although Lefort departed from the organization in 1958 as a result of a disagreement with Castoriadis about the structure and purpose of *Socialisme ou Barbarie* (Lefort wanted a less formal and more spontaneous model), these early themes continued to motivate their thought for years to come.

As Carlo Invernizzi Accetti explains in Chapter 4, Lefort's understanding of the democratic "form of society" grew out of his critique of totalitarianism. For Lefort, the distinctive feature of modern democracies is that they recognize and assume the constitutive division on which they are constructed; unlike totalitarian societies, they do not attempt to cover up divisions with substantive representations of Truth or Unity. This inscribes the domain of the political within a framework of indeterminacy, thereby configuring it as a perpetual process of experimentation and self-critique. Drawing on Lefort's writings on human rights, Accetti proceeds to show that Lefort can be read as offering a practical alternative both to the eschatological fantasies of revolutionary Marxism and to the "reformism" of neo-Kantian political theory. Recognizing and accepting the constitutive division of the social implies approaching politics as an irreducible struggle between the need to institutionalize forms of power and constantly subverting and revising them to carve out further spaces for critique.

Whereas Lefort uses a modern notion of democracy to critique totalitarianism, Castoriadis instead grounds his critique in the direct democracy of Ancient Athens. As Brian Singer argues in Chapter 5, Castoriadis's most significant contribution to radical democratic theory lies in an elaboration of the philosophical dimensions of the project of "autonomy" or "auto-institution." In what Castoriadis calls a heteronymous society, there is no room for social division: under heteronomy the laws and norms of society are derived from an extra-social origin such as tradition, religion, nature, or a despot, which guarantees their truth. Autonomy, in contrast, is premised on the public questioning of its instituted arrangements, an idea that ensures divisions will continually re-emerge. Ancient Athens was the first society to engage in such questioning via its democratic institutions. Although Castoriadis recognizes a second project of auto-institution emerging in modern Europe, Singer concludes that the merits of Castoriadis's thought may be tied to his focus on ancient Greece, a matter that separates him from Lefort regarding the question of alterity.

Although briefly a member of *Socialisme ou Barbarie*, Guy Debord was primarily affiliated with the Situationist International (SI). There are debates about the SI's role in the May 1968 uprising, but there is no doubt that the uprising perfectly represented the SI's playful, interruptive conception of radical politics, which was centred on what Debord called the "construction of situations." As Devin Penner explains in Chapter 6, although Debord is not generally considered a radical democratic thinker, there are tendencies in his thought that lead in this direction. Centrally, the concept of play provides the underlying political ethos for the situation and all of Debord's other practical concepts. While recognizing that play always requires rules, organization, and discipline, the Situationists went on to emphasize the participatory, creative, anti-hierarchical, and anti-authoritative nature of play. With this in mind, it is not surprising that Debord and the Situationists are cited in recent writings on the relationship of play and New Social Movements. Indeed, although Penner acknowledges the tension in Debord's thought between a relatively closed and dogmatic Marxism and a more open politics of play, he argues that Debord's ideas about the interruptive nature of the situation still help us to think about the practice associated with a radical politics of division.

The final three chapters turn to three theorists whose contributions to radical democratic theory are relatively recent: Jacques Rancière, Étienne Balibar, and Miguel Abensour. In the 1960s both Rancière and Balibar were staunch Marxists, students of Louis Althusser. Rancière came to break with Marxism (particularly its Althusserian and structuralist incarnations), however, because its political framework was unable to deal with the popular and spontaneous character of the May 1968 uprising. Breaking with Althusser, Rancière turned to the archives of nineteenth-century workers' writings in an attempt to better understand how it was that ordinary people came to be "emancipated." Stemming from these years in the archives in particular, Rancière came to rethink emancipation, arguing that it has nothing to do with "the freeing power of awareness," but rather is the process of assuming and demonstrating one's equality. It is this understanding of emancipation, and the reframing of experience that accompanies it, that could be said to be the uniting thread in Rancière's eclectic range of work. His rethinking of emancipation is certainly at the heart of his startling reimagining of "politics." In Chapter 7, however, Rachel Magnusson argues it is important to resist the temptation to approach these writings on politics as if they offered a new theory of politics. Rather, Magnusson contends that Rancière's originality in political thinking comes from the way he presents and mobilizes indeterminacy to open up space for expressions and demonstrations of equality. In this sense, it is the *political* nature of Rancière's rethinking and rewriting of politics that is most fascinating for those of us concerned with radical democracy.

Rather than coming to a radical democratic position *against* Marxism as Arendt, Lefort, and Rancière had, Balibar arrives at a radical democratic position *through* Marxism. Indeed, in Chapter 8, James Ingram shows that Balibar's distinctive contribution to radically democratic theory depends on an openness that seeks to address Marxism's blind spots. After reconstructing the strategies of Balibar's explicitly Marxist work – in particular, his 1976 defence of the idea of the dictatorship of the proletariat – Ingram's chapter is organized around the three perspectives Balibar has used to analyse politics in his mature thought: emancipation, transformation, and civility. Although the first is straightforwardly radically democratic, affirming the "autonomy of politics" and insurrectionary struggles to expand the scope of citizenship, the second and third reflect Balibar's ongoing engagement with Marxian problematics, and especially his interest in the background conditions of politics. Balibar's main contribution to radical democratic theory, Ingram argues, is to complicate and enrich the idea of democracy, so that, rather than appearing as the solution to the challenges of politics, society, or history, it seems both partial and endlessly problematic.

In Chapter 9, Martin Breaugh situates Abensour – a close collaborator of Lefort's – in the latest wave of the return to political philosophy in France. Centrally, Abensour refuses to reject or suppress politics in the way that many canonical thinkers do; instead, his rethinking of various political events leads him to explore the link between politics and emancipation. Totalitarianism was one of the crucial political experiences that forced Abensour to reconsider politics as integrally bound to the project of emancipation and its inverse, the critique of domination. This negative critique of totalitarian domination is complemented by attempts to conceive politics more positively as emancipation via Abensour's notion of "insurgent democracy," which he develops through an engagement with Marx's notion of "true democracy" and his reconception of utopia as a "spirit" rather than as a blueprint or specific political program. In both cases, Abensour emphasizes the importance of plurality, difference, division, and conflict against the anti-democratic and totalizing logic of oneness. Thus, Breaugh concludes, Abensour offers something "more difficult and more exhilarating" than a hypothetical proposal for change or a resignation to the status quo. He offers instead something we hope all chapters of this volume offer: "an invitation to think and act in concert with others and without sacrificing the quality of our liberty, an exhortation 'to make political liberty synonymous with a living critique of domination.'"[43]

NOTES

1 For one recent attempt to highlight the opposition between these two models, as well as to mediate between them, see Hubertus Buchstein, "Reviving Randomness for Political Rationality: Elements of a Theory of Aleatory Democracy," *Constellations* 17, no. 3 (2010): 435–54.

2 Jürgen Habermas, *The Theory of Communicative Action*, vol. 1, *Reason and the Rationalization of Society*, trans. Thomas McCarthy (Boston: Beacon Press, 1984), 398. For Habermas's key work on deliberative democracy, see idem,

Between Facts and Norms: Contributions to a Discourse Theory of Law and Democracy, trans. William Rehg (Cambridge, MA: MIT Press, 1996).

3 On the call for a new deliberative form of representation, see, for example, Nadia Urbinati and Mark Warren, "The Concept of Representation in Contemporary Democratic Theory," *Annual Review of Political Science* 11, no. 1 (2008): 387–412.

4 For one articulation of this deliberative shift, see, for example, Philip Pettit's account of the distinction between responsive and indicative modes of representation: "In responsive representation, the fact that I am of a certain mind offers reason for expecting that my deputy will be of the same mind ... In indicative representation things are exactly the other way around. The fact that my proxy is of a certain mind offers reason for expecting that I will be of the same mind." Philip Pettit, "Representation, Responsive and Indicative," *Constellations* 17, no. 3 (2010): 427.

5 See, for example, William Connolly, "A Critique of Pure Politics," *Philosophy and Social Criticism* 23, no. 5 (1997): 1–26; Bonnie Honig, *Political Theory and the Displacement of Politics* (Ithaca, NY: Cornell University Press, 1993); Chantal Mouffe, *The Democratic Paradox* (London: Verso, 2000); Andrew Schaap, *Political Reconciliation* (New York: Routledge, 2005); James Tully, *Strange Multiplicity: Constitutionalism in an Age of Diversity* (Cambridge: Cambridge University Press, 1995).

6 See, for example, the following collections: Adrian Little and Moya Lloyd, eds., *The Politics of Radical Democracy* (Edinburgh: Edinburgh University Press, 2009); Lars Tønder and Lasse Thomassen, eds., *Radical Democracy: Politics Between Abundance and Lack* (Manchester: Manchester University Press, 2005).

7 The following intellectual history was first developed by Miguel Abensour in the graduate seminar, "Le retour de la philosophie politique en France," which he taught in 2001–02 at the University of Paris VII – Denis-Diderot.

8 It is important to note, however, that Althusser himself can be seen as breaking with his prior scientific and orthodox structuralist commitments with his discovery of the unique materialist tradition, particularly the work of Machiavelli and Spinoza. See, for example, Miguel Vatter, "Machiavelli After Marx: The Self-Overcoming of Marxism in the Late Althusser," *Theory & Event* 7, no. 4 (2004).

9 Cornelius Castoriadis, "A Thoroughgoing Shakeup of All Forms of Social Life," in *Postscript on Insignificancy* [E-Book], trans. and ed. Anonymous (2011), 57; available online at http://www.notbored.org/PSRTI.pdf.

10 Louis Althusser, *For Marx*, trans. Ben Brewster (London: Verso, 2006), 34–5.

11 Ibid., 111.

12 Althusser and a number of students in his seminar at l'École normale supérieure, including Balibar and Rancière, contributed to a four-volume work of Marxist philosophy entitled *Lire le Capital,* which was first published in 1965. Althusser's and Balibar's contributions were the only ones to make the English translation of this work, which was first published in 1970; see Louis Althusser and Étienne Balibar, *Reading Capital,* trans. Ben Brewster (London: Verso, 1997). Rancière's rejection of Althusserian Marxism was forcefully announced in a 1974 book entitled *La leçon d'Althusser,* translated into English as Jacques Rancière, *Althusser's Lesson,* trans. Emiliano Battista (New York: Continuum, 2011).
13 Michel Crozier, *The Bureaucratic Phenomenon* (Chicago: University of Chicago Press, 1964), 7.
14 Ibid., 8.
15 Michel Crozier, "French Students: A Letter from Nanterre-La Folie," *National Affairs,* no. 13 (1968): 156.
16 Ibid.
17 Ibid., 159.
18 Gad Horowitz, "The Foucaultian Impasse: No Sex, No Self, No Revolution," *Political Theory* 5, no. 1 (1987): 65.
19 Michel Foucault, "Politics and the Study of Discourse," in *The Foucault Effect: Studies in Governmentality,* ed. Graham Burchell, Colin Gordon, and Peter Miller (Chicago: University of Chicago Press, 1991), 53.
20 Ibid., 71.
21 Pierre Clastres, *Society Against the State: Essays in Political Anthropology,* trans. Robert Hurley (New York: Zone Books, 1987).
22 Pierre Clastres, "Power in Primitive Societies," in *Archeology of Violence,* trans. Jeanine Herman (New York: Semiotext(e), 1994), 91.
23 Alexandr Solzhenitsyn, *The Gulag Archipelago, 1918–1956: An Experiment in Literary Investigation,* trans. Thomas Whitney (New York: Harper & Row, 1974); Claude Lefort, *Un homme en trop: réflexions sur "L'archipel du Goulag"* (Paris: Éditions du Seuil, 1976).
24 Mark Lilla, "The Legitimacy of the Liberal Age," in *New French Thought: Political Philosophy,* ed. Mark Lilla (Princeton, NJ: Princeton University Press, 1994), 12.
25 On this tradition see, for example, Mark Lilla, ed., *New French Thought: Political Philosophy* (Princeton, NJ: Princeton University Press, 1994).
26 Pierre Manent, "The Return of Political Philosophy," *First Things,* no. 103 (May 2000): 22.
27 See, for example, Pierre Manent, *A World beyond Politics? A Defense of the Nation State,* trans. Marc LePain (Princeton, NJ: Princeton University Press, 2006).

28 James Ingram, "The Politics of Claude Lefort's Political: Between Liberalism and Democracy," *Thesis Eleven* 87 (November 2006): 34.
29 Mouffe, *Democratic Paradox*, 2–3.
30 Marcel Gauchet, *The Disenchantment of the World: A Political History of Religion*, trans. Oscar Borge (Princeton, NJ: Princeton University Press, 1997), 192.
31 Ibid., emphasis added.
32 Ibid.
33 John Rawls, *Political Liberalism* (New York: Columbia University Press, 1995), xxiii.
34 Gauchet, *Disenchantment of the World*, 194.
35 Pierre Manent, *Tocqueville and the Nature of Democracy*, trans. John Waggoner (Lanham, MD: Rowman & Littlefield, 1996), 8.
36 Karl Marx, *Critique of Hegel's "Philosophy of Right,"* trans. Annette Jolin and Joseph O'Malley (Cambridge: Cambridge University Press, 1972), 137.
37 Pierre Lévêque and Pierre Vidal-Naquet, *Cleisthenes the Athenian: An Essay on the Representation of Space and Time in Greek Political Thought from the End of the Sixth Century to the Death of Plato*, trans. David Ames Curtis (New York: Humanity Books, 1996), 22.
38 Aristotle, *The Politics*, trans. Carnes Lord (Chicago: University of Chicago Press, 1995), 1294b7–10.
39 Cornelius Castoriadis, "The Greeks and Modern Political Imaginary," in *World in Fragments: Writings on Politics, Society, Psychoanalysis, and the Imagination*, trans. and ed. David Ames Curtis (Stanford, CA: Stanford University Press, 1997), 93.
40 For a recent attempt to trace the anti-political tendency in political thought, see Dick Howard, *The Primacy of the Political: A History of Political Thought from the Greek to the French & American Revolutions* (New York: Columbia University Press, 2010).
41 Initially the Arendtian influence on the French tradition of radical democratic thought could be considered something of a subterranean current, as her appropriation was not necessarily explicitly identified. It is perhaps most clearly expressed by Claude Lefort in his "Hannah Arendt and the Question of the Political," in *Democracy and Political Theory*, trans. David Macey (Cambridge, UK: Polity Press, 1988), 45–55. Elsewhere Lefort would write that, after reading Arendt's *The Origins of Totalitarianism*, he "was filled with admiration for and felt very close to the thought of the author"; see Claude Lefort, "Thinking with and against Hannah Arendt," in *Social Research* 69, no. 2 (2002): 447. Castoriadis, meanwhile, cites Arendt even less, yet it is highly revealing that at one point he identifies her as one of "the most remarkable authors"; see Cornelius Castoriadis, "Reflections on

Racism," in *World in Fragments: Writings on Politics, Society, Psychoanalysis, and the Imagination*, ed. and trans. David Ames Curtis (Stanford, CA: Stanford University Press, 1997), 27. More recently, radical democratic readers in France have been far more upfront about Arendt's influence. See, for example, Miguel Abensour, *Hannah Arendt contre la philosophie politique?* (Paris: Sens & Tonka, 2006); and Étienne Tassin, *Le trésor perdu: Hannah Arendt, l'intelligence de l'action politique* (Paris: Payot, 1999).

42 Miguel Abensour's contribution does not follow the same format as the other chapters. It was originally published in France for an edited volume on the thought of Pierre Clastres. See Miguel Abensour, ed., *L'esprit des lois sauvages: Pierre Clastres ou une nouvelle anthropologie politique* (Paris: Éditions du Seuil, 1987). The book is currently out of print, and his chapter is translated here for the first time in English.

43 Max Blechman, back cover blurb for Miguel Abensour, *Democracy Against the State: Marx and the Machiavellian Moment*, trans. Max Blechman and Martin Breaugh (Cambridge, UK: Polity Press 2011).

Part I

The Forebearers of the Return of Radical Democracy

1 Hannah Arendt: Plurality, Publicity, Performativity

CHRISTOPHER HOLMAN

Introduction

As was suggested in the introduction to this volume, a large number of the normative concerns that would come to define the tradition of radical democratic thought in France were anticipated in the political philosophy of Hannah Arendt. The French thinkers included in this volume who productively engaged with Arendt's works can be seen as providing an earlier articulation of those contemporary interpretations of Arendt that have come to emphasize the agonistic and performative elements in her work, as opposed to the deliberative and rationalistic ones. Indeed, it is this primary opposition that structures most current debates on Arendt, many readers finding a conflict in her thought between a communicative and dialogical understanding of politics and a heroic and extraordinary one. Bhikhu Parekh, for example, claims that Arendt affirms two contradictory models of politics, one a highly individualistic agonal model in which the individual attempts to distinguish herself from her peers and through this separation achieve glory, and the other a participatory model in which the individual attempts to contribute to the realization of public freedom within a civic community.[1] For Maurizio Passerin d'Entrèves, Arendt's theory of action contains a tension between what he calls expressive and communicative models: "Communicative action is oriented to reaching understanding and is characterized by the norms of symmetry and reciprocity between subjects who are recognized as equal. Expressive action, on the other hand, allows for the self-actualization or self-realization of the person, and its norms are the recognition and confirmation of the uniqueness of the self and its capacities by others."[2] When Arendt stresses the expressive model, politics appears as the great and noble performances of individuals, whereas when she stresses the communicative model, politics appears as collective deliberation between equals within a shared public realm. The fact that there are both democratic and elitist strains in Arendt's thought is taken to be a consequence of her inability to integrate these two models, the expressive and communicative.[3] Following d'Entrèves, Seyla Benhabib reads in Arendt a tension between a performative or agonal politics and a democratic or associative one. It is the former politics that gives the impression of Arendt as an elitist, to the extent that the expression of performative political acts is seen to be extraordinarily uncommon: "Agonal action is episodic and rare; only some human actions attain that quality of 'shining forth' and 'manifesting a principle' that Arendt associates with agonal action."[4] The fact that throughout history there have been so few deeds deserving of remembrance, of being recounted throughout time as a consequence of the radiance of their glory, separates these deeds from those that constitute the everyday and normal practice of politics: "Such action is rare; it transcends and in many ways transfigures everydayness and our understanding of ourselves. But the many small gestures and doings that constitute human everydayness do not usually attain such dimensions of brilliance of expression and intensity of passion."[5] In sum, the debate between the agonistic and deliberative forms of democratic theory that was pointed out in the Introduction to this volume thus seems to play itself out within the scholarly literature on Arendt as well.

What I attempt to argue in this chapter,[6] however, is that the deliberative critics of agonal action are incorrect to suggest that Arendt's affirmation of a politics of the extraordinary necessarily implies a degradation of the ordinary and everyday. It is in fact true that Arendt concedes the historical rarity of great and glorious action, writing that "[p]olitics as such has existed so rarely and in so few places that, historically speaking, only a few great epochs have known it and turned it into a reality."[7] Agonal action is in fact rare. Arendt's point, though, is just that it should not be. The recognition of the exceptionality of agonal action produces for Arendt an ethical imperative to reorganize human reality such that all citizens are able to express themselves gloriously. In the face of the episodic appearance of greatness in the world, Arendt desires not a retreat into an everyday deliberative politics that preserves equality through the denial of creative expression to all or most, but a qualitative reorganization of the nature of everyday politics. In Hanna Pitkin's words, "[a] general theory of ongoing free citizenship would have to suit people's everyday concerns, their ordinary low-profile interests and conflicts, without succumbing to triviality, apathy, or privatization. What was needed was a vision of 'normal,' ongoing, ordinary politics that was not really normal or ordinary: not in accord with the now conventional understanding of politics, nor like the now ordinary practice of politics – petty, banal, and quotidian."[8] For Arendt the relevant question is how are we to construct a political order capable of democratically institutionalizing a form of agonistic practice that in fact would manifest greatness in the everyday? The key to the answer to this question is to be found in the specific composition of the human species, in the fact that humanity is a fundamental plurality, a body of people who are by their very nature different and unique. It is this recognition of difference and uniqueness that structures Arendt's political theory.

In short, for Arendt, it is precisely the conflictual interaction of non-identical individual subjects that serves as the mechanism by which great political beginnings are initiated, an interaction that can be generalized through a specific form of institutionalization. The institutionalization of agonal, yet everyday, democratic practice is possible only to the degree that the political world is ontologically structured as a world divided. I thus begin the chapter with a brief summary of the specific way in which Arendt theorizes this social division. I then demonstrate the manner in which Arendt grounds her account of the possibility of human freedom in social division, in the creative confrontation between unique political subjects. Finally, I note Arendt's recognition of the need for this process's political objectification in an institutional order, and her identification of the revolutionary council tradition as the most appropriate such order in the current historical context. Arendt's specific theorization of the nature of council organization, I suggest, overcomes the opposition between deliberative and agonistic political modes, demonstrating the degree to which performative political values can be expressed through everyday discursive practices.

Plurality as Multiplicity of Appearance: The Arendtian Account of Human Difference and Equality

As suggested above, Arendt's political ontology is grounded first of all in the recognition of the fact of human plurality, one form of that multiplicity of appearance that characterizes all life on earth. Human plurality is the specific form of appearance that social division takes in the Arendtian case. All beings are meant to appear, but they appear to other beings who are themselves appearances. To this degree, "nothing, that is, insofar as it appears, exists in the singular; everything that is, is meant to be perceived by somebody."[9] Spectators are thus never mere subjects. Every subject, to the degree that it is an appearance, is also an object: "Living beings, men and animals, are not just in the world, they are *of the world*, and this precisely because they are subjects and objects – perceiving and being perceived – at the same time."[10] Following the bio-zoological work of Adolf Portmann, Arendt maintains that there exists an innate impulse in all organisms towards self-display: "*whatever can see wants to be seen, whatever can hear calls out to be heard, whatever can touch presents itself to be touched*. It is indeed as though everything that is alive ... has an *urge to appear*, to fit itself into the world of appearances by displaying and showing, not its 'inner self' but itself as an individual."[11] This biological urge to self-display achieves its highest form of expression in the human species, which is seen as unique to the extent that its members share not only the capacity to appear, but also the desire and capacity to do so in particular ways. The specifically human capacity of self-presentation is distinguished from mere self-display "by the active and conscious choice of the image shown; self-display has no choice but to show whatever properties a living being possesses."[12] The realization of this impulse to self-presentation is achieved through the unique human faculties of speech and action.

Human uniqueness exceeds otherness, which marks the relation between inorganic beings, and distinctness, which marks the relations between organic beings, to the extent that humans are able to further distinguish themselves from one another by means of speech and action: "In man, otherness, which he shares with everything that is, and distinctness, which he shares with everything alive, becomes uniqueness, and human plurality is the paradoxical plurality of unique beings."[13] Human plurality is a paradoxical plurality in that, in their utter uniqueness, human beings reveal themselves to be equal, not to the degree to which they share equivalent properties, but to the degree to which they share an ontological capacity to express their uniqueness: "Plurality is the condition of human action because we are all the same, that is, human, in such a way that nobody is ever the same as anyone else who ever lived, lives, or will live."[14] A primary social division between all human subjects is thus the precondition upon which Arendt thinks about human equality. This equality grounded in the manifestation of uniqueness, though, in its specifically human appearance, depends upon active initiative. According to Arendt, a life in which an individual no longer initiates speech and action for the purpose of appearance, and hence differentiation, is no longer a properly human life.[15] But what precisely does it mean to initiate? For Arendt to initiate is above all to begin something, "to set something in motion."[16] But to begin something is to bring into existence not just something that did not exist before, but something whose present existence cannot be traced back to any prior determinations that constitute moments of a causal sequence culminating in the logical appearance of the new thing. To initiate is thus not to create only the new, but the radically new: "It is in the nature of beginning that something new is started which cannot be expected from whatever may have happened before. This character of startling unexpectedness is inherent in all beginnings and in all origins."[17] It is precisely because the radically new springs from what appears to be nothing at all that it seems miraculous: "whenever something new occurs, it bursts into the context of predictable processes as something unexpected, unpredictable, and ultimately causally inexplicable – just like a miracle. In other words, every new beginning is by nature a miracle when seen from the standpoint of the processes it necessarily interrupts."[18] What distinguishes, though, "the 'infinite' improbabilities on which the reality of our earthly life rests and the miraculous character inherent in those events which establish historical reality is that, in the realm of human affairs, we know the author of the 'miracles.' It is men who perform them – men who because they have received the twofold gift of freedom and action can establish a reality of their own."[19] Human beings have the capacity to initiate such miracles precisely to the extent that each human is a unique beginning: "The miracle of freedom is inherent in this ability to make a beginning, which itself is inherent in the fact that every human being, simply by being born into a world that was there before him and will be there after him, is itself a beginning."[20]

Freedom as Performative Human Creation

The human being is thus the being whose essence it is to begin, and in this sense Arendt can be seen as anticipating that emphasis on human creation that will be highlighted by later radical democrats, most notably Cornelius Castoriadis.[21] For Arendt as opposed to Castoriadis, however, this capacity for beginning is capable of being actualized only in a certain sphere of human existence.[22] Although a discussion of Arendt's schematization of the *vita activa* is beyond the scope of this chapter, it should be noted that Arendt organizes human activity into a hierarchically arranged tripartition, the specifically human value of each triadic moment being defined by its ability to facilitate, as opposed to merely contribute to, the expression of human freedom. The tripartition is created through the implicit combination of two separate theoretical axes – specifically, Locke's alleged distinction between the labour of our body and the work of our hands, and Aristotle's distinction between *poiesis* and *praxis*. The three activities that define the *vita activa* are: labour, that cyclical movement of regeneration which corresponds to the biological life-process of the organic body; work, that fabrication of human objects which creates an independent and stable world of things marked off against the species, testifying thereby to the unnaturalness of human existence; and action, pluralistic human intercourse mediated by speech and aiming at the initiation of radical beginnings. According to Arendt, ultimately neither labour nor work can be identified with freedom, labour to the extent that it destroys plurality by uniting many into one through the reduction of human activity to processes concerned with merely bio-cyclical regeneration, and work to the extent that, as a process of conscious fabrication it is always carried out within an instrumental continuum whose goal is predetermined.

The freedom of action lies in its self-containedness, in the fact that it is carried out for its own sake. It is in this sense that action can be characterized as performative human activity, undertaken to the degree that it possesses its own specific intrinsic value.[23] Indeed, Arendt's emphasis on the performative dimension of action leads her to recharacterize the latter in aesthetic terms, as an art not of making but of performing. She identifies the theatre, for example, as the most political of all aesthetic forms, as through it the acting realm of human beings is transposed into art, into an intrinsically desirable creative expression: "The specific revelatory quality of action and speech, the implicit manifestation of the agent and speaker, is so indissolubly tied to the living flux of acting and speaking that it can be represented and 'reified' only through a kind of repetition, the imitation or *mimesis*, which according to Aristotle prevails in all arts but is actually appropriate only to the *drama*, whose very name (from the Greek verb *dran*, 'to act') indicates that playmaking actually is an imitation of acting."[24] The drama is thus an aesthetic representation of action, itself considered as the generation of new beginnings by a being who herself is a new beginning, a being who in acting reveals her singularity to the world.

Again, even though they share the general capacity to initiate activities that upset automatic processes, all individuals are radically unique, and this to the extent that they possess speech: "If action as beginning corresponds to the fact of birth, if it is the actualization of the human condition of natality, then speech corresponds to the fact of distinctness and is the actualization of the human condition of plurality, that is, of living as a distinct and unique being among equals."[25] Only a unique subject can initiate unique actions, and the subject reveals its uniqueness through the production of individualized significations: "In acting and speaking, men show who they are, reveal actively their appearance in the human world."[26] Such revelation, though, does not take the form of the presentation of fixed identifiable markers that outline the complete structure of the subject. The subject does not reveal herself as a "what," but as a "who," and to be a "who" is to be no more than a being with the ontological potential to initiate beginnings. Action is not the expression of an identical and previously constituted self that exists before the initiation of speech. The revelation of such a self would be no more than the revelation of a "what." The self, considered as a "who," constitutes itself through its action, for, in Bonnie Honig's words, "[p]rior to or apart from action, this self has no identity; it is fragmented, discontinuous, indistinct, and most certainly uninteresting."[27] In transcending its "what" character in the creation of itself through the production of unique significations, the subject reveals itself to be one in a perpetual state of becoming. Indeed, it is precisely for this reason that, for Arendt, we can only really know someone after they are dead, for only then does the subject cease its movement and present itself as an object capable of being grasped in its completeness.[28]

Because the uniqueness of the subject is revealed in the subject's self-presentation in the world of appearance, and because appearance always demands spectators, revelation always "implies an at least potential recognition and acknowledgement."[29] The theatricality of action is once again invoked: "the theatre is the political act par excellence; only there is the political sphere of human life transposed into art. By the same token, it is the only art whose sole subject is man in his relationship to others."[30] The political realm is that in which freedom is actualized, in which individuals can display their virtuosity through acting: "Performing artists – dancers, play-actors, musicians, and the like – need an audience to show their virtuosity, just as acting men need the presence of others before whom they can appear; both need a publicly organized space for their 'work,' and both depend upon others for the performance itself."[31] In no way, however, can this performative recognition be reduced to a process of thematization, precisely because of the indeterminate nature of the significations produced by the subject through speech. Again, the subject does not have the capacity for complete self-presentation. If we as subjects are incapable of presenting the totality of ourselves, others are incapable of grasping us as totalities through the consideration of that which we present to them. Speech aims not at the presentation of a "what"-content, but at the revelation of a "who"-capacity. The actor has to be disclosed as the one who is attached to the act, for unless the agent is revealed as being behind the act, the action loses its specificity and becomes merely instrumental. Here human togetherness, the necessary precondition for mutual acknowledgment through signification, is not recognized and speech is degraded to "mere talk."[32] If subjects do not recognize the "who-ness" of the one behind the act, the sense of uniqueness that characterizes human being-ness is lost, as is the potential for the generation of beginnings that arises as a consequence of the interpenetration of the wills of "whos" in their relations.

Arendtian Agonism: Action as Non-identical Exchange

For Arendt the significations produced by unique subjects is what constitutes opinion. The trajectory of group action is determined by the exchange of opinion between unique "who"s who have constituted themselves into a group for the purposes of political creation. This exchange perhaps received its first articulation in Homeric impartiality, which further demonstrates the extent to which the value of action is self-contained within itself, as opposed to within a particular determinable end. For Homer it did not matter whether the great deed was performed by his ancestors or by his ancestor's enemies; the deed was great because it aspired to immortality as a consequence of its own logic: "Impartiality, and with it all true historiography, came into existence when Homer decided to sing the deeds of the Trojans no less than those of the Achaeans, and to praise the glory of Hector no less than the greatness of Achilles."[33] For Arendt this impartiality was rooted in the Greek discovery that the world is viewed from a multiplicity of different perspectives: "In a sheer inexhaustible flow of arguments, as the Sophists presented them to the citizenry of Athens, the Greek learned to exchange his own viewpoint, his own 'opinion' ... with those of his fellow citizens. Greeks learned to *understand* – not to understand one another as individual persons, but to look upon the same world from one another's standpoint, to see the same in very different and frequently opposing aspects."[34] In recognizing the multiplicity of opinion through the "representation" of the perspectives of others, individuals manage to take account of the plurality of appearance and to produce a ground for the construction of a system of political judgment.[35]

Determinations regarding human action are thus marked above all by the reciprocal exchange of opinions between non-identical equals. Exchange takes this form as a consequence of the fact of human multiplicity and division: "If it is true that a thing *is* real within both the historical-political and sensate world only if it can show itself and be perceived from all its sides, then there must always be a plurality of standpoints to make reality even possible and to guarantee its continuation."[36] Whereas concepts of rational and absolute truth present themselves as modes of knowing appropriate to individuals considered in the singular, opinion presupposes the existence of plural individuals relating to one another as equals. Indeed, all claims of absolute truth in the human sphere are attacks on the political, which necessarily depend upon the existence of opinion: "every claim in the sphere of human affairs to an absolute truth, whose validity needs no support from the side of opinion, strikes at the very roots of all politics and all governments."[37] Political thinking is representative to the extent that the subject must attempt to represent in her mind the opinions or standpoints of those to whom she relates: "The more people's standpoints I have present in my mind while I am pondering a given issue, and the better I can imagine how I would feel and think if I were in their place, the stronger will be my capacity for representative thinking and the more valid my final conclusions, my opinion."[38] Political thinking is thus above all discursive: it aims at negotiating the multiplicity of opinions for the sake of the generation of trajectories of political action, the latter being possible only through the exercise of power, which "corresponds to the human ability not just to act but to act in concert."[39]

Political action is that which affects change in the world, and yet such change can occur only when individuals are willing and able to act together: "What makes man a political being is his faculty of action; it enables him to get together with his peers, to act in concert, and to reach out for goals and enterprises that would never enter his mind, let alone the desires of his heart, had he not been given this gift – the gift to embark on something new."[40] Above all, individuals must constitute themselves as a "we" through their organization into a political body that aims to produce new modes of being and that is marked by the mutual negotiation of interest or opinion regarding a topic, for "every topic has as many sides and can appear in as many perspectives as there are people to discuss it."[41] Such negotiation is practised in the public sphere, that space common to all in which citizens may present themselves to others and that allows for the expression of the multiplicity of opinion. Hence, "[b]eing able to persuade and influence others, which was how the citizens of the polis interacted politically, presumed a kind of freedom that was not irrevocably bound, either mentally or physically, to one's own standpoint or point of view."[42] The space of appearance necessary for political negotiation is produced wherever and whenever individuals come together to speak and act with one another, and dissolves and disappears only when power is degraded – that is, when individuals disperse.[43] Indeed, the only requirement for the production of power is the togetherness of people in a public space of appearance: "What keeps people together after the fleeting moment of action has passed (what we today call 'organization') and what, at the same time, they keep alive through remaining together is power. And whoever, for whatever reasons, isolated himself and does not partake in such being together, forfeits power and becomes impotent, no matter how great his strength and how valid his reasons."[44]

Although actors may come together to solve a particular problem they all seek to overcome, this coming together is always marked by a certain form of conflict, to the extent that all the subjects who organize to articulate the political task lack an absolute identity of mind. Articulating a specific interest thus does not mean effacing difference, but, in Lisa Jane Disch's words, "coming to understand how different we may be apart from our concern with the specific matter at hand."[45] Arendt writes that "[p]olitics deals with the coexistence and association of *different* men. Men organize themselves politically according to certain essential commonalities found within or abstracted from an absolute chaos of differences."[46] In presenting to others one's own opinions, which are never fixed but the product of a subject in flux, and representing to oneself others' opinions, which also are never fixed, and because the specific combination of subjects related to is always variable, one contributes to the construction of a fundamentally new "we." "We" is the community formed for the purposes of political creation, but precisely because every member of the political community is non-identical, with respect to both her own being and that of her fellows, the specific constitution of "we" is never given. "We" thus assumes a variety of forms to the extent that the constitution of each "we" is the coming together of an always unique body of always unique subjects. The "we" created for the purpose of initiating beginnings is thus in every instance itself a radical beginning. In coming together to exchange opinions, political actors form a new beginning, a never before seen "we." This specific organization of people cannot be traced back to prior organizations. As a new arrangement, the individuals who constitute "we" act in an entirely new way, to the extent that the interpenetration of their significations produces entirely new political permutations.

The disclosure of the identity of the actor through speech and the birth of new beginnings through action initiates an unprecedented process that emerges as the unique life-story of the new or reborn individual, a story that necessarily affects and is affected by the stories of all other individuals with whom the actor comes into contact. In this sense actors cannot be understood to function as perfectly autonomous authors or producers, but at best can be isolated and identified as agents who initiate specific actions, which nevertheless are carried out within a plural context.[47] Because action always depends upon others, every actor is at the same time a sufferer: "To do and to suffer are like opposite sides of the same coin, and the story that an act starts is composed of its consequent deeds and sufferings."[48] The chain reaction of events produced by every action is what constitutes the latter's boundlessness and marks its unpredictability. Action cannot be pre-mapped, for every act "always establishes relationships and therefore has an inherent tendency to force open all limitations and cut across boundaries."[49] The consequence of action's unpredictability is this: because the outcomes of the act cannot be predetermined, it is impossible to conceptualize an image of the specific organization of reality that will constitute the end of the act, and because there exists no conception of an end, there logically can exist no conception of a means – in the purely instrumental sense – for the actors know not where they mean to end. One is free with respect to means only when one is convinced that one knows what one is doing, but the end of history can never be known, and if one cannot know the end of history, one is not justified in interpreting history within a means-end continuum.

Action thus produces unpredictable results. The coming into existence of such results, however, cannot be reversed, and hence the second element that constitutes the indeterminacy of action: its irreversibility. The remedy for these two elements lies in the human being's unique capacities for forgiveness and promise: "The two faculties belong together in so far as one of them, forgiving, serves to undo the deeds of the past, whose 'sins' hang like Damocles' sword over every new generation; and the other, binding oneself through promises, serves to set up in the ocean of uncertainty, which the future is by definition, islands of security without which not even continuity, let alone durability of any kind, would be possible in the relationships between men."[50] The continuation of action is only possible if individuals can be forgiven for that which they did unknowingly. Arendt states: "We've all been taught to say: Lord forgive them, for they know not what they do. That is true of all action. Quite simply and concretely true, because one *cannot* know."[51] Promise, meanwhile, is that faculty which keeps individuals together for the sake of acting in concert, and it is in fact only in this instance that the idea of sovereignty achieves "a certain limited reality."[52] Here sovereignty lies in the individual's limited escape from the unpredictability of the future, an escape guaranteed precisely through the individual's communion with her peers. It is thus radically distinct from sovereignty as it is traditionally understood in the philosophical tradition, an understanding that, in fact, must be completely rejected if action is to be affirmed.

The Function of Political Objectification

As I have attempted to detail, for Arendt the ideal form of political interaction is that which is able to maximize the conflictual interaction between non-identical significations for the sake of the determination of action oriented towards changing the world. It is hence a type of agonism rooted in the expression of the uniqueness of beings that is most adequate to the creation of the radically new.[53] The agonistic conflicts within the public spaces that relate individuals to one another look towards the production of events – "occurrences that interrupt routine processes and routine procedures"[54] – the historical accumulation and objectification of which constitutes history. Whereas all other forms of biological existence are marked by a repetitive and circular movement, the temporal trajectory of the human species is rectilinear.[55] Just as human rectilinear movement cuts across cyclical organic life, interrupting the latter's repetitive movement, so too do the acts that characterize this rectilinear movement disrupt existing human trajectories through the initiation of new routes and paths. Hence, "[h]istory has many ends and many beginnings, each of its ends being a new beginning, each of its beginnings putting an end to what was there before."[56] These acts that interrupt already existing processes or sequences are the extraordinary – that which forms the subject matter of history. The task of history is to preserve the remembrance of these interruptions, which are not permanent in the way that the objects of a cycle are. According to Arendt, the historiographical impulse can be traced to Herodotus's observation that the goal of history is the preservation of the impermanent deeds of human life.[57] Creation can be guaranteed an empirical reality only if its productions become objectified: "In order to become worldly things, that is, deeds and facts and events and patterns of thoughts or ideas, they must first be seen, heard, and remembered and then transformed, reified as it were, into things – into sayings of poetry, the written page or the printed book, into paintings or sculpture, into all sorts of records, documents, and monuments."[58] For the historian the great is that which, as a consequence of its interruption of history's expected trajectory, is deserving of having its substance preserved forever through remembrance, achieved by way of a variety of forms of objectification.

I have already noted that, for Arendt, great action deserving of remembrance has been historically quite rare. I have also suggested that this is not evidence of Arendt's non-concern with the quotidian issues of everyday politics, but the starting point for the construction of an ethical imperative that seeks to generalize great action such that all citizens are capable of acting creatively and performatively on a regular basis. The challenge is to think of the conditions that would allow for a mode of institutionalization that permits everyday performative expression. We have already seen that political action requires for its preservation a form of objectification. Initially this objectification took a poetical form: great deeds were preserved in the works of poets and artists. Poetical objectification was transcended, however, with the construction of the polis, which achieved the desired generalization of the performative impulse. The function of the polis was to allow all citizens to achieve glory: "its foremost aim was to make the extraordinary an *ordinary occurrence of everyday life*."[59] The polis both allowed for the multiplication of the potential for action and provided a ground for the preservation of this action. Citizens henceforth no longer needed a Homer to immortalize their deeds, as Arendt notes that Pericles pointed out: "The *polis* – if we trust the famous words of Pericles in the Funeral Oration – gives a guaranty that those who forced every sea and land to become the scene of their daring will not remain without witness and will need neither Homer nor anyone else who knows how to turn words to praise them; without assistance from others, those who acted will be able to establish together the everlasting remembrance of their good and bad deeds, to inspire admiration in the present and future ages."[60] The polis ensured that individuals would never lack a space within which they were able to appear, where they were able to be seen and heard, and potentially achieve glory. Hence the double function of the polis: both to overcome the fleetingness of action through a mode of objective preservation, and to valorize the everyday through the expansion of the realm of performance such that all citizens, through their very activity, were capable of acting greatly. Arendt's celebration of the polis, though, is no romantic Grecophilic retreat into a long-lost and irrecuperable time. Passerin d'Entrèves is correct to note that the polis refers not to the specific political structure of the Greek city-state, but rather is a metaphor for any public-political realm in which individuals are able to show themselves to one another in speech and deed.[61] According to Arendt, within the context of late modernity, that mode of political organization most amenable to the actualization of the human potential for beginning is the revolutionary council tradition, which she investigates in some detail in what is probably her most neglected theoretical work, *On Revolution*.

Political Objectification and the Revolutionary Tradition

According to Arendt, revolutions are the only political events that in their essence directly refer us to the problem of beginnings.[62] Prior to the American and French revolutions, the idea that the flow of history could be interrupted and restarted was unknown, the latter becoming recognized only at some point during revolutionary history itself. These revolutions functioned as stories whose central narrative was the emergence of freedom, the idea of radical beginning thus coinciding with the emergence of the idea of freedom as the organizing principle of action. For Arendt freedom is the right to positive participation in political affairs. It is as such to be distinguished sharply from the essentially negative right of liberty, which is nevertheless a condition of freedom. Unfortunately, the concept of freedom increasingly has been separated from considerations of political action, and associated instead with "[t]he more or less free range of non-political activities which a given body politic will permit and guarantee to those who constitute it."[63] Needless to say, such a separation and association constitute a violation of the spirit of the concept, which should be substantively concerned with "participation in public affairs, or admission to the public realm."[64] What is significant about Arendt's account of freedom in *On Revolution*, though, is that it makes overt what was only implicit in her prior account of the nature of politics ideally considered – that is, that free public action is understood, to the degree it is considered as a performative end-in-itself, as an intrinsically gratifying and pleasurable endeavour. The emphasis on action as glory is thus supplemented by the emphasis on action as joy. According to Arendt, the content of political life is "the *joy and gratification* that arise out of being in company with our peers," out of "acting together and appearing in public," out of "inserting ourselves into the world by word and deed, thus acquiring and sustaining our personal identity and beginning something entirely new."[65] For Arendt the American political tradition, in particular, at least as it existed in its revolutionary and pre-revolutionary period, had a robust concept of public happiness. The Americans knew that to be free one had to participate in the affairs of public life, but also that this civic participation was not a sacrificial act but a good-in-itself; participation in public affairs was seen to generate a unique happiness that could not be achieved elsewhere. The Americans understood "that the people went to the town assemblies, as their representatives later were to go to the famous Conventions, neither exclusively because of duty nor, and even less to serve their own interests, but most of all because they enjoyed the discussions, the deliberations, and the making of decisions."[66]

In *On Revolution* Arendt is concerned with thinking about the possibility of constructing a set of political orders capable of institutionalizing the actualization of public happiness. It is the need for institutionalization within revolutionary movements that produces perhaps the most significant tension within, and often the degradation of, the revolutionary spirit. The latter was in fact the case in the American Revolution. The problem is that of foundation: we know that, for Arendt, unlike strength, which belongs to individuals, power comes into existence whenever individuals bind together into a "we" for the purposes of action. When individuals attempt to preserve the power created through a collective generative act, the process of foundation – "of constituting a stable worldly structure to house, as it were, their combined power of action" – has begun.[67] The "we" are a beginning for the purpose of making beginnings, yet if they are to preserve this capacity for making beginnings, they must produce a stable foundation for the principle of action that united them. They attempt to preserve that capacity through the act of political ordering, which is always motivated by the "love of freedom, and this both in the negative sense of liberation from oppression and in the positive sense of the establishment of Freedom as a stable, tangible reality."[68] Power thus demands foundation for its perpetuation, which is the prerequisite for the indeterminate continuation of the potential for action: "The grammar of action: that action is the only human faculty that demands a plurality of men; and the syntax of power: that power is the only human attribute which applies solely to the worldly in-between space by which men are mutually related, combine in the act of foundation by virtue of the making and the keeping of promises, which, in the realm of politics, may well be the highest human faculty."[69] According to Arendt, within the context of revolutionary history it was only in America that action prior to the Revolution – specifically, the formation of public civic structures – was able to generate a power capable of being preserved through promise.

The Americans recognized not only the need for foundation and its preservation, but also that this preservation could be achieved only through augmentation. In the political realm, foundation, preservation, and augmentation are all closely connected for, to the extent that it is necessary to preserve foundation, this preservation depends for its actualization on augmentation.[70] The American Founding Fathers recognized this triangular relation in the Roman political tradition, and consciously attempted to replicate it within their own historical context, in, for example, their assertion of the need for constitutional amendment: "This notion of coincidence of foundation and preservation by virtue of augmentation – that the 'revolutionary' act of beginning something entirely new, and conservative care, which will shield this new beginning through the centuries, are interconnected – was deeply rooted in the Roman spirit and could be read from almost every page of Roman history."[71] Amendment ultimately is seen to be justified to the extent that it makes possible the reproduction of the ontological condition of human life, which is in fact its own end. According to Arendt, the American revolutionaries recognized that the authority of the body politic flows from the very act of foundation itself, not from some divine or transcendent source: "it is futile to search for an absolute to break the vicious circle in which all beginning is inevitably caught, because this 'absolute' lies in the very act of beginning itself."[72] It is paradoxically, then, the creation of a stable foundation that allows for the perpetuation of what is ultimately the fundamental condition of human existence, the creation of the radically new or the upsetting of stability. Needless to say, only very specifically ordered institutional arrangements can provide a ground capable of negotiating this paradox.

The apparent tension in the revolutionary spirit is that the greatest event in the process of revolution is the act of foundation, which requires both the building and the preservation of stable structures to house action, the latter marked by the creation of something that is always radically new. In the current political context, these two moments, the concern with stability and the concern with the radically new, have become isolated and posited as opposites – in, for example, the opposition between conservatism and radicalism. For Arendt, if the revolutionary tradition is to be recollected in some meaningful sense, this opposition must be resolved into some sort of coherent unity of opposites: "Terminologically speaking, the effort to recapture the lost spirit of revolution must, to a certain extent, consist in the attempt at thinking together and combining meaningfully what our present vocabulary presents to us in terms of opposition and contradiction."[73] The failure of post-revolutionary American thought to comprehend and remember this unity of opposites was preceded by the failure of the Revolution to produce a lasting institution: specifically, the republic that was to represent the culmination of the Revolution did not allow for the perpetuation of the qualities and modes that were necessary to bring it about in the first place. The institutions of the American republic at the federal and state levels overwhelmed the town councils at the local level, as practically speaking only the representatives of the people were granted access to a space of action. For this reason, "the Revolution, while it had given freedom to the people, had failed to provide a space where this freedom could be exercised."[74] Because it was assumed that the revolutionary impulse towards political creation would continue to express itself unabated regardless of the specific structure of the political medium within which it was being expressed, the recognition of the fundamental need to create institutions specifically oriented towards active citizen participation was lost, and the concern became one of the need for foundation as such, the latter producing the Constitution and its new institutions, which focused not on freedom but on liberty, and not on participation but on representation. The loss of those institutions capable of affirming active political life generated a failure of thought to preserve the truths of the revolutionary spirit, the three principles to which the latter looks: public freedom, public happiness, and public spirit, which, when forgotten, are replaced just with civil liberties, private welfare, and public opinion.[75] The recuperation of the elements of the revolutionary spirit thus depends upon the production of a form of institution capable of allowing for the former's continual expression. If the orders of the American republic were incapable of sustaining and expressing the revolutionary spirit, of providing a space for the perpetuation of the creative impulse, the question then becomes, what form of institution is so capable? As mentioned briefly above, for Arendt the answer is to be found in the revolutionary council tradition.

The Revolutionary Council System

Arendt's political ontology – her understanding of the nature of the human essence as beginning and the political as the institutionalized sphere responsible for the actualization of beginning – is not adequately comprehensible without her account of the nature of the revolutionary council system. If the decline of the American Revolution was associated with the eclipse of participatory modes through the rise of complex systems of political representation, the Revolution's early use of councilist political forms was a concrete affirmation of the desire for political freedom and civic participation. The use of these forms, though, was certainly not unique to the American case. According to Arendt, "the council system seems to correspond to and to spring from the very experience of political action."[76] The council system invariably springs up in revolutionary situations as a consequence of the immanent nature of revolution itself – "that is, out of the experiences of action and out of the resulting will of the actors to participate in the further development of public affairs."[77] To the extent that parties and their intellectuals generally have not understood the nature of political action as radical creation, the appearance of councils has always been from their perspective unforeseen: "Each time they appeared, they sprang up as the spontaneous organs of the people, not only outside of all revolutionary parties but entirely unexpected by them and their leaders."[78] Because these appearances contradicted virtually all of the modern era's previous understandings of the nature of politics, the general tendency in intellectual history has been to marginalize or simply ignore the potential of councils to function as a legitimate and practicable form of political organization. Historians, political actors, theorists, and the revolutionary tradition itself have "failed to understand to what extent the council system confronted them with an entirely new form of government, with a new public space for freedom which was constituted and organized during the course of the revolution itself."[79] Arendt gives herself just this task of comprehending the meaning and significance of the spontaneous emergence of the revolutionary council system, ultimately seeing it as an affirmation of her political ontology – as an expression of the desire for the actualization of the human essence as beginning. She maintains that "[i]t was nothing more or less than this hope for a new form of government that would permit every member of the modern egalitarian society to become a 'participator' in public affairs, that was buried in the disasters of twentieth-century revolutions."[80]

The emergence of revolutionary councils occurred in 1870–71 as seen in the Paris Commune, in 1905 as seen in the self-organization of workers in Russia into soviets, in 1917 as seen in the reorganization of workers' soviets, in 1918–19, as seen in the German soldiers' and workers' councils, and in 1956 as seen in the new council system in Budapest. Arendt, though, traces the appearance of councils back to the eighteenth century in France and America during the beginning of revolutionary history. The council experience in France was short lived, as the spontaneous rise of a "communal council system" during the Revolution was crushed by Robespierre, who attempted to substitute for it a party machinery capable of manufacturing identical opinion.[81] The ward system in revolutionary America was more successful than the French council system, as a consequence of America's more embedded civic understanding of the goods of public freedom and happiness, as well as the system's achievement of an articulate theoretical expression, as seen primarily in the thought of Thomas Jefferson. For Jefferson the problem with the Constitution was that, although it rooted all power in the citizens, it did not give them a means to express this power in the public realm: "the danger was that all power had been given to the people in their private capacity, and there was no space established for them in their capacity of being citizens."[82] According to Jefferson, the United States should have been divided into a multitude of wardships, "little republics" that would provide all citizens with a space for direct participation in public affairs, thus providing a level of democratic involvement not achievable through simple electoral activity. On Arendt's interpretation, "[t]he basic assumption of the ward system, whether Jefferson knew it or not, was that no one could be called happy without his share in public happiness, that no one could be called free without his experience in public freedom, and that no one could be called either happy or free without participating or having a share in, public power."[83] If Jefferson was unclear on the precise structure, organization, and substance of councils – indeed, this is a recurrent criticism of all theorists of council organization – it was precisely because he was theorizing not just how to reform existing institutions, but a radically new form of government. It is for precisely the same reason that Arendt never published detailed analyses of the potential or actual structure of council systems. In John Sitton's words, "[h]er purpose instead is simply to sketch a political structure to illustrate the possibility of realizing alternative public principles: direct democracy, the experience of public freedom and public happiness in the modern world, an arena for proper opinion formation, and a polity not based on the notion of sovereignty."[84] The very attempt to fabricate in advance the ideal form of the structure that will realize the performative activity must necessarily violate to a certain degree the essence of this activity. Arendt, though, always aware of this danger, nevertheless provides some broad and tenuous formulations regarding council organization and its relation to her political ontology.

For Arendt what is most striking about revolutionary history is that, throughout such a diversity of human conditions, precisely the same phenomenon – the appearance of councils – arose again and again. In each case council members had no interest in the party system or the machinations of the professional revolutionists who comprised its bureaucracy. What they desired above all was the direct participation of all citizens in the affairs of state. Indeed, council participation actually cut across all party divisions: party membership played no role in the determination of the suitability of political participants, as the councils attracted members from all party factions. More important than this integration of diverse partisans, though, was that the councils "were in fact the only political organs for people who belonged to no party."[85] What the councils objected to, above all, was the production and maintenance of an artificial gap between the revolutionary leaders who possessed objective knowledge of the historical situation, and the ignorant masses who were to apply this knowledge passively through their directed activity. The councils affirmed the general capacity of citizens to think and act for themselves. What is more, precisely because council members understood that public participation in political affairs – thinking and acting for oneself – was an intrinsic, self-expressive good, they also understood that the council system transcended all instrumental considerations. As spaces of freedom, the councils refused to see themselves as mere temporary organs of revolution, but tried to establish themselves as permanent and enduring political structures. What they aimed at was the radical reconstruction of the nature of politics, which they recognized, in contradistinction to the professional revolutionists, as a necessary and enduring dimension of human existence.

According to Arendt, an analysis of both the 1917 Russian Revolution and the 1956 Hungarian Revolution is capable of producing a general outline of what a political order structured according to the logic of councils might look like.[86] In both cases, councils sprung up all over the revolutionary field independently of one another – in Russia, in workers', soldiers', and peasants' councils; in Hungary, in students', workers', soldiers', and civil servants' councils. Also in both cases it took only a few days to a few weeks for councils to spring up, for "accidental proximity" to be transformed into a "political institution."[87] The councils were transformed into a political institution as a consequence of being linked up to one another through their mutual integration into a coordinated system that included higher councils on a regional and national level. These higher councils, though, did not have the authority to overwhelm the initial councils or their ability to function as media for the expression of action: "The common object was the foundation of a new body politic, a new type of republican government which would rest on 'elementary republics' in such a way that its own central power did not deprive the constituent bodies of their original power to constitute."[88] Although Arendt's ideal council system took the form of a hierarchical pyramid composed of both lower and higher councils, this system would escape authoritarianism to the extent that political authority would be generated not from the top or the bottom of the pyramid, but from each layer of the pyramid. From the lowest levels, political equals would choose from among themselves delegates to move above, who would then confront as equals delegates from the higher levels, and so on: "Their title rested on nothing but the confidence of their equals, and this equality was not natural but political, it was nothing they had been born with; it was the equality of those who had committed themselves to, and now were engaged in, a joint enterprise."[89] Here political equality is not associated with a necessary affirmation of a universal and homogeneous capacity – that each can do what the other can – but with a desire to act, and hence solves what Arendt takes to be one of the most serious problems of modern politics: the reconciliation of equality and authority.

Arendt's most detailed historical account of the factual appearance of the council system is the study of the Hungarian Revolution that she undertakes in the essay "Totalitarian Imperialism." For Arendt the Hungarian Revolution was an interruption of the automatic and repetitive motion of totalitarianism, stimulated by nothing other than the attempt by individuals to actualize their creative desire to act in the world. Arendt writes that, "[i]f there was ever such a thing as Rosa Luxemburg's 'spontaneous revolution' – this sudden uprising of an oppressed people for the sake of freedom and hardly anything else, without the demoralizing chaos of military defeat preceding it, without coup d'état techniques, without a closely knit apparatus of organizers and conspirators, without the undermining propaganda of a revolutionary party, something, that is, which everybody, conservatives and liberals, radicals and revolutionists, had discarded as a noble dream – then we had the privilege to witness it."[90]

The Revolution was produced as a consequence of the increasing intensification of a series of spontaneous events: a relatively small student demonstration swelling in size and proceeding to overturn a Stalin statue in Budapest; a group of students departing for a local radio station the next day to attempt to broadcast their program; a large crowd gathering, which the police would attempt to break up; the crowd attacking the police and taking their weapons; workers leaving their factories to join the crowd; the army called in to help the police, but instead joining sides with the people and arming them further. In the end, "[w]hat had started as a student demonstration had become an armed uprising in less than twenty-four hours."[91]

What marked the Revolution was the production of solidarity among all social strata that participated, even though the uprising was initiated by communists, who themselves never resorted to stale dogmas or attempted to raise themselves up as leaders of the people. What was more, the non-communists did not react against or oppose the uprising simply because it had been begun by communists: "It was as though ideology, of whatever shade and brand, had simply been wiped out of existence and memory the moment the people, intellectuals and workers, communists and non-communists, found themselves together in the streets fighting for freedom."[92] The main problem after the Hungarian uprising was not how the people were to establish freedom – for freedom was realized in their spontaneous acting together – but how to institutionalize and hence preserve it. The solution to this problem was found in the creation of a council system, "the same organization which for more than a hundred years has emerged whenever the people have been permitted for a few days, or a few weeks or months, to follow their own political devices without a government (or a party program) imposed from above."[93] The emergence of councils demonstrated not only the extent to which individuals desired political action, but also the extent to which they were capable of channelling this desire into the construction of permanent institutional orders able to actualize this performative desire: "nothing indeed contradicts more sharply the old adage of the anarchistic and lawless 'natural' inclinations of a people left without the constraint of its government than the emergence of the councils that, wherever they appeared, and most pronouncedly during the Hungarian Revolution, were concerned with the re-organization of the political and economic life of the country and the establishment of a new order."[94] The council system required "no special conditions for its establishment except the coming together and acting together of a certain number of people on a non-temporary basis."[95] The motivation for this coming together was nothing more than the desire of individuals to express their essence as beings capable of radically beginning. It is for this reason that "[t]he councils say: We want to participate, we want to debate, we want to make our voices heard in public, and we want to have a possibility to determine the political course of our country."[96]

In the final instance, democratic councils are those political organs that are thought to provide a space for the mediation of individual political wills and an institutional foundation for radical beginning, thus universalizing the capacity to create new political modes and orders – and hence the possibility of experiencing public happiness. The council system is the political form that most adequately affirms Arendt's political ontology, to the extent that it represents an order of institutionalization capable of generalizing the human capacity for performative creation, providing a space for both the expression of unique human wills and the realization of equality via this very process of generalization. Most simply, it is within the council system, Arendt believes, that freedom and equality are affirmed simultaneously.

NOTES

1 Bhikhu Parekh, *Hannah Arendt and the Search for a New Political Philosophy* (London: Macmillan, 1981), 177.
2 Maurizio Passerin d'Entrèves, *The Political Philosophy of Hannah Arendt* (London: Routledge, 1994), 85.
3 Ibid., 96.
4 Seyla Benhabib, *The Reluctant Modernism of Hannah Arendt* (Thousand Oaks, CA: Sage Publications, 1996), 127.
5 Ibid., 130.

6 For a more detailed elaboration of the themes presented in this chapter, see Christopher Holman, *Politics as Radical Creation: Herbert Marcuse and Hannah Arendt on Political Performativity* (Toronto: University of Toronto Press, 2013).
7 Hannah Arendt, "Introduction into Politics," in *The Promise of Politics*, ed. Jerome Kohn (New York: Schocken Books, 2005), 119.
8 Hanna Pitkin, *The Attack of the Blob: Hannah Arendt's Concept of the Social* (Chicago: University of Chicago Press, 1998), 114.
9 Hannah Arendt, *The Life of the Mind*, vol. 1, *Thinking* (San Diego, CA: Harcourt, 1978), 19.
10 Ibid., 20.
11 Ibid., 29.
12 Ibid., 36.
13 Hannah Arendt, *The Human Condition*, 2nd ed. (Chicago: University of Chicago Press, 1998), 176.
14 Ibid., 8.
15 Ibid., 176.
16 Ibid., 177.
17 Ibid., 177–8.
18 Arendt, "Introduction into Politics," 111–12.
19 Hannah Arendt, "What Is Freedom?" in *Between Past and Future: Eight Exercises in Political Thought* (New York: Penguin Books, 1993), 171.
20 Arendt, "Introduction into Politics," 113.
21 See, for example, Linda Zerilli, "Castoriadis, Arendt, and the Problem of the New," *Constellations* 9, no. 4 (2002): 540–53.
22 For a critique of this element of Arendt's thought, see Christopher Holman, "Dialectics and Distinction: Reconsidering Hannah Arendt's Critique of Marx," *Contemporary Political Theory* 10, no. 3 (2011): 332–53.
23 For one attempt specifically to highlight the performative nature of Arendt's concept of action, see Douglas Torgerson, "Farewell to the Green Movement? Political Action and the Green Public Sphere," *Environmental Politics* 9, no. 4 (2000): 1–19.
24 Arendt, *Human Condition*, 187.
25 Ibid., 178.
26 Ibid., 179.
27 Bonnie Honig, "Toward an Agonistic Feminism: Hannah Arendt and the Politics of Identity," in *Feminists Theorize the Political*, ed. Judith Butler and Joan Scott (New York: Routledge, 1992), 219.
28 Hannah Arendt, "Understanding and Politics (The Difficulties of Understanding)," in *Essays in Understanding, 1930–1954: Formation, Exile, and Totalitarianism*, ed. Jerome Kohn (New York: Schocken Books, 1994), 309.

29 Arendt, *Life of the Mind*, vol. 1, *Thinking*, 46.
30 Arendt, *Human Condition*, 188.
31 Arendt, "What Is Freedom?" 154.
32 Arendt, *Human Condition*, 180.
33 Hannah Arendt, "The Concept of History," in *Between Past and Future: Eight Exercises in Political Thought* (New York: Penguin, 1993), 51.
34 Ibid.
35 It should be noted, however, that, with the 1971 publication of "Thinking and Moral Considerations," there is a shift in the nature of Arendt's account of judgment, which is no longer understood in terms of an active exercise oriented towards the mediation of opinion for the sake of the stimulation of action, but rather as a retrospective and contemplative consideration of past deeds. Ronald Beiner provides an excellent account of the nature of this shift, which is seen to be rooted in an alleged impasse of the will, in the philosophical tradition's incapacity to affirm radical creation. See Ronald Beiner, "Hannah Arendt on Judging," in *Lectures on Kant's Political Philosophy*, ed. Ronald Beiner (Chicago: University of Chicago Press, 1992); Hannah Arendt, "Thinking and Moral Considerations," in *Responsibility and Judgment*, ed. Jerome Kohn (New York: Schocken Books, 2003). Although Arendt did not live to complete what would have been her major work on judgment, the third volume of *The Life of the Mind*, much can be gleaned from her lectures on Kant's third critique. See Hannah Arendt, *Lectures on Kant's Political Philosophy*, ed. Ronald Beiner (Chicago: University of Chicago Press, 1992).
36 Arendt, "Introduction into Politics," 175.
37 Hannah Arendt, "Truth and Politics," in *Between Past and Future: Eight Exercises in Political Thought* (New York: Penguin, 1993), 233.
38 Ibid., 242.
39 Hannah Arendt, "On Violence," in *Crises of the Republic* (New York: Harcourt Brace Jovanovich, 1972), 143. For Arendt, power must be firmly distinguished from strength, violence, authority, and force. Strength refers to the energy of movement inherent in a singular object or person, violence to the instrumental use of implements designed to multiply strength, authority to the voluntary recognition of a relation of obedience, and force to the quanta of energy released by natural or social movements (143–5).
40 Ibid., 179.
41 Arendt, "Introduction into Politics," 167.
42 Ibid., 168.
43 Arendt, *Human Condition*, 199–200.
44 Ibid., 201.

45 Lisa Jane Disch, *Hannah Arendt and the Limits of Philosophy* (Ithaca, NY: Cornell University Press, 1994), 44.
46 Arendt, "Introduction into Politics," 93.
47 Arendt, *Human Condition*, 185.
48 Ibid., 190.
49 Ibid.
50 Ibid., 237.
51 Hannah Arendt, "'What Remains? The Language Remains': A Conversation with Günter Gaus," in *Essays in Understanding, 1930–1954: Formation, Exile, and Totalitarianism*, ed. Jerome Kohn (New York: Schocken Books, 1994), 23.
52 Arendt, *Human Condition*, 245.
53 Ibid., 41.
54 Arendt, "On Violence," 109.
55 Arendt, "Concept of History," 42.
56 Hannah Arendt, "The Tradition of Political Thought," in *The Promise of Politics*, ed. Jerome Kohn (New York: Schocken Books, 2005), 43.
57 Arendt, "Concept of History," 41.
58 Arendt, *Human Condition*, 95.
59 Ibid., 197; emphasis added.
60 Ibid.
61 Passerin d'Entreves, *Political Philosophy of Hannah Arendt*, 76–7.
62 Hannah Arendt, *On Revolution* (New York: Viking Press, 1965), 13.
63 Ibid., 22.
64 Ibid., 25.
65 Arendt, "Truth and Politics," 263; emphasis added.
66 Arendt, *On Revolution*, 115. Needless to say, however, Arendt was quite aware of the degradation of the concept of joy after the American Revolution, as represented, for example, in the Declaration of Independence's substitution of the term "happiness" for "public happiness," the former seen as a condition of existence to be enjoyed in private life. Government eventually would come to be understood as the means to ensure the happiness of a society of individuals, which was achieved through the production of a given state of private welfare, rather than through an active process capable of generating an intrinsic public happiness (124–5).
67 Ibid., 174.
68 Hannah Arendt, *The Life of the Mind*, vol. 2, *Willing* (San Diego, CA: Harcourt, 1978), 203.
69 Arendt, *On Revolution*, 175.
70 Ibid., 202–3.

71 Ibid., 203–4.
72 Ibid., 205.
73 Ibid., 226.
74 Ibid., 238.
75 Ibid., 223.
76 Hannah Arendt, "Thoughts on Politics and Revolution: A Commentary," in *Crises of the Republic* (New York: Harcourt Brace Jovanovich, 1972), 231–2.
77 Ibid., 231.
78 Arendt, *On Revolution*, 252.
79 Ibid., 253.
80 Ibid., 268.
81 Ibid., 249–50.
82 Ibid., 256.
83 Ibid., 258–9.
84 John Sitton, "Hannah Arendt's Argument for Council Democracy," in *Hannah Arendt: Critical Essays*, ed. Lewis Hinchman and Sandra Hinchman (Albany: State University of New York Press, 1994), 308.
85 Arendt, *On Revolution*, 267.
86 Ibid., 270.
87 Ibid., 271.
88 Ibid.
89 Ibid., 282.
90 Hannah Arendt, "Totalitarian Imperialism: Reflections on the Hungarian Revolution," *Journal of Politics* 20, no. 1 (1958): 8.
91 Ibid., 26.
92 Ibid., 27.
93 Ibid., 28.
94 Arendt, *On Revolution*, 275.
95 Arendt, "Totalitarian Imperialism," 31.
96 Arendt, "Thoughts on Politics and Revolution," 232.

2 Politics *à l'écart*: Merleau-Ponty and the Flesh of the Social

PAUL MAZZOCCHI

Rooted in the traditions of phenomenology and existentialism, Maurice Merleau-Ponty was constantly engaged in a radical interrogation of the inherited truths of Western philosophy. This initially took the form of an attempt to elaborate a philosophy of perception outside the Cartesian philosophical dualisms that dominated Western thought; later, it morphed into a critique of philosophy for its failure to interrogate adequately the category of being. These projects helped Merleau-Ponty attain intellectual prominence in the 1950s and '60s, and led one admirer and critic to label him "a truly great philosopher, the last in France before that giant of a philosopher Derrida."[1] It is, then, no surprise that there has been an enduring interest in his philosophy. But politics has been a much thornier issue for Merleau-Ponty scholarship, and has often been peculiarly absent from discussions of his work.[2]

Part of the problem lies in the fact that only two book-length texts of his are specifically works in political philosophy, and these are often considered his less "rigorous" works.[3] By bracketing out these works, Merleau-Ponty's thought is subjected to an implicit "break" thesis that treats his political writings as an "interregnum" that interrupted his philosophical writings or his return to philosophical concerns in his later works as a "retreat" from politics.[4] This thesis results in two tendencies: on the one hand, the many inquiries into his philosophy largely neglect his political writings and concerns;[5] on the other, the few inquiries into his political thought are often framed around questions about his relationship to, and ultimate "retreat" from, Marxism.[6] Although the philosophical approach is content to ignore Merleau-Ponty's politics, the political approach is content to reduce his philosophical writings to his political writings, thus contending that he retreated into a political liberalism or reformism[7] that was mirrored by an ontology of "harmony"[8] in his late works. This political reading operates via the simplistic binary of Marxism/liberalism, and suggests that any divergence from Marxism is a de facto acquiescence to liberalism and a move away from radical politics. That Merleau-Ponty broke with Marxist orthodoxy by no means suggests that he simplistically moved into the opposing camp (either politically or philosophically). Merleau-Ponty continued to view Marxism as an important source of inspiration[9] for both philosophical and political concerns – not as *the* philosophy of history, but as a source with myriad tools for critical social analysis. That said, under the pressure of a number of perceived errors in the roots of Marxian thought, Merleau-Ponty sought other sources for political-philosophical inspiration, including the work of Machiavelli.[10]

Breaking with the simplistic divisions that animate these approaches, this chapter aims to read Merleau-Ponty's ontology through the lenses of his critical political engagement with Machiavelli and Marx. My purpose in doing so is to explore Merleau-Ponty's contribution to the radical democratic tradition[11] via his social ontology. Although Machiavelli rightly acknowledges the centrality of division to political community, he appears to present a static conception of social relations, rooted in a hierarchical structure that owes something to the sorts of dualisms from which Merleau-Ponty sought to extricate philosophy. Marxism aims to eliminate these hierarchical human relations, but falls into its own dualism, and ultimately slides into a theory of the absolute subject that elides relationships of alterity. In attempting to correct these errors, Merleau-Ponty turned to developing his ontology of the flesh: a non-dualist theory of being that de-centres the subject via a multifaceted conception of alterity and intersubjectivity. In politicizing Merleau-Ponty's theory of the flesh, I aim to show how it challenges and sublates the contributions and shortfalls he found in the work of Machiavelli and Marx. In drawing out the neglected democratic import of Merleau-Ponty's philosophy, I conclude by showing briefly how a number of his key motifs are used in the works of Claude Lefort and Miguel Abensour.

Existential Motifs in Machiavelli and Marx

Merleau-Ponty's political thought is informed by the existential contention that the world is governed by "paradox, division, anxiety, and decision."[12] These conditions contradict the idea that "universal reason" can exist and that the world is predestined for a certain order or harmony.

Consequently, Merleau-Ponty proclaims the need to break with the rationalist tradition and its assertions of a closed or complete solution to the problem of human coexistence. But the existential contention that the world is governed by division and contingency does not reduce it to a meaningless flux. By the assertion "that unity and reason do not *exist*,"[13] existentialism intends to open the human world to the potential of human relations between self and others. Indeed, the dislocated world of human existence was not something simply to be swept aside for the sake of an ideal or rationalist politics; rather, it was the very characteristic out of which the political project of human community needed to be constructed. Because Machiavelli and Marx were attuned to the complicated nature of existence, Merleau-Ponty saw something particularly valuable in their political thought.

Machiavelli's work starts from the recognition of the conflictual nature of social life, attesting this to the contingency that rules and destabilizes it. In and of itself, this recognition is not unique, but, unlike previous thinkers, Machiavelli, Merleau-Ponty argues, does not attempt to overcome conflict or division. His originality lies in the fact that, "having laid down the source of struggle, he goes beyond it without ever forgetting it. He finds something other than antagonism in struggle itself."[14] In Machiavelli's description of the irrationality, violence, and death of collective life, Merleau-Ponty sees an immersion of self in others: the fear and aggression I subject the other to is the same fear and aggression I live in, am subject to, and am inspired by. Hence, "[t]he evil that I do I do to myself, and in struggling against others I struggle equally against myself."[15] We find here a circuit between self and others, in which our immersion in, and engagement with, a world of struggle subjects us all to a "common situation."[16] The coercive power of a prince must emerge to stabilize the community and prevent conflicts from becoming "insoluble," but this is not a stunting of them. The prince aims to contain, though not end, struggle and division and his authority has its limits and its goals. For Machiavelli, this division marks the starting point of "a human community emerging from" a collective life characterized by difference; recognition of this allows "us to estimate the task we are faced with if we want to bring some truth to [politics]."[17] Indeed, to iron over the struggle endemic to social life would be to subject the human community to a truly oppressive politics that seeks to annihilate difference. In a dislocated world, the prince attains "mastery of his relationships with others ... [and] clears away obstacles between man and man and puts a little daylight in our relationships – as if men could be close to one another only at a sort of distance."[18] Herein lies Machiavelli's radical humanism: he assesses politics on the basis of the relationship it creates between humans, rather than on the principles that are used in governing. Merleau-Ponty takes this as the leitmotif of any (immanent) critique: we must assess, not the values a regime purports to uphold, but the concrete relations existing among people in the light of these values.[19]

Yet Merleau-Ponty finds Machiavelli's solution to the problem of human existence somewhat lacking. In the first place, his operationalization of division appears to fall into the sort of dualistic ontology that Merleau-Ponty criticizes in Jean-Paul Sartre's work. In Sartre's account of the self/other relation, the objectifying gaze of the self – the idea that my subjectivity derives from objectifying others – negates the potential for ethical relationships. This view is predicated on a dualistic ontology under which I am able to see only the other's body – which is merely an object to me – and not the other's mind/"subjectivity." Consequently, the other is either objectified by me, or a subject that objectifies me; one cannot, on Sartre's account, be both subject and object.[20] Machiavelli's conception of the exercise of political power in *The Prince* renders a world in which some are subjects and others are only objects or objectified. Merleau-Ponty argues that this is rooted in an immutable conception of human nature that presents two types of people: "those who live through history and those who make it."[21] The latter exhibit a "natural art of commanding" and are capable of exercising political virtue. But this presents an absolute opposition, for, as Machiavelli describes the different "humours" of the body politic, "[t]he people do not wish to be commanded or oppressed by the nobles, and the nobles desire to command and oppress the people."[22] We thus have a division between those who wish to rule and are capable of doing so, and those who wish merely not to be oppressed. Unfortunately, Merleau-Ponty argues, Machiavelli leaves us no criteria for assessing the historic/political men, aside from "evoking a power which would not be unjust."[23] By redefining the problem of political virtue and human community, he leaves a void that will be filled by arbitrary powers founded in opportunism.[24]

Marxism offers a possible transcendence of Machiavelli's political void and social hierarchy in the person of the proletariat. Experiencing the conditions of capitalism as powerlessness and detachment from other individuals, the comprehension of alienation posited the very conditions out of which a collective subject could emerge. The increasing tendency of society towards proletarianization situated the proletariat as a universal subject: because the processes of objectification and alienation "transcend national, historical and ethnic peculiarities," the proletariat is capable of recognizing "itself in the others who face the same problems, the same enemy, and join in the same struggle against the same oppressive machinery."[25] Moreover, as a non-class or pure negativity, the proletariat suppresses its own existence – and the existence of classes in general – as the final stage of its own becoming. Thus, in the very modes of its (non-)being-in-the-world, the proletariat possesses the possibility of "community and communication." In Merleau-Ponty's words, "it is the sole authentic intersubjectivity because it alone lives simultaneously the separation and union of individuals."[26] For Marxism, this humanization of social relations represents the very meaning of history: the proletariat has been shaped by history, and represents a determinate solution to the continual struggles that have prevented the problem of human coexistence from being resolved. In these terms, the whole gives meaning to the contingent events that have marred history.[27] Far from being the closure of the political universe, Georg Lukács argues that the proletariat – as a pure negativity – creates itself as a self-critical power capable of "a life which makes attempts, corrects itself, and progresses as it goes."[28]

Yet, ultimately, Merleau-Ponty argues that, like Machiavelli's, the Marxist solution to the problem of human coexistence is a failure. To begin with, Merleau-Ponty argues that the "pure proletariat is a limit-case"[29] and one that is "without historical equivalents."[30] This approach – represented by Lukács – treats the proletariat as *the* identical subject-object of history, a being that acts only by acting on, and realizing, itself; in these respects, it is conceived of as the first objective possibility of the entrance of an (absolute) subject into history. But for Merleau-Ponty this is little more than the desire that the proletariat be capable of carrying out such a form of praxis.[31] Consequently, the whole closure of history via the proletariat's "becoming" is a pure myth, and the being of the proletariat is simultaneously projected backward and forward in history irrespective of its actual manifestations or existence.

Merleau-Ponty credits Lukács with attempting to preserve "a Marxism which incorporates subjectivity into history without making it an epiphenomenon."[32] But, he argues, Lukács posits this subjectivity as the incarnation of pure negativity in history. The proletariat can become the absolute historical subject that creates the means for suppressing all classes only by producing its own *non-being* as the being of society; in the process, it inaugurates "a transparent society, internally undivided and classless."[33] Against this, Merleau-Ponty argues that being always contains a partial positivity: for "nothingness" to exist, it must itself participate in being. In particular, historical subjects cannot exist as pure negativity, but must exist positively to affect history. This is true of the proletariat, too: "The proletariat *is* the revolution, the Party *is* the proletariat, the leaders *are* the party. This is not an identity in difference but, like being, is being."[34] Moreover, he asks Lukács, "[c]an one continue to think that negativity remains identical once it has acquired a historical vehicle?"[35] Merleau-Ponty finds the transparency and self-contained character of such a being to be dubious, citing Max Weber's emphasis on "the opaqueness of social reality as a 'second nature' [that] seems to postpone infinitely the limiting concept of transparent social relationships and therewith the categorical definition of history as the genesis of truth."[36] The social as second nature blurs the very "essence" of the proletariat as a pure non-being or being, positing it as merely the existence of a class in its historically specific intersubjective constellation. Consequently, if this "negative" and "critical" power becomes a positive, historical being, then self-criticism becomes nominal: the identical subject-object of history negates the possibility of opposition or plurality by positing no other outside of it, and asserting its own identity as the conditions of society itself.[37]

The full import of these problems comes to the fore in Sartre's "ultrabolshevism," which emerges at the very point that Lukács' subjectivist variant of Marxism trails off: that the proletariat is a being without historical equivalents. Although the proletariat "is not verifiable, debatable, or living," Sartre uses it as "a category delegated to represent humanity."[38] Hence, he changes it from a historical movement and incarnation of nothingness to the philosophical representation of it – to a consciousness to be created. Possessing the "gaze of the least-favoured," the idealized proletariat is the only being capable of realizing a true humanity by virtue of its own nothingness. But if the proletariat is a non-existent non-being, then it "must be invented. One must here create from nothing the milieu of a common enterprise or history, and one must even create the subjects of this enterprise: the Party."[39] For Sartre, if the proletariat does not exist but its idealization represents humanity's aims, then its power and authority "must pass to the Party which fights in its name."[40] Moreover, if its existence is entirely predicated on the pure action of the Party, then the Party's actions are unquestionable and attain the force of objective dictates. Ultimately, Sartre treats the Party and the proletariat as identical. Without the Party there is no proletariat, while the Party remains the *a priori* apparatus intended to create the proletariat because it does not exist. The decisions of the Party bring the proletariat into existence and, hence, are the decisions of the proletariat itself. This identity of Party and proletariat leads to the absolute exclusion of anything outside this identity, and denies a pluralistic subject(ivity); indeed, the historically fragmented nature of the proletariat must be suppressed as a historical reality and as a part of its identity in the making. To open the possibility of "other decisions" is to break the Party's identity and, consequently, the proletariat's potential being. This demands the negation of all internal dissent: the opposition – like the other – must be expelled. Or, like the proletariat itself, it must simply obey, which is to say conform and identify. Hence, in Sartre's hands, the "permanent revolution" "becomes the permanent anxiety of the Party," and it attempts through a falsified self-criticism to purify itself and make real the identity that cannot exist without it.[41]

Merleau-Ponty's Late Ontology: The Flesh of the World

Merleau-Ponty's late ontology has often been considered a philosophical retreat from political considerations. As I hope to show, we should read his "retreat" as a philosophical sublation of the errors he saw in Machiavelli's and Marx's own approaches to politics. Indeed, it should be acknowledged that his ontology of the flesh came on the heels of his intense critical engagement with Marxism, which he saw as the heir to the political dilemmas posed by Machiavelli. In these respects, we need to probe how the dilemma of preserving division/difference can be affected without imposing a dualistic ontology that would translate into hierarchical and monadic political relations.

In his early writings, Merleau-Ponty was centrally concerned with developing a theory of the embodied mind against Cartesian bifurcation. His central argument was that, rather than being an object largely divorced from and peripheral to experience and knowledge, the body is "on the side of the subject," for "it is our *point of view on the world*."[42] In these terms, he saw the body as the medium of our existence in the world and the pivot upon which our relationship to objects of cognition and experience revolves. Our ability to know objects is predicated on our embodied approach to them, and our body and soul thus meld in an intentional act that transcends their Cartesian separation. But in Merleau-Ponty's unfinished last work, *The Visible and the Invisible*, there is something of a "shift" that draws into question this focus on the body.

This comes to the fore in his working notes, where he states, "[t]he problems posed in [*Phenomenology of Perception*] are insoluble because I start there from the 'consciousness'-'object' distinction."[43] Operating at the level of phenomenology, Merleau-Ponty's early work sought to transcend the binaries that informed Cartesian and post-Cartesian thinking through an interrogation of subjectivity. Here, he suggests that this focus continued to contain a dualistic residue, not because it failed to transcend a one-sided notion of subjectivity, but because it focused on the subject as such. This subject, while in-the-world, was still opposed to "thing-ness." In criticizing this, Merleau-Ponty argues that the philosophy-of-consciousness approach had taken him to the endpoint of its logos: for it, the intentionality of consciousness creates a situation in which "there is no exchange, no interaction between consciousness and the object."[44] To rework philosophy, this insight needed to be brought to "ontological explication."[45]

Hence, with *The Visible and the Invisible*, Merleau-Ponty's focus shifts from the epistemological and cognitive dilemma of exploring the embodied character of mind and its relationship to the objects of perception to a more general consideration of ontology. Rejecting the binary epistemological alternatives of subject or object, he seeks to draw into question the very essence of the "being-object" and "being-subject" that traditionally had informed philosophy.[46] In doing so, he turns to an exploration of "experiences that have not yet been 'worked over,' that offer us all at once, pell-mell, both 'subject' and 'object,' both existence and essence, and hence give philosophy resources to redefine them."[47] In these respects, he aims to get to the core of brute or savage being – that is, being "behind or beneath the cleavages of our acquired culture"[48] and "before" the thinking subject of Cartesian inspiration. This endeavour required a rejection of philosophy's heretofore-accepted concepts and the adoption of a new terminology.

The terminology of "subject" and "object" limited philosophy's ability to express being as something that is not simply one or the other. To overcome this, Merleau-Ponty introduces his concept of the "flesh." In his words, "[t]he flesh is not matter, is not mind, is not substance."[49] To describe it as any of these terms would be to put it into opposition with some other category of being. To break up such closed categorizations, Merleau-Ponty proposes that we think of the flesh as an "'element,' in the sense it was used to speak of water, air, earth, and fire, in the sense of a *general thing*, midway between the spatio-temporal individual and the idea, a sort of incarnate principle that brings a style of being wherever there is a fragment of being."[50] In these respects, the flesh is intended as a non-identical ontological category. It is unnameable as a "substance," because naming it would subject it to the principle of identity and limit its being, potential becoming, and relationality. The flesh is neither a specific substance nor a compound of substances, but is present in all things that have "being." As flesh, the relationship between beings embodies simultaneously identity (they are made of the same "stuff") and non-identity (there is no superposition of one over the other, for these beings retain an *écart* – a distance, separation, or dehiscence). This disorients the traditional epistemological leitmotifs of a human subject or seer (for example, a cogito) coming to have knowledge of an external and differentiated object or a thing seen (for example, a piece of wax).[51] Rather, both of these entities are "flesh," and "the world is made of the same stuff as the body."[52] We will get a better understanding of this relationship if we interrogate it through the traditional language of "object" and "subject."

Beginning with the "object" as flesh, Merleau-Ponty rejects any notion of the object-in-itself. Rather, he aims to grasp how an object appears to a subject that is a being-in-the-world, negating the very in-itself of the object. The object is always there *for-us*. In his work on Gestalt psychology, Merleau-Ponty rejects any atomistic conceptions of objects, emphasizing perspective and totality in perception: the object always appears to us as "a figure on a background" and "is always in the middle of something else, it always forms part of a 'field.'"[53] In these terms, the object's appearance – colour, size, perspective, and so on – is structured through its relations with other objects contained in that field of vision. This understanding was epitomized in the works of Impressionist painters who – in rejecting the classical distinction between colour and outline – emphasized the extension and melding of colours and objects into one another. This blurred the atomized being of objects and conveyed the relational character of perception.[54] In the language of the flesh, Merleau-Ponty describes this relationality as a "dimension of variation" and an overlapping. In the context of the colour red, he notes that "this red is what it is only by connecting up from its place with other reds about it, with which it forms a constellation, or with other colours it dominates or that dominate it, that it attracts or that attract it, that it repels or that repel it."[55] This is an overlapping of flesh upon flesh that encompasses both identity and difference: while made of the same "stuff," these colours or fleshes maintain a certain *écart* in their layering or folding over onto one another. Indeed, they never become homogeneous; rather, each flesh is determined *through* its relations within a specific constellation. In these terms, the flesh is a living but malleable relation in which each visible is pregnant with the being of other visibles, and the categories of inside and outside (like subject and object) are sublated.[56]

If we turn to the "subject" as flesh, Merleau-Ponty views it as not opposed to, outside of, or substance-ly different than the object: my flesh – like the flesh of the world – is perceptible/visible. It is also visible/sensible to itself and to others.[57] In these terms, flesh is distinct from the traditional notion of consciousness, "which only thinks its object by assimilating it, by constituting it, by transforming it into thought."[58] By the nature of its being composed of the same stuff as the world, the flesh has no need to transform, translate, or reflect the "external" world: the flesh has an *inherence in-the-world,* being simultaneously *in* and *of* the world. But the body-as-flesh has the distinct quality of being able to draw the things of the world into communication and sensibility with itself. The body is capable of moving itself, and through the look, "it holds things in a circle around itself." Moreover, this look "radiates," "envelops," and "palpates" the visible world – that is, the body extends beyond itself, reaching into the world of which it is already a part. This extension is a result of the corporeal character of the flesh, and it "clothes" the world in its flesh. Essentially, as a visible flesh itself, the body "uses its own being as a means to participate in theirs [that is, the objects], because each of the two beings is an archetype for the other, because the body belongs to the order of the things as the world is universal flesh."[59] Again, this is a non-identical identity in which identity and difference co-mingle, relating to each other as similar in their being but never reducing the other to the self/same. In these terms, the flesh is an opening in (or up to) the world: the flesh extends beyond the confines of its own being, and enters into a communion with the seen, in much the same way as the objects in the field of vision do with one another in a constellation. Moreover, while our flesh radiates via the look, it never fully reaches the seen – for it never "becomes" it, nor can it totally grasp the seen which always contains parts that evade the look. This distance is what establishes the "other" as truly other – as more than the projection or continuation of the self.[60]

Yet, in dividing the flesh for explanatory purposes into the traditional categories of subject and object, we risk obscuring much of Merleau-Ponty's point: neither is merely "subject" or "object." As flesh applied to flesh, the subject-object relationship gives way to a situation in which "the seer and the visible reciprocate one another and we no longer know which sees and which is seen."[61] The relationship is not one between opposed beings/substances; rather, it is a relationship *within* being. In these respects, it is a de-centring of subjectivity. By describing the relationship of "seer" to "seen" as an intertwining or chiasm, Merleau-Ponty conveys that the "truth" of their being lies in neither one nor the other, but in their communion. Neither is a pure in- or for-itself; rather, they are beings with-and-through each other, and the object is "a being of which my vision is a part, a visibility older than my operations or acts,"[62] and vice versa. This defies the traditional "for-oneself"/ "for-the-other" distinction: "there is Being as containing all that" or a "co-functioning" relationship of reversibility.[63] The perceptible/visible world is itself formed across the relational intertwining in which seer is seen, and seen also sees. The look of my flesh and the look or façade of the flesh facing me palpate each other and allow for this mediated visibility to take place. In essence, things look at me looking at them in a relationship of mutual – though jarring – recognition.

At the level of a savage or pre-reflective ontology, there is no *a priori* opposition between these beings. Indeed, as a relationship of flesh to flesh, neither body nor world dominates or fully envelops the other; they neither coincide nor fuse. Rather, each participates in – and, in effect, extends and subtends – the being of the other. This participatory aspect is hedged in the terms of intertwining; Merleau-Ponty says that it is "as though [my look] were in a relation of pre-established harmony with [the visible things]."[64] This de-centring and sublation of the subject/object dichotomy occurs because the very notion of the flesh is not oppositional, as expressed in being as an *opening* in the world. This distinguishes the flesh from the "closed" cogito, which perceives the world from a position of interiority, as ideas within the mind. As an opening, the flesh is capable of corporeal relations with the "outside," relations characterized by the openness – the mutual palpation and penetration – of the flesh. In Merleau-Ponty's words, "there is a reciprocal insertion and intertwining of one in the other."[65] In a different language and with different results, Merleau-Ponty here reiterates his previous contention that "the relationship between human beings and things is no longer one of distance and mastery such as that which obtained between the sovereign mind and the piece of wax in Descartes's famous example."[66] The de-centred relationship of intertwined flesh dislocates and dissociates the traditional categories of subject/object, human/world, inside/ outside, with each taking on attributes of its binary "other."

What should equally be emphasized is that the flesh is not identical with itself. Because we experience and live the world from within as "beings who are embodied and limited," we are capable of seeing only from particular vantage points.[67] In *The Visible and the Invisible*, Merleau-Ponty finds that the relationship of reversibility dislocates identity to an even greater degree, for it also dislocates the identity of the body-subject as flesh. In the relationship of reversibility, my own being/identity is fragmented and partial because it is mediated through my relationship to the object in a constellation. But Merleau-Ponty also contends that the body-as-flesh is non-identical with itself. The full import of this idea emerges through the example of touch. The body is a sensible among sensibles. This characteristic constitutes what Merleau-Ponty calls the body's "double belongingness," or its concomitant existence at the level of object (a "thing amongst things") and subject (a thing that "detaches itself upon [things], and, accordingly, detaches itself from them"). Moreover, touch contains a paradox of immanence and transcendence: my hand "is felt from within," as a synesthetic aspect of my corporeal being and as something that is present as a sensible part of myself; but, simultaneously, like all my senses and the very nature of flesh-as-being, my hand is also "accessible from without" as my sentient being that palpates the world outside, and touches it while also being touched by it.[68] In essence, then, the body-as-flesh is always in the process of transcending itself, as an opening palpating the world, but always simultaneously felt as an immanent sensible.

As with perception, we find with touch that the relationship of reversibility blurs the identities of sentient and sensible. But Merleau-Ponty emphasizes "that it is a reversibility always imminent and never realized in fact." This emerges in the case of my left hand "touching my right hand touching the things."[69] In this situation, my right hand is simultaneously touching and touched (the touching-touched). But the ability to touch my right hand's touching of the things always evades my left hand: either my right hand becomes touched, in which case "its hold on the world is interrupted," or my right hand "retains its hold on the world, but then I do not really touch *it* – my right hand touching, I palpate with my left hand only its outer covering."[70] My hands never usurp each other: my left hand never touches the things touched by the right hand, nor does the left hand co-opt the touch of the right hand. But my left hand does transform the touching into the touched, in a relationship that can be reversed when the right hand lets go of the world and touches my left hand in turn. The point is that they "never reach coincidence; the coincidence eclipses at the moment of realization."[71] Perceiving or touching necessitates an *écart* that also separates my body – as a sentient-sensible – from itself, cutting it in two. In the case of one hand touching the other, rather than coinciding, there is an overlapping, and the hands alternate between touching and touched. Hence, while the two hands belong to the same body, their relationship illustrates that, as an opening, my body-as-flesh is not identical with itself: the unity of my body with itself is broken.

We might deem this an alienation, but it is an alienation that is an affirmative principle of the flesh. The flesh is always de-centred by virtue of its openness and its inherence in the world. In this vein, Merleau-Ponty does not see this imminent-but-unrealized character to be a failure, but the perennial condition of being. Indeed, because the body-as-flesh is not a pure interiority, but a being-in-the-world *open* to other beings-in-the-world, it is continually in the process of its own short-circuited becoming.[72] Consequently, the flesh is a hyperdialectics of being, envisaging "without restriction the plurality of the relationships and what has been called ambiguity."[73] The flesh, then, is a vertiginous conception of the subject, always contained in myriad constellations. As Merleau-Ponty states, "[t]he perceiving subject is not this absolute thinker; rather, it functions according to a natal pact between our body and the world, between ourselves and our body. Given a perpetually new natural and historical situation to control, the perceiving subject undergoes a continued birth; at each instant it is something new. Every incarnate subject is like an open notebook in which we do not yet know what will be written."[74] *Écart* plays into an openness that gives us access to the world and its/our indeterminate and vertiginous being.

But this de-centred and vertiginous existence is also contained in the relationship between beings. As with things, in the relation of self to others, we no longer know who sees and who is seen, who is subject and who is object; again, it as though "they were in a relation of pre-established harmony." Their being composed of the same "stuff" is the means to their intertwined communion: I can see and be seen by, touch and be touched by, speak to and hear, the other as flesh of my flesh, and vice versa, because we are sensible and open to one another. These relations and experiences are not possible in the "mute" and "solipsist" world of opposed and closed substances mired in their own particular being. The flesh as non-identical "claim[s] no monopoly of being and institutes no death struggle of consciousnesses."[75] Indeed, there is no *a priori* opposition that would necessitate my subsumption or conquering of others as objects for my own self-realization. The non-identity of the object-for-me opens it up to other perspectives, and I have no need of a monopoly on the objects of the world. The world is a non-identical depth open to multiple perspectives, and "the field open for other Narcissus, for an 'intercorporeity.'"[76] This absence of the death struggle is contained in the idea that the flesh's opening "is more dispossession than possession."[77] This once again emphasizes the relationship of non-identical identity: my flesh positively subtends, but never possesses or consumes, the being of others. As a whole, we belong to the same visible world: "as overlapping and fission, identity and difference, it brings to birth a ray of natural light that illuminates all flesh and not only my own."[78] But even when Merleau-Ponty states that "we function as one unique body," he is not operating in terms of a pure identity, for the body is never identical with itself, and this reversible relationship of self-to-self operates equally at the intercorporeal level. The other creates "within me an other than myself, a divergence (*écart*) by relation to … what I see, and thus designate it to me myself."[79] Far from being an autonomous entity, the flesh-as-being is split within itself, simultaneously impartial and formless in its very essence and pregnant with and formed by the others with which it coexists.

Reading the Flesh through and against Machiavelli and Marx

On an abstract level, Merleau-Ponty's ontology of the flesh runs parallel to Machiavelli's division of the social and the affirmative character that the maintenance of division brings to politics. But Machiavelli's conceptualization of the specific nature of the social relationship – particularly as mobilized by Claude Lefort – presents problems. Lefort describes Machiavelli's social division as "natural" because it is pre-political. Indeed, these beings are immediately opposed to one another and, as Lefort summarizes, "in [the grandees] the people encounter their *natural* adversary, the Other who constitutes them as the immediate object of its desires."[80] Moreover, he continues, "one class only exists by the lack that constitutes it opposite the other."[81] In this context, the relationship is presented as one of opposition. Derived from the opposed natural desires/dispositions of the respective beings, with their separate "lacks" constituting a wholeness, each being is the negation of the other. This is a conflict that cannot be transcended. Hence, the "solution" to their conflict lies in the prince. The prince – or, more generally, the "empty place" of power that he occupies – rises above the social division, giving the "image" of a higher unity that masks, but never supersedes, the division.[82]

In the first place, the ontology of the flesh moves beyond the relatively atemporal character of Machiavelli's ontology and its failure to acknowledge the "plurality of relationships" that the hyperdialectic of being posits. By asserting that the division of rich/poor or ruler/ruled (as embodied in the being of the grandees and the plebeians) is a "universal" and natural relationship – part of the "immutable" character of humans, and reproduced in the cyclical character of history[83] – Machiavelli appears to collapse the ontic experience of this division into a permanent feature of social ontology. In other words, he takes a specific incarnation of being as a universal and transhistorical fact. Throughout his work, Merleau-Ponty posits the transient nature of being and intersubjective relations. In this vein, he argues, "[h]istory is other people; it is the interrelationships we establish with them, outside of which the realm of the ideal appears as an alibi."[84] In the context of his existential rejection of an ultimate solution to the division, anxiety, and decision that characterize the social, Merleau-Ponty sees the potential for human community and mutual recognition through the creation of new modes of action. But, in rejecting reference to the ideal, he demands that we look at "the real relationships between people in our societies." In these respects, he finds that, "for the most part, these are master-slave relationships." But the existence of these relationships is no reason for their acceptance, and he calls for us to think outside of the trap of adopted customs to "prepare the ground for those rare and precious moments at which human beings come to recognize, to find, one another."[85] We should read Merleau-Ponty's return to ontology in this context.

With the specific project of *The Visible and the Invisible*, Merleau-Ponty attempts to give an account of a savage or wild being; such an ontology would be capable of moving "below" or "outside" contemporary social structures and conventions. In light of this, he suggests that Machiavelli fails to get to an unsullied analysis of being, but still operates at the level of a post-reflective philosophy tainted by preconceived social and cultural categories. The flesh is rooted in a phenomenological ontology that aims to grasp the *essence* of being, bracketing out what we "already know" or think we know about it to allow being to appear to us as it *is*, as being-*qua*-being. In this vein, Merleau-Ponty finds the essence of being contained in its openness to the world and others, in the flesh's interactive presence in which the other is always the subtending and extension of the self. This openness, in conjunction with its temporal foundations, means that the flesh is a fluid constellation, and militates against any notion of being and intra-being relations as absolute and fixed: the non-identity of the self with itself and with others opens it up to different relations and ways of being/becoming across time and space. In these respects, our being is informed by our interrelations with the world: it is constructed out of the complex but contingent interaction of various beings whose identities are determined through their interrelations.

For Machiavelli this sort of fluid interaction is ontologically absent and a political non-starter. He posits two atemporal beings or dispositions that constitute an essentially closed self/other difference as opposition, but fails to truly posit the self/other relation as a de-centring. His division of the social is purely one of opposition, whereby the being of the grandees is contained in its attempt to constitute the other as an object, and the being of the plebeians is contained in its desire merely not to be objectified. But in these respects, there is the assertion of subjectivity *by* the two beings *against* each other, but seemingly no intersubjectivity *between them.* "Interaction" is manifested through – and limited to – a play of forces, and the assertion of self versus other, in the "place of politics." But this is competition, not interaction. The being of each is irreconcilably opposed to the being of the other by definition; the only "solution" is a masking of this struggle, or its mediation through the prince or place of power, not through the intercorporeity of these classes. Here we have a case of mutual exclusion, whereby the Sartrean notion of subjectivity is embodied in "the political" as an open realm that facilitates the arbitrary alternation of subjects objectifying the other. The being or subjectivity of each is hence not reconcilable with/through the being of the other. At his most democratic, in *The Discourses*, Machiavelli argues that a mixed constitution – giving the core social factions a share in the constitution – is ideal. But this is still structured around the opposed social wills of those who want to oppress (the grandees) and those who want merely not to be oppressed (the plebeians). Here the opposition of irreconcilable wills is merely institutionalized as a system of checks or mediations on the power and disposition of the other.[86]

For Merleau-Ponty we are not two opposed entities constituting a whole or in need of a mediating sphere; rather, we are pregnant with others, as non-identical beings open to and de-centred by our relationship with them. This does not necessitate the superposition, consumption, or constitution of the other, but posits the constellative being of self and others. This constellative intersubjectivity rejects treatment of others as merely the negation of the self, as a "disjunction" in which self and other are irreconcilable modes of being and, consequently, "form a system of reciprocal exclusions." It also rejects any form of synthesis (imaginary or otherwise) of our modes of being-in-the-world. The ontology of the flesh suggests that I "[exist] between others and myself, between me and myself, like a hinge, the consequence and the guarantee of our belonging to a common world."[87] By acknowledging our belonging to a common world – our common belonging to the world of being – we recognize that the other "engages with the things in my world in a style that is at first mysterious to me but which at least seems to me a coherent style because it responds to certain possibilities which fringed the things of the world."[88] This implies an openness to other modes of being-in-the-world, and demands the attempt to form a "unity across incompossibles such as that of *my* world and the world of the other."[89] Hence, these other modes of being-in-the-world are not the negation or counterpoint of my own. Rather, they surprise, disorient, and disjoint my own being. Indeed, we are "enslaved" to one another not in the sense of a possessive hold that aims to oppress or master nor as an accident irrelevant to our own essential being. We live under the gaze of the other as part of our being, "born" of this communion and shaped by the presence of others.[90] This de-centring of being through the relationship of reversibility "presupposes a transformation of myself and of the other as well":[91] the other's mode of being comes to affect mine and be a part of my own existence, and vice versa. In these respects, Merleau-Ponty suggests that politics cannot be founded merely on the recognition of the "divided" character of the social or the non-identity of the social with itself, but on the interactive character and the constellation of being in which my world and the world of the other collide. For Merleau-Ponty, otherness is expressed in the direct relation between the different beings that comprise the social, and what must be assessed is the relationship that exists between them.

In contradistinction to Machiavelli's atemporal and hierarchical treatment of social relations, Marx grasps the historicity of being, and posits the political project of overcoming objectifying social relations. This is the core insight in *Capital*: it shows that the alleged "permanent" features of human/social nature "are really the attributes (and the masks) of a certain 'social structure,' capitalism, which is evolving towards its own destruction."[92] For Marx, being is always historical, and history is constituted by subjects' attempts to realize themselves through the process of externalization via labour, a process that also comes to shape their relationship to others and to nature. But two important contentions emerge from this. First, different modes of externalization embody forms of being-in-the-world and forms of giving meaning to the world. Second, this self-realizing act often takes place at the expense of excluding or coming into conflict with others over the use of the world of objects, ultimately turning others into objects as well.[93] By taking "the merely momentary for the eternal," political economy and scientism naturalized historically specific modes of domination.[94] Merleau-Ponty draws on Marxism in rejecting dualistic manifestations of social relations, in which "some men exercise their absolute right as subjects in which case the others submit to their will and are not recognized as subjects."[95] Hence, rather than viewing these divisions as an "end" to be accepted and affirmed, Marx posits the emergence of a subject, the proletariat, that is capable of transcending these boundaries and inaugurating truly human social relations among people. Thus, Marx attempts to institutionalize human community through the being of a subject whose own powerlessness in the structure of human relations can herald a regime "capable of suppressing exploitation and oppression."[96]

Yet, rooted in the mythical character of the proletariat as the intellectually deduced idea of experience no longer contained in experience itself,[97] Merleau-Ponty sees the negation of the negation to be enacted by the proletariat as a future positivism.[98] This is the result of a dualistic residue (or ambiguity) in Marx's work that emerged in hyperbolic fashion among latter-day Marxists. Consequently, the ontology of the flesh starts out from an entirely different position than the opposition (posited by Sartre, yet relevant to Lukács) between positivity and negativity, or being and nothingness. The Sartrean world is one that is "opaque and rigidified," haunted by the "open and uncompleted meanings" that characterize the absolute subjectivism of nothingness; Sartre overcomes this through the completed meanings that emerge through the pure action and absolute freedom of the Party-as-Cartesian-subject. The flesh, in dispensing with the language of being/nothingness, presents a world filled with density and movement.[99] As Merleau-Ponty states, "[o]ur point of departure shall not be *being is, nothingness is not* nor even *there is only being* – which are formulas of a totalizing thought, a high-altitude thought – but: there is being, there is a world, there is *something* ... there is cohesion, there is meaning."[100] This implies that the flesh attempts to sublate these oppositions. With respect to positivity and negativity, we find the flesh as something that is partial and incomplete, something that exists positively but is always continually remaking itself and its relations to/in the world. Merleau-Ponty's hyperdialectic rejects pure negation and pure realization as idealizations that ignore that "the only surpassings we know are concrete, partial, encumbered with survivals, saddled with deficits."[101] To say that the flesh exists positively is to say that it has an inherence in a world and a historical situation that subtends its absolute freedom or realization. But the flesh is still an openness to a field of meanings and directions that are never pre-ordained or complete, and it allows for a freedom and movement within this field, within the world as depth. In this sense, Merleau-Ponty argues that being cannot be closed in some absolute subject or in the absolute closure of historical meaning. In de-centring the being of the "subject" and "object," there can be no identity between the two: by stripping the subject and the object of their determinacy, the ontology of the flesh rejects the possibility of their identity. Consciousness (embodied or otherwise) cannot constitute the "object" as its own: the flesh's inherence in the world sublates the opposition between subject/object and being/world, producing in each characteristics of the other and eliminating the absolute freedom of the Cartesian subject.

Directly related to this is Merleau-Ponty's contention that we must "relativize the Marxist idea of a pre-history which is going to give way to history – of an imminence of the complete, true Society in which man is reconciled with man and nature."[102] The de-centred character of the flesh rejects the very idea that "there are beings who are living definitions, whose existence is fully included in their essence."[103] Neither a subject nor society is capable of sustaining or producing this identity: the relationship of reversibility implies not only that they always retain a dehiscence from one another and never become identical, but that this relationship exists between each and itself. Moreover, there cannot be a subject that is pure presence to itself because our being is fundamentally subtended and shaped by our relationships with others; a subject purported to have a completed essence is ultimately the elision of the other that is outside this essence. This elision ultimately destroys social relations themselves, positing in their stead the relationship of the self with itself – the illusory self-critical being of an identical subject-object. Sartre ostensibly posits several subjects (proletariat, militant, Party), but, for him, these subjects – like the proletariat and bourgeoisie – are ultimately for-itselfs whose perspectives conflict and are incapable of meshing. By reducing them to the identity of the Party, Sartre ultimately negates the complex sphere of the interworld. As the absolute assertion of the I and the objectification of all that is non-I, there is consequently no intersubjectivity: "There is no longer any ordered passage from one perspective to another, no completion of others in me and me in others ... the Other can thus be present to the I only as its pure negation."[104] In eliding the other, Sartre's ultrabolshevism ultimately destroys the dehiscence and difference that characterizes the constellative being of the social.

For Merleau-Ponty, we are always already social and intertwined with others.[105] The ontology of the flesh discloses to us the different perspectives and meanings that inhabit a world of depth, a world characterized by the openness of being rather than the closed and possessive battle of for-itselfs. If the flesh is "more dispossession than possession," then different perspectives, meanings, and identities need no longer be conceived of as irreconcilable and in need of coincidence; rather, the flesh facilitates "the meshing of two experiences which, without even coinciding, belong to a single world." Hence the political dilemma of the other is not about the negation of the self, but about constructing a human community open to multiple subjects, perspectives, and modes of being-in-the-world. In this vein the other is always more than a latent potential of my own being: always already instituted in social relations, the other comes to form a central aspect of my own essential being. In *Adventures of the Dialectic*, Merleau-Ponty asserts, in embryo, the hyperdialectic of being: "There is dialectic only in that type of being in which a junction of subjects occurs, being which is not only a spectacle that each subject presents to itself for its own benefit but which is rather their common residence, the place of their exchange and of their reciprocal interpretation."[106] In other words, my very identity is formed not in the interiority of my own being, but in that junction or meeting place (the interworld) of other subjects that my being-as-flesh opens onto, palpates, in which I am a hinge to my own and their being, and vice versa. Hence, meaning – which is continually open, as a constellation always in the process of formation, yet never realized – is created through our participation in the world, with and through others.[107] In these respects, Merleau-Ponty demands that we judge societies on the basis of the relations they attempt to create between genuine subjects, between the self and others, all of whom are capable of being-in-the-world in their own way.

Merleau-Ponty's Legacy of Ambiguity and His Ambiguous Legacy

Merleau-Ponty's premature death prevented him from potentially elaborating on the direct political import of the ontology of the flesh. Yet his ontology is loaded with implications that come to the fore if we read it in unison with his political engagements. Thus, although the insufficiencies of Machiavelli and Marx may have paved the road for Merleau-Ponty's "retreat" into philosophy, they also provide a means for drawing his ontology back into the political web. I have sought to recuperate a political core in Merleau-Ponty's work, but its specifically radical democratic import has been noticed only occasionally[108] – usually through the medium of his student and literary executor, Claude Lefort. Although I draw a distinction between the two regarding the reading of Machiavelli, Lefort grasps the very ambiguity that Merleau-Ponty sees as so politically important in Machiavelli's work.

In his political philosophy, Lefort draws a distinction between politics (a realm of competitive division and indeterminacy: the originary division of the social) and the political (conceived of as a regime, or the realm of "law," where politics represents its symbolic image of itself).[109] For Lefort, what separates democracy from totalitarianism is the manner in which each objectifies itself. Through the mechanisms of violence and repression, totalitarianism seeks to abolish the conflictual sphere of politics and to represent society via the political as a whole that is identical to itself. Drawing on Merleau-Ponty's savage ontology, Lefort argues that democracy acknowledges social division and refuses to efface the gap/*écart* between politics and the political. This relationship, with its sustained gap, is a transposition of what occurs in Merleau-Ponty's ontology of the flesh when the left hand touches the right hand. That democratic society is incapable of realizing itself – or exhausting its symbolic image – is what leaves its very being open to the alterity of the self with itself: democracy recognizes the reversibility that is "always imminent and never realized in fact," and aims to preserve the *écart* that differentiates being from objectification so that "the coincidence eclipses at the moment of realization."[110] In political terms, we find democratic contestation is symptomatic of the very being of politics as always caught up in a process of becoming – a becoming, a difference, and a division that totalitarianism aims to deny. Thus the political milieu that emerges via Machiavelli in Merleau-Ponty's ontology is one in which society's separation from itself opens up ambiguity as the constant need to test society against its own symbolic representation.[111]

Less noted is the influence that Merleau-Ponty's work has had on Miguel Abensour. Although this often emerges through the medium of Lefort, Abensour offers his own specific inflection on Merleau-Ponty. In mobilizing the concept of savage being, Abensour cites Lefort's description of Merleau-Ponty's "flesh of the social": "*raw being* ... vertical being, not the 'flattened' being offered to the dreams of a sovereign consciousness, it is the *savage spirit*, the spirit that makes its own law ... because submitted to being, it ever awakens at the contact of the event to contest the legitimacy of established knowledge."[112] The savage spirit is at the base of the work of both Lefort and Abensour, but Abensour takes it in a more anarchistically inclined direction to correct what he sees as an ambiguity in Lefort's savage democracy. Although the state (as a fixed ordering) appears to be in an irreconcilable tension with democracy (as a regime of indeterminacy), savage democracy confirms only the *possibility*, not the *necessity*, of democracy's being an insurgent action *against* the state. As Abensour states, "[i]sn't the 'savage' exposed to being confined and thus reduced to a mode of being, a mode of expression, to an epochal style characterized above all by a crisis of foundations, without drawing all the consequences from this crisis?"[113] To push this savage ontology to its logical conclusion, Abensour argues that democracy – as the expression of the indeterminate character of the demos – exists only *against* the state (conceived of as the alienation of the demos's power: its separation from the originary subject that institutes it). Hence the "savage" character of democracy lies less in a mode of being, than in the form of a rupture or break that attempts to delimit modes of being. It is for these reasons that Abensour introduces the name "insurgent democracy": "the term clearly signifies that the advent of democracy is the opening of an agonistic scene which has the State as a 'natural' and favoured target; or else that democracy is the play of a 'permanent insurrection' against the State, against the unifying, integrating, organizing State-form."[114]

Abensour also turns to Merleau-Ponty to introduce an innovative concept of institution to combat a central criticism directed at his work: if politics is defined by its anarchic and disruptive indeterminacy, it ignores or minimizes the problem of institution, for anarchy would be only a disturbance devoid of sustainability.[115] Redefining institution, Merleau-Ponty describes it as "those events in an experience which endow the experience with durable dimensions, in relation to which a whole series of other experiences will make sense, will form a thinkable sequel or a history – or again the events which deposit a sense in me, not just something surviving or as a residue, but as the call to follow, the demand of a future."[116] Here, institution refers to the sedimentation of experience into a coherent field of meaning that embodies the conditions of possibility for praxis. This sedimentation brings into being not a reification, but the means of transforming and giving new expression to the experiences that institution draws together: as the instituting-instituted (as the flesh of its flesh), it is an opening that creates the conditions of possibility for its own transformation. Borrowing this conception, Abensour refuses to equate institution with laws or the "governing machine," instead positing it as an experiential and practical *matrix*, possessed by an "imaginative dimension, one of anticipation, which in itself has the potential to engender customs, or rather attitudes and behaviours, consistent with the emancipation it announces."[117] In these respects, it is the bringing forth of a way of existence that does not determine or limit action, but facilitates and opens it as possibility. Although democracy's insurgent moment aims to avoid the political taking on a permanent and alien form, the reconceptualization of institution allows Abensour to treat insurgence as more than the singular moment of its coming: it is the opening and openness to insurgency as persistent moments of creation and the new.[118]

The rather open, and ambiguous, character of Merleau-Ponty's thought shows through in both the political reading I have given and in the different inflections on democratic thought supplied by Lefort and Abensour. In fact, rooted in the Machiavellian and Marxian poles, Merleau-Ponty's work betrays two divergent impulses: on the one hand, towards the affirmation of struggle and division in politics (Machiavelli); on the other, towards a commitment to an emancipatory and egalitarian politics of alterity (Marx). Although these impulses might be somewhat unresolved in Merleau-Ponty's work, far from having retreated into the realm of abstract ontology, the very existence of this tension is indicative of the political orientation of his ontology and of his place within the democratic return to political philosophy in post-war France.

NOTES

1 Louis Althusser, *The Future Lasts Forever: A Memoir*, trans. Richard Veasey (New York: New Press, 1998), 178.

2 Diana Coole summarizes this, and a number of other faulty trends, in *Merleau-Ponty and Modern Politics after Humanism* (Lanham, MD: Rowman

& Littlefield, 2007), 1–17. Coole's work supplies a political reading of Merleau-Ponty, but from a different perspective than I focus on here.

3 Even Coole states that *Humanism and Terror* and *Adventures of the Dialectic* "are not among his best [books]." See Diana Coole, "Philosophy as Political Engagement: Revisiting Merleau-Ponty and Reopening the Communist Question," *Contemporary Political Theory* 2, no. 3 (2003): 332.

4 This tendency is pointed out by Martin Jay, *Downcast Eyes: The Denigration of Vision in Twentieth-Century French Thought* (Berkeley: University of California Press, 1993), 299–300; and Coole, *Merleau-Ponty and Modern Politics*, 1–17. It appears to be rooted in Jean-Paul Sartre's recounting of his relationship with Merleau-Ponty. Yet, in letters exchanged between the two, Merleau-Ponty explicitly rejects the idea that there is a break or change in his thinking or a retreat from politics. See Jon Stewart, "Philosophy and Political Engagement: Letters from the Quarrel between Sartre and Merleau-Ponty," and Sartre, "Merleau-Ponty Vivant," both in *The Debate between Sartre and Merleau-Ponty*, ed. Jon Stewart (Evanston, IL: Northwestern University Press, 1998).

5 By way of example, it is notable that the pre-eminent English-language book on Merleau-Ponty's philosophy – M.C. Dillon, *Merleau-Ponty's Ontology* (Evanston, IL: Northwestern University Press, 1992) – contains no references to Merleau-Ponty's relationship to Marxism or to his political writings. A more recent monograph – Lawrence Hass, *Merleau-Ponty's Philosophy* (Bloomington: Indiana University Press, 2008) – aims to connect Merleau-Ponty's philosophical work to contemporary post-structuralist thought, but neglects Merleau-Ponty's own political writings. Moreover, as Diana Coole points out, only two of the thirteen essays in *The Cambridge Companion to Merleau-Ponty*, ed. Taylor Carman and Mark Hansen (Cambridge: Cambridge University Press, 2005), deal with Merleau-Ponty's politics.

6 This approach is front and centre in Barry Cooper, *Merleau-Ponty and Marxism: From Terror to Reform* (Toronto: University of Toronto Press, 1979); Martin Jay, *Marxism and Totality: The Adventures of a Concept from Lukács to Habermas* (Berkeley: University of California Press, 1984), chap. 12; Sonia Kruks, *The Political Philosophy of Merleau-Ponty* (Atlantic Highlands, NJ: Humanities Press, 1981); and Mark Poster, *Existential Marxism in Postwar France: From Sartre to Althusser* (Princeton, NJ: Princeton University Press, 1975), 151.

7 See, in particular, Cooper, *Merleau-Ponty and Marxism*; and Kruks, *Political Philosophy of Merleau-Ponty*. In a more recent essay, Martin Plot follows this trend in reducing Merleau-Ponty's work to a variant of parliamentary

democracy; see "Our Element: Flesh and Democracy in Merleau-Ponty," *Continental Philosophy Review* 45, no. 2 (2012): 235–59.

8 Kruks, *Political Philosophy of Merleau-Ponty*, chap. 7.

9 Coole, *Merleau-Ponty and Modern Politics*; idem, "Philosophy as Political Engagement"; and Bernard Flynn, "The Development of the Political Philosophy of Merleau-Ponty: Humanism and the Rejection of Terror," *Continental Philosophy Review* 40, no. 2 (2007): 135. Coole sees a more direct and continuing link to Marx than does Flynn.

10 Flynn, "Development of the Political Philosophy of Merleau-Ponty," 135.

11 More adequate readings of Merleau-Ponty's philosophy and politics are rendered by John O'Neill, *Perception, Expression, and History: The Social Phenomenology of Maurice Merleau-Ponty* (Evanston, IL: Northwestern University Press 1970); and James Schmidt, *Maurice Merleau-Ponty: Between Phenomenology and Structuralism* (New York: St. Martin's Press, 1985). That said, both neglect Merleau-Ponty's relationship to the radical democratic tradition.

12 Maurice Merleau-Ponty, *Humanism and Terror: An Essay on the Communist Problem*, trans. John O'Neill (Boston: Beacon Press, 1969), 187.

13 Ibid., 188.

14 Maurice Merleau-Ponty, "A Note on Machiavelli," in Maurice Merleau-Ponty, *Signs*, trans. Richard McCleary (Evanston, IL: Northwestern University Press, 1964), 211.

15 Ibid., 212.

16 Ibid., 212–15.

17 Ibid., 214.

18 Ibid., 217.

19 Merleau-Ponty, *Humanism and Terror*, xiii–xv.

20 Jean-Paul Sartre, *Being and Nothingness: An Essay on Phenomenological Ontology*, trans. Hazel Barnes (New York: Washington Square Press, 1966), part 3. For explications of this divide between Sartre and Merleau-Ponty, see Hass, *Merleau-Ponty's Philosophy*, 104–6; Jay, *Downcast Eyes*, 306–11; and Jack Reynolds, *Merleau-Ponty and Derrida: Intertwining Embodiment and Alterity* (Athens: Ohio University Press, 2004), chap. 5.

21 Merleau-Ponty, "Note on Machiavelli," 221.

22 Niccolò Machiavelli, *The Prince*, trans. Peter Bondanella (Oxford: Oxford University Press, 1984), chap. 9.

23 Merleau-Ponty, "Note on Machiavelli," 221.

24 Ibid., 221–2.

25 Merleau-Ponty, *Humanism and Terror*, 113–17.

26 Ibid., 116–17.

27 Ibid., 129–31.
28 Merleau-Ponty, *Adventures of the Dialectic*, trans. Joseph Bien (Evanston, IL: Northwestern University Press, 1973), 137.
29 Merleau-Ponty, *Humanism and Terror*, 177.
30 Merleau-Ponty, *Adventures of the Dialectic*, 204.
31 Ibid., 54, 64. See also Coole, *Merleau-Ponty and Modern Politics*, 82; and Jay, *Marxism and Totality*, 373.
32 Merleau-Ponty, *Adventures of the Dialectic*, 41.
33 Maurice Merleau-Ponty, "Materials for a Theory of History," in *In Praise of Philosophy and Other Essays*, trans. John Wild and James Edie (Evanston, IL: Northwestern University Press, 1963), 104.
34 Merleau-Ponty, *Adventures of the Dialectic*, 89.
35 Merleau-Ponty, "Materials for a Theory of History," 106.
36 Ibid., 106.
37 On these themes, see James Miller, *History and Human Existence: From Marx to Merleau-Ponty* (Berkeley: University of California Press, 1979), 220–1.
38 Merleau-Ponty, *Adventures of the Dialectic*, 168–71.
39 Ibid., 164.
40 Ibid., 135–7.
41 Ibid.
42 Maurice Merleau-Ponty, *Phenomenology of Perception*, trans. Colin Smith (New York: Routledge, 2002), 235–9; idem, "An Unpublished Text by Maurice Merleau-Ponty: A Prospectus of His Work," in Maurice Merleau-Ponty, *The Primacy of Perception and Other Essays on Phenomenological Psychology, the Philosophy of Art, History and Politics*, trans. Arleen Dallery (Evanston, IL: Northwestern University Press, 1964), 3–5, emphasis in original.
43 Maurice Merleau-Ponty, "Working Notes," in *The Visible and the Invisible*, ed. Claude Lefort, trans. Alphonso Lingus (Evanston, IL: Northwestern University Press, 1968), 200. As Martin Dillon argues throughout *Merleau-Ponty's Ontology*, this comment does not signal a break with his earlier writings on the body; rather, we should view it as a development and deepening – if not an immanent self-critique – of ideas present, in embryo, in these earlier writings.
44 Maurice Merleau-Ponty, "Institution in Personal and Public History," in *In Praise of Philosophy* (Evanston, IL: Northwestern University Press, 1963), 107.
45 Merleau-Ponty, "Working Notes," 165–7, 183.
46 Maurice Merleau-Ponty, *The Visible and the Invisible*, ed. Claude Lefort, trans. Alphonso Lingus (Evanston, IL: Northwestern University Press, 1968), 22–3.

47 Ibid., 130.
48 Ibid., 121.
49 Ibid., 139.
50 Ibid.
51 Ibid., 139–41.
52 Maurice Merleau-Ponty, "Eye and Mind," in Merleau-Ponty, *Primacy of Perception*, 163.
53 Merleau-Ponty, *Phenomenology of Perception*, 4; see also idem, "Working Notes," 206.
54 Maurice Merleau-Ponty, *The World of Perception*, trans. Oliver Davis (New York: Routledge, 2004), 37–43.
55 Merleau-Ponty, *Visible and the Invisible*, 132.
56 Ibid., 132–3.
57 Merleau-Ponty, "Eye and Mind," 162.
58 Ibid., 162–3.
59 Merleau-Ponty, *Visible and the Invisible*, 137.
60 Ibid., 134–8; Merleau-Ponty, "Eye and Mind," 162–3.
61 Merleau-Ponty, *Visible and the Invisible*, 139.
62 Ibid., 123.
63 Merleau-Ponty, "Working Notes," 214–15.
64 Merleau-Ponty, *Visible and the Invisible*, 133.
65 Ibid., 138.
66 Merleau-Ponty, *World of Perception*, 51.
67 Ibid., 54.
68 Merleau-Ponty, *Visible and the Invisible*, 133–8.
69 Ibid., 147.
70 Ibid., 148.
71 Ibid., 147.
72 Ibid., 133–4, 147–8.
73 Ibid., 93–5.
74 Merleau-Ponty, "Unpublished Text," 6.
75 Maurice Merleau-Ponty, "The Philosopher and His Shadow," in Merleau-Ponty, *Signs*, 170.
76 Merleau-Ponty, *Visible and the Invisible*, 141.
77 Merleau-Ponty, "Philosopher and His Shadow," 170.
78 Merleau-Ponty, *Visible and Invisible*, 142.
79 Merleau-Ponty, "Working Notes," 224.
80 Claude Lefort, *Machiavelli in the Making*, trans. Michael Smith (Evanston, IL: Northwestern University Press, 2012), 141.
81 Ibid., 140.

82 Bernard Flynn, *The Philosophy of Claude Lefort: Interpreting the Political* (Evanston, IL: Northwestern University Press, 2005), 5–23.
83 Merleau-Ponty, "Note on Machiavelli," 221.
84 Maurice Merleau-Ponty, "The Primacy of Perception and Its Philosophical Consequences," trans. James M. Edie, in Merleau-Ponty, *Primacy of Perception*, 25.
85 Merleau-Ponty, *World of Perception*, 66–8.
86 Niccolò Machiavelli, *Discourses on Livy*, trans. Harvey Mansfield and Nathan Tarcov (Chicago: University of Chicago Press, 1996), book I, chaps. 2–5, 46.
87 Merleau-Ponty, "Institution in Personal and Public History," 108.
88 Maurice Merleau-Ponty, *The Prose of the World*, ed. Claude Lefort, trans. John O'Neill (Evanston, IL: Northwestern University Press, 1973), 142–3.
89 Merleau-Ponty, "Working Notes," 214.
90 Maurice Merleau-Ponty, "Reading Montaigne," in Merleau-Ponty, *Signs*, 207.
91 Merleau-Ponty, *Prose of the World*, 142–3. This point is also made by Diana Coole in *Merleau-Ponty and Modern Politics*, 246–7.
92 Maurice Merleau-Ponty, "Marxism and Philosophy," in *Sense and Nonsense*, trans. Hubert and Patricia Dreyfus (Evanston, IL: Northwestern University Press, 1964), 126.
93 Merleau-Ponty, *Humanism and Terror*, 101–2.
94 Merleau-Ponty, "Marxism and Philosophy," 126.
95 Merleau-Ponty, *Humanism and Terror*, 110–11.
96 Merleau-Ponty, "Note on Machiavelli," 222.
97 Dick Howard, *The Marxian Legacy* (London: Macmillan, 1977), 216.
98 Maurice Merleau-Ponty, "Philosophy and Non-Philosophy since Hegel," *Telos* 29 (September 1976), 95, 105.
99 Ibid., 143–4.
100 Merleau-Ponty, *Visible and the Invisible*, 88.
101 Ibid., 95.
102 Maurice Merleau-Ponty, "Everywhere and Nowhere," in Merleau-Ponty, *Signs*, 131.
103 Merleau-Ponty, *Adventures of the Dialectic*, 168.
104 Ibid., 204–5.
105 David Michael Levin, "Justice in the Flesh," in *Ontology and Alterity in Merleau-Ponty*, ed. Galen Johnson and Michael Smith (Evanston, IL: Northwestern University Press, 1990), 36–40.
106 Merleau-Ponty, *Adventures of the Dialectic*, 204.
107 Ibid., 199–205.

108 It is worth noting that the radical anti-essentialism at the root of Merleau-Ponty's work is mentioned, but not explored, by Ernesto Laclau and Chantal Mouffe, *Hegemony and Socialist Strategy: Towards a Radical Democratic Politics* (London: Verso, 1987), 146.

109 See, in particular, Claude Lefort, "The Question of Democracy" and idem, "The Permanence of the Theologico-Political?" in *Democracy and Political Theory*, trans. David Macey, (Cambridge, UK: Polity Press 1985).

110 Merleau-Ponty, *Visible and the Invisible*, 147.

111 It should be noted that Lacan's work played a formative role for both Merleau-Ponty and Lefort.

112 Abensour, *Democracy Against the State*, 109–10.

113 Ibid., xxxii.

114 Ibid., xxxiii–xxxiv.

115 Ibid., xxv.

116 Maurice Merleau-Ponty, *Institution and Passivity: Course Lectures from the Collège de France (1954–1955)*, (Evanston, IL: Northwestern University Press, 2010), 77.

117 Abensour, *Democracy Against the State*, xxvii.

118 Ibid, xxviii.

3 The Counter-Hobbes of Pierre Clastres

MIGUEL ABENSOUR[1]

Translated by Martin Breaugh and Devin Penner

The preliminary question to which we will try to respond is this: can we interpret the work of Pierre Clastres from the point of view of political philosophy without doing it violence? Interpreters are free to choose their approach, one would think. The question is then more precise: to what extent does the work of Clastres – in what it says, in its aims, in what it invites and allows us to do – question the point of view of political philosophy.

In our time, we certainly encounter ethnologist-philosophers; confronted both in terms of their own position and practice with the problem of knowledge of the other, the ethnologist is necessarily engaged in a relationship with philosophy. But, in the case of Clastres, the relationship to philosophy goes beyond the specific requirements of contemporary ethnology. Influenced by an early study in religious anthropology, by the study of ritual and religious life, Clastres makes us meditate on the metaphysical and religious universe of the Guarani Indians in *Le grand parler* (The Great Speech).

Furthermore, and this is perhaps the originality of Clastres in this ethnological-philosophical rapport, his philosophy has a particularly strong relationship to – is pregnant with – the tradition of political philosophy. This is not because he speaks from inside this tradition, but rather from a place that beckons to it. It remains to measure the effects. Clastres undertakes works of political anthropology: the subtitle of *Society Against the State* is *Essays in Political Anthropology*. Taking seriously primitive societies, in particular their political existence, he is dedicated to revealing the philosophy of Indian leadership starting from his first text, "Exchange and Power" (1962): "far from giving us the lacklustre image of an inability to resolve the question of political power, these societies astonish us by the subtlety with which they have posed and settled the question. They had a very early premonition that power's transcendence conceals a mortal risk for the group, that the principle of an authority which is external and the creator of its own legality is a challenge to culture itself. It is the intuition of this threat that determined the depth of their political philosophy."[2] What he means is that we do not know how to read primitive societies, that they have a depth that is not rivalled by our tradition.

An initial response might already be provided to our question: an essay on Clastres' work from the point of view of political philosophy is legitimate, at a basic level, to the extent that his work is the site of a permanent confrontation between political philosophy and political anthropology. Indeed, political anthropology, in the narrow sense, is the part of social anthropology that provides space for reflection on the question of political power in societies without the state; in this case, the case of Clastres, it is a properly scientific research oriented to the question of leadership and power in the primitive societies of South America, and that aims to develop a general theory of political power in primitive societies – that is to say, societies without the state.

To develop a discourse on power in societies without the state, political anthropology cannot ignore the discourse of political philosophy, the discourse on the "living together" of men, on political matters, on the place of power in societies with the state. It can even less ignore the sense in which anthropology cannot further develop, cannot conquer its independence, by separating itself from philosophy – by avoiding philosophy, anthropology merely ends up being its unconscious reproduction. It is still necessary to separate properly the contours and premises of each. Thus, at this first level, the anthropologist, like the political philosopher, establishes a common relationship, with the only difference being that the relationship unfolds, in both cases, in reverse order.

First, for political philosophy, it is not possible to think about societies *with* the state, civil society, without turning to societies *without* the state, in a pre-civil state. As Eric Weil writes, "[i]t is only to impose its own problem that [political philosophy] is interested in 'primitive' groups, in which there no doubt exists a power, but where that power is not reflected."[3]

Second, for classical political anthropology, it is not possible to think about societies *without* the state without first turning to societies *with* the state; or, to be more precise, one can think of societies without the state only from the point of view of societies with the state. It is this movement that is at work in the classification principles of Jean William Lapierre's *Le fondement du pouvoir politique* (The Foundation of Political Power, 1968). Departing from the work of Meyer Fortes and Edward Evans-Pritchard, Lapierre proposes a continuum of five types of pre-state societies, ranging from archaic societies in which power is most developed to those that have what Lucy Mair calls "minimal government," where there is almost no political power.

In contrast to the classical political anthropology that he radically contests, Clastres at the same time maintains and upsets the relationship between societies with and without the state. He maintains the relationship: "Inevitably, discussing societies without the state involves naming the others, i.e. the societies with the state."[4] But, as is already indicated by the order of this passage, he simultaneously upsets the relationship; he upsets the sense, the very direction of the relationship, the orientation of the gaze. No more does the movement go from societies with the state to societies without the state, but instead from societies without the state to societies with the state. In short, Clastres invites us to change our perspective. Several movements can be distinguished.

Clastres begins by subverting the very term "society without the state" and, in fact, as we have seen, he refuses all models of lack, of incompleteness or of embryos. After the work of Clastres, "society without the state" no longer means a society of lack, an aborted state, or an infant form of the state, but a *society against the state*, a fully adult state that constitutes itself positively, that acquires its sociological identity in and by its refusal of the state.

After this substitution is made and the concept of a society against the state is recognized, a further distinction is necessary: society against the state does not mean society without politics or the refusal of political society, but only the refusal of a certain well-defined, regional configuration of politics. It is important to recall that politics and the state cannot be confused – suggesting the universality of politics is not tantamount to suggesting the universality and eternality of the state – or, better yet, a society against the state can take form and derive meaning from the invention of a new political relation.

Furthermore, it requires the ethnologist to disturb our habits of thought in describing the political sphere that takes shape in the struggle against the appearance of a separate political power, the state. Indeed, we are forced to question a certain critique of the state, soon degraded in a mystifying refrain, which had taught us that, if there is a state, there always was a state, so there will always be a state. Clastres asks us to reject not only the eternity of the state – according to him, the example of primitive societies sufficiently proves that the state is not eternal – but also to break with a quietist Marxist dogmatism, which Adorno already had denounced in *Negative Dialectics* under the question: contingency of the antagonism? "Economics is said to come before dominion, which must not be deduced otherwise than economically ... The primacy of economics is to yield historically stringent reasons why the happy end is immanent in history."[5]

To accommodate the new thinking of Clastres, multiple questions emerge: what is the configuration of the political universe oriented against the state? What are the devices of primitive society that allowed it to ward off the state? With these devices discovered and interpreted, how do we think anew the question of the birth of the state? "No doubt only a close examining of the functioning of primitive societies will be able to shed light on the problem of origins."[6] And what becomes of the familiar thesis of the withering of the state, a question all the more formidable in that it is no longer possible, after studying societies against the state, to maintain the illusion of a spontaneous sociality that reduces politics to economics. "The political can be conceived apart from violence; the social cannot be conceived without the political. In other words, there are no societies without power."[7]

It is not true, then, that there was nothing to see there. Now the ethnologist can no longer hide, but is faced with the enigma of a leader without power, of a non-coercive political authority. The task for the ethnologist is to understand, to reconstruct the singular logic and operation of societies against the state. It is not about leaving a memory – is it possible to remember that which is situated on the side of "accidental"? – but about rethinking the space of privileged intelligibility that is the space of politics; it is about complicating the horizon of our thought, of adding a dimension to it. It is about moving beyond the visible boundary of the statist horizon via another horizon – an ancient horizon: the horizon of primitive societies whose anti-statist logic unfolds in multiple different ways.

A new problem has eroded the framework of existing dogmatisms. This is the Copernican revolution of Pierre Clastres, the heliocentric conversion to which he invites us: it is now possible to rotate the societies with a state around societies against the state, to ruin their centripetal narcissism, to decentre them and confront them with a logic that is heterogeneous to them – that of the multiple choice that in the same movement reveals and accuses the "fury of the One." "Judge that which comes after by that which came before," writes Clastres, not flatly, as if history should sew up the before and after even though there is a gap between them, not to feed a nostalgia of the before (the savage politics Clastres describes remain far from the *topos* of the Golden Age), but to put into perspective the two forms of the political institution of the asymmetrical, discontinuous social, and that then become paradigmatic references.

This is not the place to try to measure the effects of such a significant change of perspective, work that is always to be redone, and all the less since we know that the transformation of the order of terms implies a change in the meaning of each of them. We must remember only this: there is another sensibility to political history if we assume that there was not one, but multiple births of the state – that conventional statist histories are haunted by an unwritten history of demolition, of the ruin of anti-statist systems. This idea leads to two propositions: the universality of political power, and the merely regional character of the Western conception of power. The new questions to consider are numerous: what happens when the political is rethought in the light of the primitive *politéia*? What happens when politics is thought about at a distance from coercion? How should we think differently, according to new intellectual gestures, about the question of the origin of the state? Reformulating the "true question of politics," why are primitive societies without a state?

We are now ready to clarify the relationship of Clastres' work, his new political anthropology, to political philosophy. This relationship appears to be twofold.

First of all, there is a relationship of opposition to the fundamental proposition that, according to Clastres, constitutes political philosophy – namely, the proposition that a division between masters and subjects is a constitutive dimension of society, an ontological structure of the social belonging to the very being of all human societies.[8] It follows, according to this conception, that it is an epistemological impossibility to pose the question of the origin of political domination, since, under this logic, domination – the division between the dominant and the dominated – is consubstantial with the very essence of the society. In addition, there is an absolute blindness, a non-acknowledgment of the social forms of society where this division does not appear.

But, second, the relationship between Clastres and political philosophy cannot be reduced to this one relation of opposition. Indeed, Clastres maintains a relationship of *affinity* to the countercurrents of thought that, although at the heart of a tradition that is less homogeneous than it appears, dared to think of the division between masters and subjects as problematic and that anticipated, from a logical point of view, the Copernican revolution that resulted from the discovery of primitive politics: Montaigne, La Boétie, Rousseau.[9]

Actually, there are three possible passageways between the new political anthropology and political philosophy.

First is a positive relationship to the countertendencies that have been able to practically recognize otherness, rather than merely find incomprehensibility. This relationship is all the more justified because each of the three cases selected – Montaigne, La Boétie, Rousseau – developed their political thought from reflecting on the primitive world as depicted in the ethnographic literature of their time. Again, it should be said that this relationship is not merely about clarifying the tradition that inspired Clastres. Indeed, it may be seen in another sense: it shows that ethnological experience makes possible a different reading of the works that belong to this tradition. Consider, for example, Clastres' reading of La Boétie: "Freedom, Misfortune, the Unnameable."[10]

Second is a complex and ambivalent relationship to the authors who Clastres salutes for their passionate interest in the "dark and mysterious" question of power. Clastres nevertheless distances himself from these thinkers because so much of their thought appears to rest on a non-reflective identification of politics with violence and coercion. In this regard, Clastres' confessed relationship to Nietzsche, thinker of discontinuity and "misfortune," and more precisely to the *Genealogy of Morals*, remains to be explained.

Finally, there is a relationship of overt opposition to the thinkers who assume or even claim that power is equivalent to violence, and therefore affirm the upmost need for the state as a separate power, as a figure of the One external to society. With this in mind, I have chosen in this chapter to focus on the relation to Thomas Hobbes. Why privilege a relation of opposition? Because, in a sense, the relation of opposition is the most inventive one; if the relation of affinity allows a better appreciation of where Clastres is situated in the tradition of political philosophy, the relation of opposition appears to present more theoretical interest because it is the place where we are best able to see how the ethnological experience has shaken the tradition of political philosophy, and to locate the presuppositions that it attacks and that it aims to ruin.

In what way does the ethnological detour make possible a new approach to politics? Or, more modestly, in what way does it prepare the initial foundation for a new approach, more in the form of interrogation than of dogmatic theses? Ethnology is perhaps "the unique bridge between Western civilization and primitive civilizations."[11] Yet we cannot confuse that which occurs on each of the two sides, or mechanically transpose an idea from one side to the other, or imagine a place from where we can look down on both sides. Ethnology is irrevocably a science after the division of Western and primitive civilizations. If, thanks to the ethnological detour, we can begin working on the emerging questions of the primitive world, we must acknowledge that we can pose these questions only because we are after the "misfortune" and can address them only from this place. In his "Savage Ethnology," Clastres seems to define more precisely the place of our query: "The question of power in this kind of society, posed properly, breaks with the academicism of simple description … and points familiarly to men of our society: the dividing line between archaic societies and 'western' societies is perhaps less a matter of technical development than of the transformation of political authority. Here, as well, is an area that would be essential for the sciences of man to learn to inhabit, if only to better occupy its own place in Western thought."[12]

But Clastres immediately warns against the illusion of a knowledge, of a mastery, that claims to occupy both sides. Knowing how to sojourn into the primitive world means challenging "the ruse of a knowledge that is to become absolutely abolished in silence." This is a place where people cannot live as masters. This is why anyone who drifts between the two sides is doomed to be a second-rate philosopher.

The Counter-Hobbes of Clastres and Its Challenges

For demanding thought like that of Clastres, there is in some sense an internal need to encounter Hobbes, at some point in his journey to tackle Hobbes's political science – his "wolfish science" – and to make this meeting a cross-examination of Clastres' own theses on primitive politics. What emerges from this confrontation is a true "counter-Hobbes." Two main texts bring to light the challenges that Hobbes represents to Clastres: "Savage Ethnography" (1969), and "Archeology of Violence: War in Primitive Societies" (1977).[13]

In his 1962 text, "Échange et pouvoir: philosophie de la chefferie indienne" (Exchange and Power: The Philosophy of Indian Leadership), Clastres begins to address the question of the disjunction of power and leadership in primitive society. Then, in 1969, Clastres encounters Hobbes for the first time in a discussion of the importance of the empirical phenomenon of war in the Yanoama Indian tribe; in 1977 he encounters Hobbes a second time in introducing the issue of war to his problematic in an attempt to rehabilitate war. On this issue, Clastres does not give in to the fascination of war or show any complacency for warrior values. It is indeed a rehabilitation of war: Clastres, in fact, is convinced that we cannot think about primitive society without thinking about war at the same time. Further, war is not to be considered a secondary phenomenon at the margins of primitive society, but a massive event inscribed at the very heart of such society, as a crucial part of its refusal of the state. The new political anthropology defines itself as one where the prevalence of war is finally recognized. Clastres' fundamental 1977 text seeks to end the silence of ethnological literature on war and consequently to contest the thesis according to which primitive societies were societies against violence, non-violent societies. Primitive societies were violent societies – their social being was a "being-for-war." "It thus seems well established that one cannot think of primitive society without also thinking of war which, as an immediate given of primitive sociology, takes on a dimension of *universality*."[14] The new political anthropology thus strives to fight against all epistemological reductions of war that follow from the naturalist approach, or from economic discourse, or again from the exchange model. This leads to the following three positive proposals: far from returning to nature, war is entirely a social fact; far from resulting from scarcity or deriving from economics, war is entirely a political phenomenon; and far from being accidental or the outcome of a failing exchange logic, war is a complete institution that follows its own logic and carries out a sociological function in primitive society. The introduction of the element of war brings about an enrichment and a complication of political anthropology.

This complication was already apparent in Clastres' 1969 text, "Savage Ethnography." Following the narrative of Helena Valero,[15] the Yanoama Indian tribe experienced, or at least seems to have experienced, a quasi-permanent state of war. Was this a confirmation of Hobbes's thesis that the state of nature is a war of all against all? Clastres soon expresses his reservations, at first empirical – the permanent war did not persist for the twenty-two years of Valero's stay – and above all conceptual. First, Hobbes's state of nature did not try to describe a moment in human history any more than did Rousseau's state of nature; second, the term "war" is not truly appropriate because in the Yanoama the opposing units are allied groups. It seems, then, that, in this initial text, the exchange model mitigated the question of war and attenuated the effects of war. Therefore Clastres concludes: "It seems clear that 'war' among the Indians must first be thought of in terms of the circulation of women, who are never killed."[16] Bloody confrontation might be substituted by the fight club, which was sufficient to exhaust vengeance. "The result is that the boundaries between peace and violence, between marriage and war, become very blurred."[17]

What remains is an issue regarding the organization of primitive society. If, on the one hand, the political existence of primitive society is defined as a disjunction of power and of leadership, and if, on the other hand, war is defined as a "provisional meeting of leadership and of authority," would not war, which is claimed to be frequent or even constant, defeat the system of division of leadership and power and lead to the death of primitive society as an undivided political form? In "Savage Ethnography," Clastres, aware of this difficulty, raises doubts about the popular view that war was likely to alter relationships of leadership and authority, to reunite what was separate: "and again, it should be looked at more closely." He has a different response in the 1977 text, "Sorrows of the Savage Warrior." Here, Clastres' methodical doubt is transformed into a refutation of the earlier hypothesis. War no longer leads to a reunification of leadership and authority: "war does not, any more than peace, allow the chief to act the chief … War does not open a new field in the political relations between men: the war chief and the warriors remain Equals; war never creates, even temporarily, division in primitive society between those who command and those who obey … The war machine, by itself, is incapable of engendering inequality in primitive society."[18] Moreover, this society of permanent war is a society against the warrior. Tragedy is the fate of the primitive warrior, along with the defence mechanism of primitive society – or indivisible society – against the eventual metamorphosis of the desire for status into the desire for power.

For the new political anthropology, this complex problem swells to a new magnitude when, in the text of 1977, war is viewed as an essential structure of primitive society. "No general theory of primitive society can economize a consideration of war."[19] "War is a structure of primitive society and not the accidental failure of an unsuccessful exchange. This structural status of violence is illustrated by the universality of war in the Savage world."[20]

The problem complicates the new order as soon as a further question arises: how do we piece together a conception of primitive society as a complete or finished society when, on the one hand, its social being is constituted by the continuous refusal of the state, and thus of division, and on the other hand, it is a society for war, an asocial state that tends towards chaos, towards a society of nothingness, and that exposes it to the emergence of division, which permanently threatens during the waging of war? In short, how do we bring together the primitive social cosmos and war?

Faced with this question, it is necessary to revise or even abandon theses of consistency, of the "positivity" of primitive politics; or, better yet, it is necessary to think *otherwise* about war – war is no longer equated with chaos, but viewed as an institution of a heterogeneous society. To put the matter differently: from the moment the ethnologist confronts the empirical phenomenon of war – when, once again, he recognizes war as consubstantial with primitive society –is he not forced to embark on a return to Hobbes? So, Clastres could not avoid this confrontation. But this path is teeming with traps. It is perilous, even contradictory, because if the ethnologist accepts Hobbes's ideas, he must agree to think that the state against primitive society emerges precisely in the dynamic of war. From this vantage point, a number of additional questions arise: in what sense can war be considered a structure, a specific logic of primitive society, without thinking of it as the very deathblow required to turn, because of the war within it, primitive society into a society with the state? How can primitive society be thought of simultaneously as social-being-for-war and as society against the state? Is it really a question of returning to Hobbes? Or is it rather about a detour imposed by Hobbes, a kind of counterexample destined to produce a significant intellectual move: to elaborate another approach to war, a conception of war as an anti-state machine and also to think about a community that takes form within the conduct of war?

Although it is necessary to pay homage to the brilliant intuition of the author of *Leviathan* – his identification of the relationship between the state and war – a momentary return to Hobbes as an ethnologist invites us immediately to change course. But we should not turn towards a reassuring notion of a peaceful "state of nature," or look for the exchange occurring "beneath" war. Instead, the return to Hobbes should provoke us to realize that the emergence of the state does not happen by itself: a social bond is instituted in war and *against* the state, so the state is not as self-evident as it is usually portrayed. Copernicus and war?

With the issues defined in this way, let us move on to the role that Hobbes plays in the thought of Clastres.

It makes sense to begin by noting the status of this reference. Clastres turns exclusively to *Leviathan* and, within that work, he privileges the famous chapter related to the state of nature: "Of the Naturall Condition of Mankind, as concerning their Felicity, and Misery." He makes no reference to the works of Hobbes before or after *Leviathan* – Clastres' aim is clearly not to deliver an interpretation of Hobbes considered in all of its complexity. Rather, Hobbes is offered as a model, as an ideal type. One could, according to Clastres, approach primitive society thorough two principal models: either the exchange model of Lévi-Strauss or the Hobbesian model of war. Yet it is through the opposition of these two models – he contests one with the other to emphasize their one-sidedness – that Clastres invites us to think about society *and* war. It follows that the relationship Clastres establishes with Hobbes is of a different nature than the one that Marshall Sahlins proposes in his unexpected parallel between *Leviathan* and Marcel Mauss's *The Gift*.

What are the components of the Hobbesian model that Clastres retains, and against which components does he especially orient his thought?

First is the state of nature as *bellum omnium contra omnes* (the war of all against all): "Hereby it is manifest that during the time men live without a common Power to keep them all in awe, they are in a condition which is called Warre; and such a warre, as is of every man against every man."[21]

Second is Hobbes's confirmation of the hypothesis about the state of nature with reference to the discovery of the "savages" of America: "It may peradventure be thought, there was never such a time nor condition of warre as this; and I believe it was never generally so, over all the world: but there are many places where they live so now. For the savage people in many places of *America*, except the government of small Families, the concord whereof dependeth on naturall lust, have no government at all; and live at this day in that brutish manner, as I said before."[22]

Third is Hobbes's qualification of this condition, the war of every man against every man, as a society of nothingness: "In such condition, there is no place for Industry; because the fruit thereof is uncertain: and consequently no Culture of the Earth; no navigation, nor use of the commodities that may be imported by sea; no commodious Building; no Instruments of moving and removing such things as require much force; no Knowledge of the face of the Earth, no account of Time; no Arts; no Letters; no Society; and which is worst of all, continuall feare and danger of violent death; And the life of man, solitary, poore, nasty, brutish, and short."[23]

Fourth is the war of all against all, as a society of nothingness, which leads either to the destruction of the human species or, to escape from this evil fate, to the state, a singular and separate power:

> The finall Cause, End, or Designe of men, (who naturally love Liberty, and Dominion over others,) in the introduction of that restraint upon themselves, (in which wee see them live in Common-wealths,) is the foresight of their own preservation, and of a more contented life thereby; that is to say, of getting themselves out from the miserable condtion of Warre, which is necessarily consequent (as hath been shewn) to the naturall Passions of men, when there is no visible Power to keep them in awe, and tye them by feare of punishment to the performance of their Convenants, and observation of [the] Lawes of Nature ... The only way to erect such a Common Power ... is to conferre all their power and strength upon one Man, or upon one Assembly of men, that may reduce all their Wills, by plurality of voices, unto one Will ... This is the Generation of that Great Leviathan, or rather (to speake more reverently) of that *Mortall God*, to which wee owe under *Immortall God*, our peace and defence.[24]

Fifth is the association of the idea of war with that of duration; we cannot speak of war if this condition occurs over time and appears as a trend, a disposition proving that it goes in a certain direction.[25]

Hobbes's blueprint is indeed a valuable model, but one against which Clastres, concerned with making sense of the savage political universe, opposes an anti-model. Clastres salutes the ingenuity of Hobbes in identifying the relationship of war and state: "With a lucidity that has since disappeared, the English thinker was able to detect the profound link, the close relationship of between war and the State."[26] But for Hobbes it is a contradictory proximity because war and state never go together. The state and war exist in a relationship of exclusion: when there is a state, there is no war; the state puts an end to or even prevents the war of all against all. Conversely, when there is war, or as long as there is war, there cannot be an active state, or the war prevents the state from forming. Again it is important to specify which of these propositions hold when they are seen in the light of the division between primitive societies and societies with the state. Clastres repeatedly insists that war completely changes its form in the context of societies with the state; if, until a certain point, the state has a tendency to favour war, no doubt war does not reinforce the power of the state.[27]

But, in the work of Clastres, it is indeed about a counter-Hobbes. The new political anthropology, as it acknowledges the prevalence of war, bases itself on two propositions that result directly from the encounter with the theses of *Leviathan*'s author. First, contrary to Hobbes and many others, primitive society is by no means a society of nothingness, a quasi-animal condition, but rather a full and complete social state. Second, and paradoxical to Hobbes's theses, it is through the state of war that primitive society leaves a quasi-animal condition, instituting a complete social state. Hobbes's colossal error, according to Clastres, was his belief "that the society which persists in war of each against each is not truly a society."[28] In the case of primitive societies, war, a properly sociopolitical activity, can be considered as the very focus of the political institution of the social. The institution of this society in its particularity – an undivided social order – transpires through the very fact of war.

The latter proposition appears essential, and makes it clear why we need to detour through Sahlins's text, which establishes a parallel between *Leviathan* and *The Gift*,[29] if we want to understand Clastres' aims fully. As a first approximation, we can say that to some extent the thought of Clastres appears to be at odds with that of Sahlins. The latter, in his own way, also encounters Hobbes, reflecting on exchange and reciprocity; however, he does not oppose Hobbes, or try to write his own counter-Hobbes. Rather, in playing with the comparison to Mauss, Sahlins tones down the classic Hobbes, the theorist of the war of all against all, to present an innocent Hobbes for whom the state of nature, the state of war, is nonetheless a political order. If Hobbes reveals the latent plan of *The Gift* – the gift is like a form of political contract and in this sense it prevents war – then Mauss's work unveils a hidden Hobbes who sees war not simply as chaos, but instead as a form of authority. Sahlins, relying on the interpretation of F.S. McNeilly,[30] proposes a nuanced Hobbes: he "rounds off" the edges, one could say, while Clastres confronts them. Otherwise conforming to a coherent plan, Sahlins sees exchange or, rather, a tendency towards exchange, in Hobbes's work and thus the birth of reason. The encounter of Clastres and Sahlins is all the more interesting insofar as both agree to see primitive society as a savage polity. But it is there, in the interpretation of savage society, that they articulate and delve into their different relationships to Hobbes.

To summarize the elements of Clastres' counter-Hobbes that appear in his critique of Sahlins, first, primitive societies, which are complete societies, have their own savage politics, a form of politics that is novel and specific to them. Second, the political institution of the savage social world is established in and through war. Third, if war – or rather the state of war – enters the dignity of the *politéia,* it is not because war in primitive societies is the result of exchange or a tendency towards exchange, or because war is a combination of war and exchange that leads to the birth of reason. War is rather a form of the political institution of the social, as it is fully a struggle among men, meaning not just a struggle of man against man, but a human struggle, a fully human institution, lifting the life of humans from a quasi-animal condition. Clastres' aim of creating a counter-Hobbes restores war to show how, in and through war, one passes from "wolf" to human.

War as an Institution of the Savage Polity

In his interpretation of Hobbes, Sahlins reworks the term "polity," which comes from Rousseau[31] and evokes the Greek term "*politéia,*" the organization of human beings in matters of political power. The term implies, according to Sahlins, the ambiguity of the state of nature: if in the state of nature war indeed constitutes an underlying structure of society, there is also another level of reality when we consider the formal structure of relations between men, specific relations of power, or better, an "organization of authority." For Sahlins, it is for this reason that Hobbes's state of nature merits the designation of "polity": "The state of nature is already a form of society." In short, the state of nature would not be a society of nothingness. As we have seen, Clastres could only welcome the idea that, through a reinterpretation of Hobbes, primitive society would be seen as a primitive polity, as a political society.

However, Clastres in fact makes a complete break with Sahlins's thought; the latter, in effect, is able to rethink the state of nature with the help of two theses that are directly contrary to the orientation of Clastres' thought. First, the state of nature, according to Sahlins, can all the more be designated a primitive polity when it has a right to wage war, but not when there is actual war. Second, presenting a connection between the English thinker Hobbes and the French sociologist Mauss, Sahlins suggests that war tends towards exchange, while the gift would be a type of repressed war initiative.

The state of nature is a savage polity for Sahlins because exchange already lies hidden beneath war. To summarize, Sahlins, departing from Mauss's softened interpretation of Hobbes, believes that the state of nature is a polity to the extent that it reduces or progressively tends to reduce war. In this sense, *The Gift*, reinterpreted by the confrontation with Hobbes, suggests a conception of the primitive polity as a *society for peace*. This peace is thanks to the institution of the gift, which is for primitive society what the state is for civilized society: "The primitive analogue of social contract is not the State, but the gift. The gift is the primitive way of achieving the peace that in civilized society is secured by the State."[32]

Again we can see the difference with the paradoxical position of Clastres. While agreeing with Sahlins that the state of nature is a real polity (as a society of abundance of a different level), Clastres reverses the reasons for, as well as the meaning and content of, this claim. The state of nature is a polity not because it tends towards peace, but, to the contrary, because war is a permanent dimension of primitive society. The permanence of war does not mean that battle is in full swing day and night, but that, at the level of formal relations between men, a given community is constituted by its enemies, by hostile relationships between communities. It is therefore about a condition, a structural state of war, as this hostile disposition proves to be constitutive of the social being of primitive society. Far from proposing a relationship between the mitigation of war and the rapid development of the primitive polity, Clastres invites us to see into these warlike conditions, into this being-for-the-war of savage society, which institute the primitive polity in its singularity and constitute its condition of possibility. It is a savage polity, according to Clastres, because war, and without undergoing any mitigation, is in its essence the very institution of the social, the instituting event of a heterogeneous society oriented against the emergence of the One.

What are the implications of this original position? The idea that war institutes the savage polity implies the priority of war over exchange. Let us look closely for a moment at the theses of Clastres' "Archeology of Violence: War in Primitive Societies." Clastres refuses to choose between Lévi-Strauss and Hobbes: Lévi-Strauss has a strong understanding of exchange, but he has forgotten war; Hobbes has a strong understanding of war, but he has forgotten exchange. Clastres' refusal to choose between them is necessary because, in his view, this opposition is not applicable to savage society: "Primitive society is a space of exchange, and it is also a place of violence: war, on the same level as exchange, belongs to the primitive social being."[33] But a new complication appears: does Clastres' refusal of the opposition permit him to think simultaneously about war and exchange by juxtaposing them, as if the juxtaposition must leave the two terms unchanged? Clastres on several occasions refuses the thesis of juxtaposition that he attributes to Lévi-Strauss – the thesis of a transactional equilibrium or a balance between the two components – by reminding that to be mistaken about war is to be mistaken about society. This renews the question: given that Clastres acknowledges the two dimensions of primitive society, war and exchange, and also refuses the idea of juxtaposing them, how can he conceptualize the two dimensions – with the help of what relations – without being mistaken about society?

Before getting to the conditions of a proper conception, let us make a clarification: "primitive society" is taken here in a double sense. On the one hand, "primitive society" denotes an original social formation, indivisible and therefore distinct from societies with coercive power (that is, societies with the state); on the other hand, "primitive society" denotes a sociological ensemble composed of primitive communities. This means that it is appropriate to think about the sociological ensemble as comprising two types of relations: intracommunity relations and intercommunity relations.

Refusing all forms of commonsense thought, Clastres from the very outset poses a dissymmetry. War and exchange cannot be juxtaposed, and Hobbes cannot be added to the exchange model, because it is not possible both to "rehabilitate war" as an essential dimension of society and maintain the idea of exchange as the essence of the social. Lévi-Strauss's error, according to Clastres, was not that he privileged exchange, but that he confused the levels on which the respective activities of war and exchange operate, placing them instead on the same plane.

War and exchange should not be thought of on a continuum that moves gradually from one to the other – when exchange increases, war decreases, and vice versa. Rather, they should be considered in terms of a *radical discontinuity*, as this is the only way to reveal the truth of primitive society. Primitive society consists of two different structures, war and exchange, which exist in a relationship of discontinuity insofar as each structure serves a specific function on its own specific plane. We could say that this discontinuity between war and exchange is, for Clastres, a *subordination of exchange to war*. This is contrary to the thought of Lévi-Strauss, for whom commerce, which is at the heart of the social, "holds sociological priority over war."[34]

We cannot understand the principle of the intelligibility of war unless we return to the social being of primitive society. According to Clastres – the Montesquieu of savage societies – the primitive community has a dual nature that gives rise to two principles: it is "at once a totality and a unity."[35]

As an autonomous totality, the primitive community integrates all the diverse unities that constitute it into one; it forms a system or a set that represents more than the simple sum of individuals, more than the addition of groups. A political totality, it etches itself into a territory as the exclusive space for exercising communal rights, and through this inscription, it establishes a communal self as the exclusion of the Other. Lacking ties to a superior totality that swallows it up, the primitive community functions, in its comprehensiveness and in its very completion, as a self-government.

As a homogeneous unity or indivisible society, the primitive community does not tolerate the appearance of any difference that is likely to produce a cleavage within it – for example, the oppositions between rich and poor, exploiters and exploited, dominators and dominated. What is distinct about primitive societies is precisely the complex devices they use to separate prestige from power in the person of the chief, and thereby prevent the emergence of a separate political power. This unity is intrinsic to the social body: it requires a whole that continues to ward off, to prevent, the manifestation of a figure of the One that is external to the community, removing itself from the community in order to embody it. Concerned with preserving itself through the refusal of social division, the primitive community operates, so to speak, through continuous *indivision*. A dual nature, two intersecting principles: each community, as it maintains indivision, can establish itself as a collective subject, as a *we* in intercommunity relations; each *we* considers itself a completed totality, finished, folded in upon itself in a relationship of equals with the other *we* equivalents. "The primitive community can posit itself as a totality because it institutes itself as a unity: it is a whole because it is an undivided We."[36] Clastres is able to adopt a two-step approach because his point of departure is the dual nature and dual principles of the savage *politéia*. This point of departure allows him to think together, and not merely juxtapose, war and exchange, with the aim of better understanding the social being of primitive society.

Now the task is to show how each of the two characteristics of the savage *politéia* – autonomous totality and homogeneous unity – thwart either the generalized exchange hypothesis (Lévi-Strauss), or the war hypothesis (Hobbes). For Clastres, taking either of these two hypotheses as the principle of intelligibility has the contrary effect of missing the sociological being of the primitive community. As an autonomously functioning and complete totality, primitive society invalidates the hypothesis of exchange; as a homogeneous unity persevering through indivision, it invalidates the hypothesis of war of all against all. To put it another way, the hypothesis of exchange or of "generalized friendship" shatters the principle of autonomy – the primitive community as a complete totality – which is to say that this hypothesis counters the logic of differentiation, of dispersion, the will of fragmentation that primitive communities achieve in and by war. In terms of the social being of primitive societies, war is a mechanism; it is also a structure to resist the logic of integrative identification. Its *telos* is completely political, preserving autonomy through fragmentation and the perpetuation of fragmentation.

As for Hobbes's hypothesis, that of generalized war, it aims to deny the principle of indivision – the primitive community as a unity – which is to say the logic that takes place in and by exchange, by posing a renewed conspiracy of division. For primitive society, exchange functions as a mechanism of resistance to division, to the emergence of the relationship of domination that necessarily results from war, since, to end, war always leaves in its wake a winner and a loser. With these two hypotheses thus refused – that of generalized friendship (Lévi-Strauss) as ruinous of autonomy and that of generalized war (Hobbes) as ruinous of indivision – the interpreter seems to be redirected to the initial question: is it adequate to think about primitive social being in terms of the coexistence of war and exchange, as the balanced co-presence of these two components on the same plane?

Clastres' thought is at the same time subtle and ambitious. Indeed, its task is to articulate positively, and in two distinct ways, the logic of difference (war) and the logic of indivision (exchange), showing how each of these two logics is, in its own way, established while preserving the double nature and double principle proper to primitive society. "The primitive social being, thus, simultaneously needs exchange and war, in order to be able to combine at once the autonomist point of honour and the refusal of division. It is to this twofold demand that the status and function of exchange and war are related, unfolding on different levels."[37] In following Clastres, we now know there is at the same time a need for war to satisfy the centrifugal logic of primitive society – war is posited as a constitutive structure of primitive society and no longer as a failure of the logic of exchange – and the impossibility of the war of all against all: the idea of a generalized war that results in a winner/loser division would undermine indivision and mark the end of primitive society as a homogeneous unity.

If, in the same movement, all primitive communities necessarily practise war and are opposed to generalized war (that is to say: the Others are all enemies), it follows that it is necessary for them to construct a classification of those who surround them, to divide the Others into two groups, friends and enemies. In this perspective, we succeed in giving sociological priority to war: war as a constitutive structure of society responds to a logic of differentiation – for instance, there is in a sense the production of permanent enemies in primitive societies. This illustrates to what extent alliances are subordinate to war; it acknowledges, in fact, that the success of the war venture depends on enclosing war within certain limits, so as to avoid the situation of generalized war. In the context of this problematic, alliance inevitably changes status: alliance takes at the same time the object of a reduction and of a partition; dissociated from the logic of exchange, it no longer appears as the goal, the end of an exchangist logic; it falls instead to the level of a simple means, a means of war. Why does a primitive society decide against alliances? Because the primitive community, the society for war, has enemies. The parting of alliances and exchange go together with the insistence on the articulation of alliance in war: alliance is no longer seen as merely satisfying exchange, but rather it responds to the complex demands of the war effort. As Clastres puts it, alliance is "an essential property of international life in primitive society: war relates first to alliance; war as an institution determines alliance as a tactic."[38]

Contrary to Lévi-Strauss, Clastres considers the articulation between war and exchange under the heading of asymmetry: the level of exchange is subordinated to the level of war in the way that tactics are subordinate to strategy. This subordination operates in a double sense: there is a sociological priority of war over alliance – the constitution of enemies comes first – according to the sociological logic of primitive society, and the primitive community needs allies because, in accordance with its own social being, it first produced enemies. This subordination so strong, Clastres claims, that exchange has no autonomy from war. The principle of reciprocity, the form taken by the primitive logic of exchange, assembles groups together into networks of alliance – networks of allies, and allies only. War is the *primum movens* – no domain of intercommunity relations is autonomous from exchange since the sphere of exchange exactly corresponds to that of alliance; or, to put it otherwise, exchange does not overflow the sphere of alliance.

At this point we can resume the critique of Lévi-Strauss: by choosing the hypothesis of "generalized friendship," one could say that, for Clastres, the author of *Tristes Tropiques*[39] had written a "bad" counter-Hobbes because of the confusion it created between two forms of exchange. In primitive society, the question of exchange – of its status, its function, and above all its relation to war – is decisive: the interpretation of savage society depends on the interpretation of the war/exchange relationship. Two types of exchange can be distinguished. One could be called "human" exchange, that of the *anthropos*, which, by the exogamous exchange of women (exchange to outside tribes), implements the incest prohibition and distinguishes human society from the animal. An entrance into culture and an exit from nature, this exchange is experienced as the distance between instinct and institution; it brings humanity to a well-ordered universe. But the exchange of women in primitive society can be interpreted not just from an anthropological perspective, but also from a political one or, more precisely, from the perspective of political intelligence. Exchange is related not only to the *anthropos*, but also to the *anthropos* as a political being.

The primitive community is the theatre for an exchange of women that takes the form of a covenant, with the aim of producing an alliance or a network of alliances between different communities in the midst of a permanent state of war. Faced with this situation of war, it is not enough for the primitive community merely to break away from the animal – it must make friends, allies – in this case, as brothers-in-law. In the logic of this "political" – and no longer only anthropological – exchange, exchange is subordinated to the alliance. Witness the recovery of the two spheres: through the mediation of alliance, exchange returns to war. Or better yet: through alliance, exchange affirms its subordination to war as instituting the savage *politéia* and, moreover, in instituting the society against the state.

Returning to Hobbes, Clastres can reconsider the essential thesis that the primitive world is not a social world, that it falls short of being social because the state of war prevents the exchange of goods and services, but also the exchange of women. According to Hobbes, men lead a quasi-animal existence – falling short of culture, they abandon themselves to their natural desires.

Yet the distinction between "anthropological" exchange and "political" exchange shows that one can make two different retorts to Hobbes. It is possible to conceive of two versions of the counter-Hobbes: encountering the author of *Leviathan*, Lévi-Strauss invokes anthropological exchange, while Clastres invokes political exchange.

In the counter-Hobbes of Lévi-Strauss, the primitive world is not a society of nothingness. It is very much a social world that remains far from animal life, particularly to the extent the incest prohibition makes necessary the exchange of women. Then, departing from this human fact, this anthropological difference – the extrapolation according to which primitive society is fundamentally a society for exchange –war is reduced to a failed exchange. "Social" is understood here to mean "human," the access to the human that invalidates Hobbes's thesis. The state of nature is a society because exchange triumphs over war.

Far more paradoxical, but also far more resolute, is Clastres' response. His counter-Hobbes has a totally new look: it grants to Hobbes the permanent state of war as a structure, to Sahlins the existence of a polity, and to Lévi-Strauss the presence of exchange. But permanent war, polity, and exchange become the objects of analysis in a radically new interpretation. First, war: the sociological reality of the state of war is beyond doubt. But far from being a society of nothingness, a miserable quasi-animal state, a chaos, the state of war is fully recognized as a social phenomenon. A genuine social cosmos can establish itself and expand in and by war. The primitive community is very much a polity but not, as Sahlins maintains, thanks to a mitigation of war; to the contrary, it is a polity at the outset, in the very execution of war. Moreover, war is the means of preserving the being of the savage *politéia*: its *conatus essendi* requires the development of a continuous logic of fragmentation that is fulfilled in war, in the determination of the enemy. The operation of war is about warning of and preventing the emergence of a unified meta-community that would both establish peace and ruin the rule of the multiple.

Next, exchange: the savage polity certainly practises exchange, but rather than operating through its own logic, it is subjugated to the logic of war. We could even say that, far from opposing exchange, war produces or creates it. It is important to emphasize, however, that war creates exchange as a tactic that is entirely subordinate to it. The play of alliances better controls the effects of war and prevents it from threatening the state of indivision proper to primitive society as a homogeneous unity.

The counter-Hobbes of Clastres is situated far from that of Lévi-Strauss, or is even its opposite. Following Clastres' theses, we could reckon that Lévi-Strauss is in some way deceived by exchange; he does offer, against Hobbes, the "wrong" exchange – that of the rupture with animality, that of anthropological difference – but that remains insignificant in political terms. As for the oppositional character, the audacity, of Clastres' theses, after them Lévi-Strauss – and this is might be the secret of his response to the author of *Leviathan* – appears to be in complete accord with Hobbes's position that a state of war does not represent a state of society. After all, is it not to share this presupposition of Hobbes that Lévi-Strauss comes to minimize war and privilege exchange in primitive society? But the innovation that ultimately distinguishes the new political anthropology is seen in Clastres' perspective: attention to politics, to the foundation of intelligibility that is the political institution of the social. Indeed, unlike traditional anthropology, what relentlessly orders Clastres' analyses is a devotion to the requirements of a political understanding of human societies. The intention behind his appeal to political categories is precisely his wish for a political reading of social formations. This can prevent "bleeding hearts" from confusing his thought with the suspect enterprises that have a weakness for warrior values. "In other words, primitive war is the means to a political end," Clastres writes.[40] "An examination of ethnological facts reveals the properly political dimension of warlike activity."[41] War, life force of primitive society, is not the derivative of an unknown war-prone human nature, nor of economics, nor of a failed logic of exchange. Politics is the foundation for the intelligibility of primitive war, which is a thoroughly political phenomenon.

This political understanding is even more remarkable insofar as it produces results that should be emphasized to better appreciate the exact nature of Clastres' counter-Hobbes. Clastres' refutation of the author of *Leviathan* is not just any refutation, but a political refutation – that it to say, a refutation that highlights the political logic at work in the institution of primitive society. Returning to Clastres' response to Hobbes to clarify and avoid forgetting any of its propositions, we can see that it is really threefold.

First, the agreement to start with Hobbes: war is indeed the permanent state of primitive society. And at no point does Clastres try to minimize his agreement on this issue by invoking a countertendency that moderates the potency of war. "War is linked to primitive society as such (and so it is universal there); it is its mode of operation … War is at the very heart of the primitive social being, war constitutes the very motor of social life."[42]

But, second, Clastres' fundamental divergence with Hobbes – and, if one thinks about it, with many of his adversaries – soon becomes apparent: the permanent state of war is in reality a state of society. Although, according to Hobbes, the life of man in the miserable state of war, subject to the "continuall feare ... of violent death," is "solitary, poore, nasty, brutish, and short," for Clastres, in this glorious state of war, the social being of primitive society comes into its own and the primitive man breathes the air of liberty. War, the foundational phenomenon, is at the very centre of primitive sociality, the means by which the social bond between its members is formed, the very element where primitive society takes shape as society and acquires its own coherence.

Third, a doubling divergence and word-by-word opposition: the state is against war, on the one hand; the war is against the state, on the other. For Hobbes, this asociality, this permanent dissolution of the social that threatens the human species with self-destruction, stirs the creation of a common power, an external unifier, that allows the reduction of all wills to a single one and leaves them to enjoy safely the endless game of self-preservation; in short, it inspires the advent of a "mortal god," the great *Leviathan*. For Clastres, by contrast, the social bond that takes shape in war positively unfolds as a permanent struggle against the One, against the emergence of all mechanisms of unification, unifying law, or instance. Primitive society, society for war, is a society against the state. This means that primitive society as a warrior society assumes a specific position in relation to the originary division of the social – it creates its own form of regulation. War by its very texture implements or develops a unique form of sociality – a social being that operates through the dispersion, partition, fragmentation, the reign of the multiple – which is directly antithetical to the form of sociality that institutes the state. The multiple against the One: "Primitive war is the work of a centrifugal logic, a logic of separation …, a logic of the multiple. The Savages want the multiplication of the multiple."[43]

The importance of this last proposition of Clastres cannot be overemphasized. It is indeed what makes a political counter-Hobbes – a critique of Hobbes carried out with the help of political categories and on the very site of the political. Clastres' refutation of Hobbes does not rely on the invocation of a vulgar naturalism or on an appeal to an original sociality. It is unlike that of Kropotkin, for example, who, in failing to consider war from a political perspective, appeals instead to a law common to all beings, animal and human – a law of mutual aid and support – that would invalidate the theses of Hobbes.[44] No natural sociality, which would exist before the political institution of society in the form of a spontaneous association, is called to the rescue by Clastres. Primitive society, taken seriously as a political society, is a fully instituted society. War is at the centre of this unique institution of the social – it is what allows the self-preservation of primitive humanity in the free operation of its heterogeneous existence against all logics aiming to totalize the multiple and reduce it to the One. Primitive society's resistance to the unifying logic tells us that the final form of the social is not to be found in a fused collectivity or in a harmonious totality. Is the savage social being, then, anti-Platonic and anti-Hegelian? Indeed, it is precisely the pluralism of primitive existence – the many social beings that comprise the primitive communities, the excess overflowing all reduction to the One – that expresses itself in war.

This is why Clastres is so thorough in describing the social institution of war, especially the relations between the intercommunal and the intracommunal; this is why he is concerned with showing how the internal indivision of the homogeneous community and the external opposition of the autonomous totality continue to combine, to reinforce each other reciprocally. External politics is necessarily related to internal politics: provoked in some way by the need to oppose Self to Others, to reassert its autonomy, the primitive community puts its identity to the test in clashes with the enemy and finds, at the same time, in this figure of the enemy, a confirmation of its identity. Thus such clashes can only strengthen its social conservatism, maintain its internal indivision, and, in doing so, oppose all social changes likely to undermine the devices that prevent the emergence of division within it. Conversely, internal politics is related to external politics: because the primitive community preserves itself through indivision – because it constitutes itself as a homogeneous "we" under the cover of division – it can at the same time consider itself as a "we" exclusive of Others and risk this exclusivity in the test of war.

Above all, the same anti-unifying logic governs the two domains: the primitive community responds to the vital necessity of maintaining independence in the sphere of external relations with war, the centrifugal logic, the "multiplication of the multiple." War is how it reaffirms its autonomy against the imposition of a unifying external law, against the threat of an integrated peace coming from outside. Primitive society responds to the vital necessity of maintaining internal indivision with a set of devices of disjunction that Clastres describes well and that are all means to fight against the emergence of a unifying moment, the figure of the one chief, which would abolish the continuous exchange of the *All Ones* and widen the deadly master-subject division.

Perhaps now, after this analysis of Clastres' counter-Hobbes, we are ready to risk the question: how do we think together war and friendship?

In the intercommunal realm, the centrifugal logic of the multiple that manifests through war is precisely the condition of possibility of "friendship," in the sense of an equality maintained between the different socio-political units constituting primitive society in its free political being. The paradox of primitive society lies in the articulation of war with friendship: it is thanks to the fragmentation that is sustained by the permanent state of war that this plurality, in its agonistic existence, can resist the unifying mechanism of the state, the appearance of an external law, the *pax incaïca* or other, that would both put an end to the war and create a fateful division between dominant and dominated societies. War is necessary to maintain "friendship," then, but, as we have also seen, generalized war is impossible because, if primitive society wants to persevere as it is, it must distinguish among the Others between allies and enemies to avoid a situation of total war – that is to say, to avoid the successful realization of the division between vanquisher and vanquished, the emergence of other figures of external domination. Once again, a connection between war and friendship is established through the mediation of alliance, a connection that is necessary to prevent the adverse effects of a war without limits.

In the intracommunal realm, we first say that "friendship," in the sense of an effective indivision, is the condition of possibility of the premises of war. Moreover, let us say that, contrary to common opinion, war does not destroy friendship or introduce into savage society the division between those who command and those who obey. "The war machine, by itself, is incapable of engendering inequality in primitive society."[45] Primitive society does not get carried away with the war machine, to avoid having warriors set themselves up as the dominant group. As Clastres insists in "Sorrows of the Savage Warrior," primitive society, society for war, is society against the warrior.

Yet questions remain. Is the type of friendship that Clastres describes for primitive society similar to what Spinoza calls "peace" in *Political Treatise*? Does Clastres' response provide enough evidence to conclude satisfactorily that friendship exists? Indeed, friendship is not a mere absence of inequality, or even an absence of division; it is equally a positive condition. So the legitimate question of J.M. Besnier would become: does the savage *politéia* as warrior society engender a *philia* (brotherly love or friendship) in the positive sense of the term?

How can this place be inhabited? Are we just left guessing about the meaning of this articulation of war and friendship?

There is no doubt that the author of the political counter-Hobbes is devoted to freedom. The proof is his insistence on the centrifugal logic of savage societies, on their legitimate distrust of the One, on their constitutive struggle against all projects of unification. What is remarkable in this sense is the identification of the antithetical nature of war: war is a relation that separates, opposes people to each other, and, at the same time, connects them together as a multiplicity resistant to totalization. Is this not how the ethnologist, in his interpretation of war in primitive society, society against the state, meets the philosopher, the thinker of ontological pluralism who sees in war "a relation between beings exterior to totality"?[46]

But, more fundamentally, this conception of war returns to the tradition of political philosophy, which reflects on the conditions of liberty at the same time as it clarifies them. This is best seen in the affinity of Clastres' work with what we have called the countercurrents of the tradition. Clastres' work is a counter-Hobbes because, contrary to the author of *De Cive*, he returns humans to a condition of political living not by beginning with the exogamic exchange of women – that is, the sign of the human – and not *despite* war, but *through* war, *starting with* war. In savage society, war is the site that best reveals the political animality of the human being. It is useless to try to reduce the sharpness of this thesis, to rely on well-known formulas of war as a continuation of the political, and vice versa. The warlike turmoil of savage society is the turmoil of primitive freedom. It is as if, for a thinking concerned about freedom, the *koinonia* (association, communion, or togetherness) could not be dissociated from conflict, the social bond could not be formed except by the *mise en forme* (shaping), the *mise en sens* (giving meaning), and the *mise en scène* (staging) of war, to appropriate the words of Claude Lefort. As Lefort writes in "L'échange et la lutte des hommes" (Exchange and the Struggle of Man): "Only the human can reveal to the human that they are human, as only they can endanger this reality. It is the promise of humanity or the threat of alienation. The Spinozist formula, 'man is a god to man,' has its negative corollary."[47]

Clastres' theses on war and friendship in savage society also have the merit, for those of us who live in societies for the state at a moment when consensus flows freely, of drawing attention to the central questions that are asked, in a similar vein to those of Clastres, about the possible relations of war and liberty (liberty as the condition of possibility for friendship) on the one hand, and of peace and servitude on the other. We are still far from praising war. It is, rather, about casting a legitimate suspicion on the very idea of peace – about a moment of necessary scepticism with respect to the project of peace – because peace finally does not carry within it all the ambiguities and all the threats of death contained in the desire for unity.

Machiavelli reminds worshippers of *pax romana* that the principle of liberty which resulted in the grandeur of the Roman Republic was located in the ongoing strife between the people and the Senate, in the tumultuous opposition between "two conflicting factions, that of the people and that of the nobles."[48]

Rousseau – who detested Hobbes's horrible hypothesis – praises *stasis*, unrest, and war among the Greeks. Freedom is the very source of human prosperity:

> Riots and civil wars greatly frighten rulers, but they do not cause the true misfortunes of peoples, which can even some respite while argument rages over who will tyrannize them … In olden times Greece flourished amid the cruellest wars; blood flowed copiously, yet the whole land was filled with men. It seemed, Machiavelli says, that amid murders, banishments and civil wars our [Florentine] Republic grew all the more powerful; the virtue of its citizens, their morals and their independence had more effect in strengthening it than all its disputes had in weakening it. A little unrest gives vigour to the soul, and what makes the species truly prosper is not so much peace as liberty.[49]

Montesquieu praises the divisions and popular uprisings in Rome, and practises, with the greatest insight, this project of suspicion towards the uncritical valuation of peace. Suspicion towards peace is the same as suspicion towards the One:

> That which is called union in a body politic is a very equivocal thing. A true union is one of harmony, by which all the social elements of the state, however opposed to each other they may appear to be, concur in promoting the general good of society, just as the discords in music concur in producing the total accord. There may be union in a state – that is to say, a harmony from which results the welfare of the people, and which is the only true peace – where all appears to be a scene of confusion ... But amid the accord of the Asiatic despotisms, as indeed of all governments which are not moderate, there is always a real separation of the social elements. The labourer, the warrior, the merchant, the magistrate, the noble, are not joined together, only in so far as some oppress others without resistance. If there is union in such a state, it is not citizens who are united, but dead bodies buried close to each other.[50]

Similarly, Spinoza, who was a thinker of unity – the best state is the one where men live in harmony – but also a thinker of democracy, warns against a solemn relationship between peace and servitude. This is because he presents a positive definition of peace, as opposed to the possible negative association of peace with the extinction of liberty:

> A commonwealth whose subjects are deterred from taking up arms only through fear should be said to be not at war rather than to be enjoying peace. For peace is not just the absence of war, but a virtue which comes from strength of mind; for obedience is the steadfast will to carry out orders enjoined by the general decree of the commonwealth. Anyway, a commonwealth whose peace depends on the sluggish spirit of its subjects who are led like sheep to learn simply to be slaves can more properly be called a desert than a commonwealth.[51]

NOTES

1 Translator's note: This work was originally published in French as "Le Contre-Hobbes de Pierre Clastres," in *L'Esprit des lois sauvages: Pierre Clastres ou une nouvelle anthropologie politique*, ed. Miguel Abensour (Paris: Éditions du Seuil, 1987), 115–44.
2 Clastres, *Society Against the State*, 44.
3 Éric Weil, "La philosophie politique," *Encyclopaedia Universalis* (Paris, 1970), 226.
4 Pierre Clastres, "Entretien avec Pierre Clastres (14 décembre 1974)," *L'Anti-Mythes*, 9 (1975): 1.
5 Theodor Adorno, *Negative Dialectics*, trans. E.B. Ashton (New York: Routledge, 1973), 321–2.
6 Pierre Clastres, "Power in Primitive Societies," in *Archeology of Violence*, trans. Jeanine Herman (New York: Semiotext(e), 1994), 92.
7 Clastres, *Society Against the State*, 23.
8 Pierre Clastres, "The Return to Enlightenment," in *Archeology of Violence*, 120.
9 Pierre Clastres, "Marxists and Their Anthropology," in *Archeology of Violence*, 137.
10 Pierre Clastres, "Freedom, Misfortune, the Unnameable," in *Archeology of Violence*, 93–104.
11 Pierre Clastres, "Entre silence et dialogue," *L'Arc*, numéro spécial consacré à Claude Lévi-Strauss (1968): 76–8.
12 Pierre Clastres, "Savage Ethnography (On Yanoama)," in *Archeology of Violence*, 35.

13 Translator's note: Both of these texts were originally published as French journal articles but also included in Clastres' 1980 collection of essays, *Recherches d'anthropologie politique*. This collection was translated into English as *Archeology of Violence* in 1994.
14 Pierre Clastres, "Archeology of Violence: War in Primitive Societies," in *Archeology of Violence*, 142; emphasis in original.
15 See Helena Valero and Ettore Biocca, *Yanoama: The Narrative of a White Girl Kidnapped by Amazonian Indians* (New York: Dutton, 1970).
16 Clastres, "Savage Ethnography (On Yanoama)," 36.
17 Ibid.
18 Pierre Clastres, "Sorrows of the Savage Warrior," in *Archeology of Violence*, 170.
19 Clastres, "Archeology of Violence," 143.
20 Ibid., 158.
21 Thomas Hobbes, *Leviathan* (London: Penguin Books, 1968), part I, chap. 13.
22 Ibid.; emphasis in original.
23 Ibid.
24 Ibid., part II, chap. 17; emphasis in original.
25 Ibid., part I, chap. 13.
26 Clastres, "Archeology of Violence," 166.
27 "[W]hen there is a State, what takes place is the exact opposite of what takes place in primitive society. Take, for instance, when we speak about war: the State prevents war, it prevents the state of war. At the very least, there is a shift in the meaning of war in the Society with the State"; see Clastres, "Entretien avec Pierre Clastres," 23.
28 Clastres, "Archeology of Violence," 166.
29 Marshall Sahlins, *Stone Age Economics* (Chicago: Aldine-Anderton, 1972), 149–83.
30 See F.S. McNeilly, *The Anatomy of Leviathan* (London: Macmillan, 1968).
31 Jean-Jacques Rousseau, "Of the Social Contract," in *Of the Social Contract and Other Political Writings*, trans. Qunitin Hoare (New York: Penguin Books, 2012), book I, chap. 4.
32 Sahlins, *Stone Age Economics*, 169.
33 Clastres, "Archeology of Violence," 152.
34 Ibid., 150.
35 Ibid., 155.
36 Ibid., 156.
37 Ibid., 159.
38 Ibid., 159–60.

39 Translator's note: Translated first as *A World on the Wane* by John Russell; a second English translation was published in 1973 under the original French title. See Claude Lévi-Strauss, *Tristes Tropiques*, trans. John Weightman and Doreen Weightman (New York: Atheneum, 1973).
40 Clastres, "Archeology of Violence," 153.
41 Ibid., 163.
42 Ibid., 163–4.
43 Ibid., 164–5.
44 Peter Kropotkin, *Mutual Aid: A Factor of Evolution* (London: Allen Lane, 1972), 83–112.
45 Clastres, "Sorrows of the Savage Warrior," 170.
46 Emmanuel Lévinas, *Totality and Infinity: An Essay on Exteriority*, trans. Alphonso Lingus (Boston: Martinus Nijhoff, 1979), 223.
47 Claude Lefort, *Les formes de l'histoire* (Paris: Gallimard, 1978), 28. Translator's note: On Lefort's distinction between *mise en forme, mise en sens,* and *mise en scène,* see also idem, *Democracy and Political Theory*, trans. David Macey (Cambridge, UK: Polity Press, 1988), 218–19.
48 Niccolò Machiavelli, *Discourses on the First Decade of Titus Livius*, trans. Ninian Thomson (London: Kegan Paul, 1883), book I, chap. 4.
49 Rousseau, "Of the Social Contract," book III, chap. 9.
50 Charles Montesquieu, *Considerations on the Causes of the Grandeur and Decadence of the Romans*, trans. Jehu Baker (New York: D. Appleton, 1894), chap. 9.
51 Baruch Spinoza, "Political Treatise," in *Spinoza: Complete Works*, trans. Samuel Shirley, ed. Michael Morgan (Indianapolis, IN: Hackett, 2002), chap. 5, § 4.

Part II

The Critique of Totalitarianism and the Emergence of Radical Democratic Thought

4 Claude Lefort: Democracy as the Empty Place of Power

CARLO INVERNIZZI ACCETTI

Intellectual Background

Claude Lefort's writings are best known for the theory that democracy is a "form of society" in which the "place of power" is represented as an "empty space." It is on this theory that I primarily focus in this chapter. To bring out the significance and also the concerns that are at stake in this formulation, however, it is useful to begin with an account of the intellectual path that brought Lefort to pose the question of democracy in the first place.

His philosophical career began in the immediate aftermath of the Second World War, as a member of the French Trotskyist party. The intellectual horizon was therefore that of Marxism; and even if the adhesion to Trotskyism implied a critique of the Stalinist regime, the core of his concerns remained distant from democracy. In the first writings he published, Lefort was interested in examining how a less deterministic reading of Marx could further the progress of the international socialist revolution, particularly in Third World countries.[1] In the space of a few years, the sharpening of his critique of the Soviet regime brought Lefort away from the intellectual horizon of Trotskyism. In 1949 he and Cornelius Castoriadis co-founded *Socialisme ou Barbarie*, a group that refused the definition of the Soviet Union as a "degenerated proletarian state." What they thought was taking shape instead was a new form of domination, characterized primarily by the concentration of capital in the hands of the state, and the formation of a new ruling class, the bureaucracy.[2]

A further break occurred during the 1970s, in the wake of the publication of Alexandr Solzhenitsyn's *Gulag Archipelago*, which convinced

Lefort to employ the category of "totalitarianism" to describe the Soviet regime. It was at this time that Lefort was also exposed to the writings of Hannah Arendt, particularly through her book on the *Origins of Totalitarianism*, which was to exercise a lasting influence on his thought. Henceforth, a large part of Lefort's intellectual effort was dedicated to the task of understanding the specificity and political significance of the "totalitarian" form of domination. This effort was also in large part one of self-critique, because Lefort did not shy away from the task of unearthing the intellectual roots of "totalitarianism" within some of the elements of the socialist ideology to which he himself had adhered. Ultimately it is through this path that he was led to the issue of democracy. His analysis of the "totalitarian" form revealed that one of the principal traits of such regimes, in both their socialist and fascist variants, was a categorical rejection of liberal democracy. To understand the nature of "totalitarianism," then, Lefort concluded that it was first of all necessary to focus on the nature of "democracy." This conviction opened the way for the development of a whole new agenda in the French philosopher's thought, which ultimately proved to be among the most fruitful in his career.[3]

It is on this latter corpus of thought that I focus in this chapter. In the light of what has been said so far, however, it might already be possible to bring out some of the elements concerning the specific perspective from which Lefort approaches the study of democracy. First of all, his audience – that is, the public with which his analyses are in dialogue: many of Lefort's writings on democracy begin by pointing out that a significant number of intellectuals who emerged from the same cultural background as he did manifest a certain "reticence" towards the question of totalitarianism, coupled with a certain "suspicion" of the democratic form, often still apprehended merely as a "bourgeois" form of domination.[4] Lefort's writings pose as an answer precisely to this "reticence" and "suspicion." By forcing the thinking parts of the political left to go through the same process of self-critique he underwent, Lefort is interested in trying to convince them that the modern democratic form, in fact, can represent an opportunity to realize many of the same normative orientations that underscored their adhesion to socialism in the first place.

The second insight on Lefort's theory of democracy that can be extracted from the account of his intellectual path concerns the content of these normative orientations. Something that Lefort never abandoned from his initial Marxist allegiance was the conviction that "human emancipation" could be achieved only through a process of radical "critique" of authoritarian and oppressive institutions. In his later writings, Lefort attempts to encapsulate this normative orientation within the context of a project of "reclaiming" the notion of democracy for radical political theory. In this sense, his can be considered properly a "radical" theory of democracy, because it understands itself as a way of reconceptualizing the project of emancipation through critique in light of the failure of "really existing socialism."[5]

The last preliminary remark, which might be useful before moving on to a substantive discussion of Lefort's theory of democracy, concerns its reception in the English-speaking world. This has occurred relatively late, and in a highly selective manner. Many of Lefort's writings – particularly the early ones, but also some of the most recent – have not even been translated yet. It was only after the publication of a study by Bernard Flynn entitled *The Philosophy of Claude Lefort*[6] that his work as a whole began to become known in the Anglo-Saxon world. As the totalizing opposition between a neo-Kantian "analytic" approach and the continental "deconstructive" approach appears to be waning, the space has finally opened for the engagement with new and different ways of thinking about democracy that do not renounce the critical perspective, but also refuse to cut themselves off from the dimension of normativity.

The Notion of a "Form of Society"

Having cleared the ground with these background remarks, one can now move on to discuss the substance of Lefort's theory of democracy. As I stated at the beginning, the most synthetic – and well-known – definition he provides identifies democracy as a "form of society" in which the "place of power" is represented as an "empty space." Each of these terms needs to be clarified.

The notion of a "form of society" refers to the fact that Lefort does not examine democracy exclusively as a "form of government" – that is, essentially, an institutional configuration determining the procedures through which collectively binding decisions are made. His approach is much more encompassing, inasmuch as it treats democracy as a mode of organization of society as a whole, which also includes a specific culture, a sensibility, and, most important, a specific way of "being" in the world and perceiving it.

This approach derives from a presupposition of social ontology according to which society is not an aggregate of pre-existing parts but a mode of organization of reality itself, which determines what is intelligible and practicable within it. Given this premise, what Lefort is interested in examining is the specific way in which democracies structure the space of the social as a whole. From this point of view, the institutional dimension is clearly important, but it does not exhaust the range of factors of political significance. On the contrary, what Lefort wants to bring out is the way in which the institutions we are used to associating with a "democratic" regime are inserted in a wider context that makes them intelligible and legitimate in the first place, thereby enabling them to function properly.

To further clarify this point, it might be useful at this stage to introduce an important conceptual distinction that will later become fundamental for the formulation of Lefort's theory of democracy: that between two different modes of apprehending the notion of the "political," respectively referred to in French using the masculine and the feminine versions of the same noun, *le politique* and *la politique*. The context in which Lefort discusses this distinction most thoroughly is his analysis of the political thought of Machiavelli in *Le travail de l'oeuvre Machiavel*,[7] a text that is worth briefly engaging because it contains a preliminary elaboration of a theme that inflects all of his subsequent political thought.

Machiavelli is commonly read as the first theorist to have affirmed the so-called autonomy of the political domain: by describing a series of specific strategies and techniques peculiar to the purpose of obtaining, exercising, and maintaining political power, he is assumed to have defined a new "sphere" of human action, distinct from morality, religion, economics, and law.[8] Lefort, however, argues that, in reality, *The Prince* achieves much more than that: through the multiple layers of ambiguity and aporia in its manifest content, it succeeds in putting the reader in contact with the experience of the "institution" of the social itself – that is, in Lefort's language, to show that the idea according to which a specific "sphere" of human endeavour exists, concerned exclusively with the means of access and exercise of political power, already presupposes a specific horizon of intelligibility within which it can appear meaningful. From this, Lefort deduces that the "autonomy" of the political presupposes a specific organization of society as a whole, not just in the way power is wielded, but in the broader sense of the way in which all human relations with each other and with the world are structured – what Lefort calls the "being" of the social. This dimension, for him, is already inherently political because it determines in advance the kinds of power relations that are possible and even thinkable within society. Moreover, Lefort points out, it is with this dimension of social existence that political philosophy traditionally has been concerned: the whole tradition of establishing a "typology" of political regimes that runs from Plato and Aristotle up to Machiavelli, Montesquieu, and de Tocqueville has not been concerned exclusively with different forms of government, but with apprehending different "forms of society" in their totality.

For this reason, Lefort suggests that it is necessary to distinguish between two different senses of the notion of the "political." The first, which he refers to through the masculine version of the term (*le politique*), corresponds to the organizational structure of society as a whole: what enables us to identify it as one in the first place, and to distinguish it from different "forms" of society. The second, on the other hand, which Lefort refers to through the feminine version of the term (*la politique*), corresponds to a specific sphere of human endeavour *within* society, which emerged historically as a consequence of a specific mode of organization of society as a whole. From this it follows that, while *le politique* is assumed to be a universal and constitutive feature of all human societies, *la politique* is a contingent reality that can stand out really only in a determined political context. In the light of this distinction, it is possible to say that, by treating democracy as a "form of society," Lefort signals that he intends to discuss it as a form of *le politique* – that is, as a mode of organization of society as a whole, not simply as a set of institutions or a technique of government. To reduce it to these latter aspects – as a lot of contemporary political science tends to do – would be to treat democracy exclusively as a form of *la politique* without taking into account that the idea that there exists a specific "sphere" of human endeavour that may be identified as "political" is already the result of a previous organization of the social space as a whole, and therefore in a sense is to misunderstand a part for the whole.

The Idea of a "Place of Power"

The notion of a "place of power" is closely connected with that of a "form of society" because it refers to the "generating principle" of the differences between such forms. In this, too, Lefort is implicitly drawing on a long tradition in the history of political thought, according to which all specific aspects of a given form of society can be traced back to a single "source," which is also the pole defining society's basic unity and coherence.

Montesquieu, for example, speaks of a fundamental *"ressort"* from which the specific laws and customs of a given social form all spring. Similarly, in de Tocqueville, there is the idea that equality of social conditions is the "generating factor" from which all the other aspects of democratic society can be deduced. Although Lefort's notion of a "place of power" cannot be reduced to either of these concepts, it is clearly with reference to this tradition that he speaks of an "organizing pole" that gives unity and coherence to society, structuring at the same time its mode of relation to itself and its internal divisions. One of the clearest explanations Lefort offers of the notion is the following:

> The fact that the space we call "society" is organized as *one* despite (or because of) its multiple divisions ... implies a reference to a place from which it can be seen, read and named. Even before we examine it in its empirical determination, this symbolic pole proves to be power; it manifests society's self-externality and ensures that it can achieve a quasi-representation of itself ... We can further specify this notion of shaping [*mise en forme*] by pointing out that it implies both the notion of giving meaning [*mise en sens*] to social relations and that of staging them [*mise en scène*]. Alternatively, we can say that the advent of a society capable of organizing social relations can come about only if it can institute the conditions of their intelligibility, and only if it can use a multiplicity of signs to arrive at a quasi-representation of itself.[9]

This is a dense quote, which shows that the notion of the "place of power" is doing a lot of work for Lefort. The way in which it is assumed to structure the social space is threefold: first of all, it provides a principle of internalization that defines society's basic unity and coherence, despite its internal divisions, and also in relation to the outside (*mise en forme*); second, it defines the basic coordinates of intelligibility within a society, what its members are capable of thinking, and therefore of doing, within the social space (*mise en sens*); third, it provides society a symbolic pole of representation through which it can dramatize for itself its own basic structure and therefore make it accessible and intelligible to its members (*mise en scène*).

Of these three notions, the most important for Lefort, and the one he refers to most often, is the third: *mise en scène*. The reason is that this is also assumed to correspond to the process through which societies ground their specific conception of what is "right" and "legitimate": by constructing a representation of themselves they subsequently strive to realize, societies obtain a conception of both what they "are" and what they "should be." Thus, the notion of collective self-representation provides the bridge between the domains of the "is" and the "ought."

Employing a vocabulary derived from psychoanalysis – in particular, from Lacan – Lefort calls this dimension of collective self-representation the "symbolic."[10]

The opposite pole to the "symbolic" is taken to be the "real," which corresponds to what society is as a matter of fact, beyond its self-representation. For Lefort, the tension between these two dimensions – that of the "symbolic" and that of the "real" – is constitutive of all forms of society. For this reason, another way in which he often refers to the notion of a "place of power" is in terms of the "constitutive division" of the social. The central idea here is that society is always, constitutively divided from itself: its symbolic representation of what it is and the factual reality behind it can never completely coincide, therefore neither fully exhausts the "being" of the social. Rather, human societies are constructed precisely around the *tension* between what they are and what they represent themselves to be. In this sense, Lefort can be identified correctly as a theorist of social division, because for him social unity is paradoxically realized precisely *through* division: by separating itself from itself, and constructing a symbolic representation of itself, society constitutes itself as one, distinguishing itself from others and assuming a specific organizational form. Moreover, the unity that results is assumed to consist precisely in the organization of the multiple layers of division *within* society. In Machiavelli, for example, we saw that the delineation of a specific "sphere" of human endeavour, distinguished from all others, was precisely the way in which the social order as a whole was structured. Thus, as Lefort himself puts it, "division merely appears as a specific mode of social relation."[11]

To clarify further how this process of social division functions to structure the social space, it might be useful to give another example. I focus in particular on Lefort's conception of the *Ancien Régime*, which in many ways constitutes the foil for his theory of democracy. Drawing in part from the historical analyses put forward by Ernst Kantorowicz, Lefort asserts that, during the *Ancien Régime*, society understood itself essentially as an incarnation of the king – meaning that its members thought of themselves, pretty concretely, as constitutive elements of the king's body.[12] In this way, society was able to identify itself as one and to distinguish itself from others: the king's body therefore functioned as a sort of totalizing "whole," simultaneously present within each specific component of society and exceeding them all collectively. At the same time, this representation also had important consequences for the internal organization of society, since the idea that every individual member constituted a specific part of the king's body assigned a very specific set of rights and duties to each in relation to the others, ultimately defining a precise hierarchy of power relations. Thus the society of the *Ancien Régime* actually functioned as if it were a "body," with the orders coming from the "head" of the state and the lower "members" executing them.

What is distinctive for Lefort about that society, however, is that its members were not *conscious* that this mode of social institution implied a process of "division": the assumption was that the individual members of the state literally *were* component elements of the king's body. Thus the king's body was not perceived as a "symbolic" representation, distinct from the "real" of society: the specific mode of social organization that prevailed depended on the fusion of these two dimensions. This is precisely what changed with the passage to democracy.

Democracy as an "Empty Space"

In the light of the above example, one can finally move on to examine what Lefort means when he says that democracy is a "form of society" in which the "place of power" is represented as an "empty space." The first thing to note is that this does not imply that what Lefort calls the "place of power" is abolished entirely. As we have seen, for him, all forms of society must necessarily have an organizing structure, because this is what enables them to identify themselves as "one" in the first place. Thus there must necessarily remain a pole of self-representation through which society constructs an image of what it is for itself.

Flynn expresses this by saying that democracy "abolishes the figure, but not the dimension, of the Other."[13] This can be interpreted as meaning that the symbolic pole in terms of which society organizes itself persists, but is emptied of its content. Paradoxically, therefore, democratic society configures itself as a form of society whose organizing structure is precisely the idea of a "non-structure." At the level of collective representations, this takes place through the effacement of the figure of the king, which means that society ceases to understand itself as a "body." However, instead of substituting this representation with another substantive image – which would assign social roles in a different pattern but following the same logic – it begins to organize itself in terms of the image of a "lack." This notion of a "lack," Lefort points out, is inseparable from the idea of something that needs to be filled. Thus democratic society must always be attempting to "fill" the "place of power" with a concrete representation of what it is. To preserve the initial "lack" means, however, to recognize that all concrete representations will necessarily be inadequate and therefore provisional. Thus, in the final analysis, democratic society must understand itself as an infinitely malleable entity, open to assuming all specific forms, on condition that none will be definitive.

At the level of the "real," this specific mode of self-representation is translated in a refusal to accept any specific organizing structure. As a matter of fact, it is inevitable that social practice will produce relations of power and therefore reciprocal social roles. However, the specificity of democratic society is taken to be that it refuses to consider any of these relations of power or social roles as definitively legitimate, thereby leaving them open to an endless process of revision and renegotiation. In this way, democracy inscribes a constant tendency towards change within the organizing structure of society itself, which ultimately implies that the movement between different social configurations becomes more important than the specific social outcomes.

It is for this reason that Lefort asserts that democracy can be understood as an "essentially historical" form of society:

> Just as the figure of power in its materiality and its substantiality disappears, and just as the exercise of power proves to be bound up with the temporality of its reproduction and to be subordinated to the conflict of collective wills ... the dimension of the development of right unfolds in its entirety, always dependent upon a debate upon its foundations and as to the legitimacy of what has been established and of what ought to be established ... Democracy thus proves to be the historical society *par excellence*, a society which, in its very form, welcomes and preserves indeterminacy.[14]

Another way in which Lefort expresses the specificity of the democratic form is through the idea that this is the only form of society that preserves and affirms the tension between the dimension of the "symbolic" and that of the "real." This means that democratic society is conscious that the normative self-representations it constructs of itself can never correspond fully to what it is as a matter of fact; and therefore that its actual mode of organization must always remain lacking in legitimacy. This constitutive "lack," or perpetual inability to live up to what it wants to be, is precisely what compels democratic society to change all the time, striving to fulfil its normative aspirations, even while remaining conscious that it can never correspond fully to its representation of itself.

Since, as we have seen, for Lefort, the tension between the "symbolic" and the "real" corresponds to the "constitutive division" of all forms of society, this amounts to another way of saying that democracy is a form of society that is constitutively organized around the consciousness of its own division from itself – and cherishes it as a value. Indeed, Lefort goes as far as to suggest that democracy is the *only* form of society that can cherish division as a value, because it seeks to preserve the "gap" between the symbolic and the real. In the *Ancien Régime*, according to Lefort's reconstruction, this gap was not even perceivable, because the assumption was that society corresponded directly to its representation of itself – as we have seen, it *was* an incarnation of the king's body. In a democratic framework, on the other hand, the consciousness and appreciation of social division are reflected at all levels of social organization: not only the separation of society from its own representation of itself, but also the separation of the state from civil society, of the executive from the legislative and judiciary powers, and of the various constituents of civil society from one another in a multitude of groups and civic associations that remain irreducible to one another. Ultimately, it is precisely the interplay among all these various social "parts" that generates the constant movement characteristic of democratic societies.[15]

The "Disincorporation" of Law, Power, and Knowledge

To clarify the way in which the multiple layers of division of society from itself function as the engine of the constant political movement characteristic of democratic societies, it is necessary to dig deeper into Lefort's theory of democracy, beyond the image of a "place of power" represented as an "empty space." For this purpose, it is useful to refer once more to what Lefort says about the *Ancien Régime*, since it and totalitarianism constitute the "foils" for his theory of democracy.

Under the *Ancien Régime*, Lefort asserts, the domains of law, power, and knowledge were "incorporated" in the figure of the king's body. By this he means that society was organized in terms of a pyramidal structure of justification, according to which all individual social practices ultimately found the source of their legitimacy in a unique principle: through his simple, bodily presence the king offered a guarantee for everything that took place in society. With the passage to a democratic form of organization, the possibility of making reference to this ultimate "ground" of legitimacy was lost. Thus the various forms of human behaviour were forced to develop the principles of their own justification autonomously. This encouraged the formation of different ends and criteria of legitimacy peculiar to different "spheres" of human endeavour. In particular, Lefort claims that the spheres of law, power, and knowledge were progressively "disincorporated" from one another through a series of conceptual transformations that marked the transition to the democratic age.

We have already seen how in Machiavelli the sphere of the political (in the sense of *la politique*) was delineated essentially as the set of strategies and techniques having to do with the access to and exercise of power over the institutions of the state. Through his work, therefore, the dimension of power assumed a self-referentiality it had never displayed before, by being detached from all "external" considerations of morality and religion. The second key moment in the transition to the democratic age, for Lefort, occurred with the various declarations of human rights that took place towards the end of the eighteenth century. These had the effect of affirming a principle of right external to that of political power, and therefore capable of limiting it from outside. In this way, they contributed to the formation of an autonomous sphere of law, organized around its own internal criteria of coherence and legitimacy.[16] Finally, the autonomization of the sphere of knowledge, for Lefort, occurred in the context of the German Enlightenment. It affirmed a principle of rationality different from that of *raison d'État*, and therefore opened the space for the possibility of a "critique" of political power based on the exercise of human reason.[17]

The consequence of all this, for Lefort, was that, between the various "spheres" of human endeavour, an overarching criterion of discrimination ceased to be available. This implied that it became impossible to adjudicate potential conflicts between them in an absolute or definitive manner, a point that Lefort expresses by saying that the "disincorporation" of the domains of law, power, and knowledge led to a "dissolution of the markers of certainty": "When an empty place emerges, there can be no possible conjunction between power, law and knowledge, and their foundations cannot possibly be enunciated. The being of the social vanishes or, more accurately, presents itself in the shape of an endless series of questions (witness the incessant, shifting debates between ideologies). The ultimate markers of certainty are destroyed, and at the same time there is born a new awareness of the unknown element in history, of the gestation of humanity in all the variety of its figures."[18]

This quote is significant because it establishes a connection between the notion of a "dissolution of the markers of certainty" and that of an infinitely renewed "questioning": an index of the fact that the separation of different "spheres" of human endeavour does not imply a lack of relations among them. On the contrary, Lefort insists that separation is only a specific mode of relation, which makes possible a reciprocal "questioning" between the "spheres." Thus, for example, within a democratic context, the conformity of power with law is more insistently examined than ever. Similarly, the foundation of legitimacy of law itself becomes the object of an endless research.

From this, Lefort deduces that the "disincorporation" of the domains of law, power, and knowledge poses the conditions for an "institutionalization" of the conflict among them. Moreover, since the possibility of making reference to a superior criterion of legitimacy is removed, this conflict must take place within the context of a radical "indeterminacy," which implies that it can never be definitively resolved. In this way, the separation of different "spheres" of human endeavour becomes the engine of a constant transformation of society, because these various spheres are forced to constantly renegotiate their relations with one another, without ever being able to reach a definitive solution.

Furthermore, Lefort adds, the "dissolution of the markers of certainty" implies that "institutionalization of conflict" is also reflected *within* the various "spheres" of human endeavour. In the field of knowledge, for example, the lack of an ultimate foundation implies that the search for truth is given over to an "endless debate." In the sphere of *la politique,* on the other hand, the competition for power takes precedence over its appropriation, because no individual or social group can claim to exercise it legitimately, in a definitive manner. This latter point is particularly important for Lefort because it effectively constitutes the sphere of *la politique* as a further representation of society's basic organizing structure at the level of the "real." This produces a sort of short-circuit between the dimensions of the "symbolic" and the "real," whereby society's "symbolic" self-understanding is redramatized at the level of the "real" in one of the specific "spheres" it generates. For Lefort, all the various institutions we commonly associate with "democracy" are precisely this – a "stage" on which society dramatizes its mode of institution for itself in order to gain access to it: "The erection of a political stage on which competition can take place shows that division is, in a general way, constitutive of the very unity of society. Or to put it in another way, the legitimation of purely political conflict contains within it the principle of a legitimation of social conflict in all its forms."[19]

Thus the relationship between the dimensions of *le politique* and *la politique* has a complex structure in a democratic society. On one hand, the existence of a specific "sphere" called *la politique* implies a specific mode of organization of society at the level of *le politique*. On the other hand, however, this overall mode of organization is obtained precisely through the constitution of the specific "sphere." Once again, therefore, division is shown to be merely a mode of relation, because, beyond their separation, *le politique* and *la politique* prove to be reciprocally constitutive of each other.

Beyond Marxism and Liberalism

Having attempted to spell out Lefort's theory of democracy in the terms he uses to formulate it, I now attempt to bring it into further relief by comparing it with some of the political philosophies from which it explicitly attempts distinguish itself. I focus in particular on two constant points of reference for Lefort: classical Marxism and contemporary liberalism. As I pointed out at the beginning of the chapter, Lefort began his intellectual career as a Marxist, and it was only gradually that he marked his distance from this starting point. The best way to bring out how he finally operated this "overcoming" is with reference to a specific text by Marx, on which Lefort commented several times throughout his career: the famous essay "On the Jewish Question."[20]

Of course, I cannot develop Marx's argument in detail here. What is important to recall, for the present purposes, is that Marx claims that modern society is based on a separation between the *state*, within which citizens are treated as "free" and "equal," and *civil society*, within which "capitalist" relations of production persist. This separation, for Marx, has the effect of masking the persistence of concrete forms of oppression behind an illusory "veil" of emancipation. Thus the real condition of human beings in society remains one of oppression, even if, at the level of political representation, they think of themselves as "free." The only way to achieve "full human emancipation," Marx concludes, is for human beings to overcome the separation between the state and civil society, by consciously appropriating the means of their self-determination, at the level not only of symbolic representation, but also of concrete social relations.

Relative to this theory, Lefort's conception of democracy can be read as a way of affirming that the separation between the state and civil society need not necessarily function exclusively as a mask for oppression, but can also contain an emancipatory potential. The reason is that, as we have seen, for him, the preservation of a "gap" between the "symbolic" and the "real" is precisely the feature that sets in motion the democratic movement of constant self-redefinition of society. Since Marx himself seems to suggest that the state corresponds to society's symbolic self-representation, while civil society is the concrete dimension of the real, this implies that the separation between them can have a transformative effect on civil society itself, by encouraging it to change to better "fit" with the representation it constructs of itself at the level of the state. Conversely, Marx's idea of definitively overcoming this distinction seems to suggest that society could reach a final state of total coincidence with its representation of itself, in which it would be definitively available to itself as a conscious subject. As well as being intellectually dubious, for Lefort this supposition is politically dangerous, because, as we will see before the end of this chapter, the idea of a society capable of consciously determining itself in all its specific parts is a necessary condition for the emergence of a "totalitarian" form of domination. It is in this sense, therefore, that Lefort finds the germ for "totalitarianism" in Marx's philosophy – which is, of course, very different from saying that this philosophy *implies*, or even leads *necessarily*, to a totalitarian form of domination.

The difference between Lefort's theory of democracy and the horizon of contemporary liberalism is not thematized in such an explicit manner in his writings. Although Lefort uses the term "liberalism" relatively often, he appears to refer to different authors and traditions in different contexts.[21] In what follows, I focus on a specific strand of contemporary liberal thought, characterized by a neo-Kantian form of constructivism such as that of Jürgen Habermas or John Rawls. Although it is unclear whether Lefort ever has this specific body of thought in mind in particular, it might be interesting to compare it with his theory of democracy because of its importance in the English-speaking academic environment.

The distinguishing feature of this neo-Kantian form of liberalism is the attempt to reconstruct the normative grounds of political legitimacy on a substantive conception of "rationality." The background assumption is therefore similar to Lefort's: that, in the context of modernity, the grounds on which legitimacy traditionally was based have been undermined. The difference, however, is that, instead of assuming this "lack" and attempting to make it into the foundation for a theory of democracy, neo-Kantian liberals seek to establish new points of reference to substitute for the ones that have been undermined. This can be seen, for example, in the works of two of the most illustrious representatives of this strand of thought. Starting from the premise that modernity corresponds to a "post-metaphysical" context, Habermas finds within the pragmatic structure of language itself the normative resources that enable him to establish the rationality of a consensus reached under the conditions of an "ideal speech situation."[22] Similarly, Rawls starts from the premise that contemporary societies are characterized by the "fact of pluralism," but then uses the artifice of an "original position" to deduce the principles on which he assumes there must be an "overlapping consensus" among reasonable individuals.[23]

My contention is that, if Lefort had considered these theories explicitly, he would ultimately have judged them "ahistorical," even though they both claim to be grounded in a theory of "modernity." The reason is that they refer to a substantive conception of "rationality," which is either assumed to be valid universally, or introduced dogmatically as appropriate for our historical condition. In both cases, therefore, the presupposition that, within the context of modernity, the possibility of making reference to "absolute" and "indubitable" points of reference has been removed is ultimately contradicted. Of course, this does not mean that Lefort would do away with the concept of "rationality" altogether – that would mean succumbing to the same temptation in reverse, simply substituting rationalism for irrationalism. His point more likely would be that, within the context of modernity, the concept of rationality itself has been pluralized and divided from itself. Different forms of rationality have emerged that are specific both to the various "spheres" of human endeavour and to the different contexts and objects to which they apply. Thus it is impossible to ground the legitimacy of the social order on a single conception of rationality without falling back into the kind of "foundationalism" that for Lefort has been rendered anachronistic by the sociological and philosophical background of modernity.

From this perspective, Lefort's theory of democracy proves to be far more daring than Habermas's or Rawls's versions of liberalism, because instead of trying to find a new substantive foundation for legitimacy, he attempts to conceive of a political order grounded precisely on the *absence* of such ultimate foundations. The crux is that, if the possibility of making reference to "absolute" foundations is removed, all existing configurations of power must necessarily become incapable of fully legitimating themselves, and therefore always open to a possibility of "critique." The idea of a society's constantly criticizing its own forms of organization therefore replaces that of a society's seeking to fulfil a fixed idea of normativity.

Here neo-Kantian liberals might object that the notion of "critique" itself already presupposes a normative criterion of legitimacy, as a "foil" against which to measure concrete social practice. However, that would be to miss the key point of Lefort's argument, which is that critique does not necessarily need to be grounded on an "external" criterion. His presupposition is that all forms of social organization must necessarily produce their own justifications to function properly. However, since in a democratic context the possibility of making reference to "absolute" grounds has been removed, these justifications are always bound to remain "partial" and "inadequate." Thus the space is opened up to criticize existing social configurations *on their own terms*, for their incapacity to legitimate themselves fully. It is this notion of critique as an immanent process of self-reflection, within the context of a radical "indeterminacy," that drives Lefort's theory of democracy – as opposed to a determinate conception of the grounds of legitimacy, based on a substantive conception of "rationality."

The Twin Risks of Modernity: Relativism and Totalitarianism

The above discussion should not give the impression that, for Lefort, once "the ultimate markers of certainty are destroyed," democracy is a foregone conclusion. It is an essential aspect of his theory that modernity is open to a plurality of different outcomes, not all of which are equally attractive. In this final section, I focus on two specific "risks" that Lefort identifies as always present for democracy in modernity.

The first is what he refers to as "relativism." This is defined as a "banalization of the recognition of the other," which occurs when the absence of ultimate points of reference undermines the drive towards political participation. It therefore corresponds to an attitude of "indifference," which is assumed to lead to a "retreat into the sphere of the private" and a "passive acceptance" of whatever occurs at the level of the political, as if this were not of immediate concern to individuals.[24] For Lefort, two underlying structural trends conspire to make this "risk" particularly worrying for contemporary democracies: the unchecked diffusion of a market-based logic of distribution, and the capillary expansion of a system of regulation legitimated in terms of an ideal of "security." Both trends are assumed to induce individuals to trade "political engagement" for "material well-being." The concern, therefore, is that they might result in an "impoverishment" of democratic politics, which would translate into a form of "stagnation," rather than the vital process of "self-critique" that is constitutive of democratic societies.[25]

The other major "risk" that Lefort sees as ever present in modernity – the degeneration into a "totalitarian" form of domination – is not entirely disconnected from this conception of "relativism." Drawing heavily on the historical analyses of Hannah Arendt, Lefort suggests that it is precisely when individuals have been "depoliticized" and confined to the private pursuit of exclusively material concerns that a "longing" for ultimate points of reference may re-emerge. If, for some reason, the system proves temporarily incapable of satisfying their material demands, individuals might seek redemption at the level of the political. At this stage, the image of the "place of power" as an "empty space" might prove "intolerable," and this paves the way for the rise to prominence of political parties that promise to refill it with substantive representations of Unity and Truth – such as the "*Volk*" or the "Proletariat."[26] In this sense, Lefort suggests that "totalitarianism" may be understood, at least in a preliminary way, as an attempt to reconstitute the intellectual and political framework of the *Ancien Régime* within the context of modernity: society acquires a "body" once more, and the various "spheres" of human endeavour are "re-incorporated" in the absolute principle of legitimacy. Correspondingly, the dimension of "division" is denied at all levels of social organization.[27]

At the same time, however, it is also important to point out that, for Lefort, "totalitarianism" cannot be reduced exclusively to a reactionary regression to the political coordinates of the *Ancien Régime*. There is something irreducibly "modern" in it, which can be traced back to the "fiction" of a society that would be fully "transparent" to itself, capable of determining itself consciously in all its specific parts. Ultimately, for Lefort, it is this "fiction" that abolishes all the "limits" to political power, and therefore distinguishes totalitarianism from classical forms of oppression such as "tyranny" or "despotism."[28] This is significant because, for Lefort, the idea of a society capable of fully determining itself in all its specific parts emerges from *within* the democratic imaginary. The idea of a society in flux, always open to being transformed by the critical endeavours of its inhabitants, might be confused for the idea of a society wholly "available" and perfectly "transparent" to them, if the idea of the "place of power" as an "empty place" is shifted from the level of the "symbolic" to that of the "real." Thus, the risk of degeneration into a "totalitarian" form of domination is assumed to be lodged in the organizing structure of democracy itself.

From this it follows that democracy, for Lefort, can never be taken for granted. On the contrary, one might conclude by pointing out that, for him, it configures itself in the form of a perpetual "test" for its members. To avoid the Scylla of relativism and the Charybdis of totalitarianism, individuals have to be able to live up to democracy, constantly formulating and defending concrete political projects, without succumbing to the temptation to seek to ground them on "absolute" foundations – a political balancing act that might not prove easy, but that represents the only hope of preserving freedom in a situation in which the certainties of the past have been radically compromised.

NOTES

1 See Claude Lefort, "L'analyse Marxiste et le Fascisme" and "Les pays coloniaux – analyse structurelle et stratégie révolutionnaire," both in *Le temps present: écrits 1945–2005* (Paris: Belin, 2007), 31–6, 49–75.

2 Claude Lefort, *Éléments d'une critique de la bureaucratie* (Paris: Gallimard, 1979).

3 Lefort published two books on democracy – *L'invention démocratique: les limites de la domination totalitaire* (Paris: Fayard, 1981) and *Essais sur le politique* (Paris: Seuil, 1986) – as well as countless other articles both in academic journals and in the general press. Only the latter book was translated entirely into English as *Democracy and Political Theory*; some chapters of the former are available in a volume entitled *The Political Forms of Modern Society: Bureaucracy, Democracy, Totalitarianism*, ed. John Thompson (Cambridge, MA: MIT Press, 1986).

4 Claude Lefort, "Question of Democracy," 9.

5 For a discussion of Lefort's political philosophy in relation to other theories of radical democracy, see Ingram, "Politics of Claude Lefort's Political."

6 Flynn, *Philosophy of Claude Lefort*. For further secondary literature on Lefort's work in English, see also Warren Breckman, Peter Gordon, and Dirk Moses, eds., *The Modernist Imagination: Intellectual History and Critical Theory* (New York: Berghahn, 2009); Olivier Marchart, *Post-Foundational Political Thought: Political Difference in Nancy, Lefort, Badiou and Laclau*, (Edinburgh: Edinburgh University Press, 2007); and Martin Plot, ed., *Claude Lefort: Thinker of the Political* (New York: Palgrave Macmillan, 2013);

as well as the "special issues" devoted to his thought by *Thesis Eleven* (2006) and *Constellations* (2012).

7 Lefort, *Machiavelli in the Making*.

8 This is the interpretation provided, albeit in different ways, by, for example, Gerhard Ritter and Leo Strauss, both of whom Lefort discusses in specific chapters of his book; see ibid., 206–18, 259–306.

9 Lefort, "Permanence of the Theologico-Political?" 218–25.

10 This notion of the "symbolic" perhaps can be brought into greater relief by comparing it to the use made by Cornelius Castoriadis of another notion drawn from Lacanian terminology: that of the social "imaginary," as outlined in his *The Imaginary Institution of Society* (Cambridge, MA: MIT Press, 1987), and discussed in Chapter 5 in this volume. Both mean to refer to the fundamental idea that society "institutes itself" through an idealizing process of "self-representation." The key difference, however, is that, while for Castoriadis the "imaginary" is an "originary" and creative "power" that constantly produces social representations in a radically unpredictable fashion, for Lefort the symbolic remains inscribed within the terms of a dialectical relationship with the existing social reality, and therefore is not posited as any sort of ontological "foundation" for society, but rather points towards the idea that society is held together by the reciprocal relations between its constitutive parts, without the need for an absolute "foundation." On this point, see, for example, Breckman, "Lefort and the Symbolic Dimension."

11 Lefort, *Machiavelli in the Making*, 372.

12 Ernst Kantorowicz, *The King's Two Bodies: A Study in Mediaeval Political Theology* (Princeton, NJ: Princeton University Press, 1997).

13 Flynn, *Philosophy of Claude Lefort*, 126.

14 Lefort, "Question of Democracy," 16–18.

15 This conception of democracy as a "form of society" in which the "place of power" is represented as an "empty space" has an interesting and complex relationship to the theory of "populism" as the essential structure of the political developed by Ernesto Laclau. As Laclau himself points out in his *On Populist Reason*, which includes a section devoted explicitly to Lefort's work, their respective theories have in common the idea that society is instituted through its self-representation, and that there remains an irreducible "gap," or tension, between this representation and its material basis, a point Laclau expresses through the idea that social unity is ultimately achieved through the hegemonic condensation around an "empty signifier." The key difference, however, is that Lefort understands the "empty place of power" as a structural feature of a *distinctive* form of

society, while Laclau understands "empty signifiers" as a discursive tool employed by *all* processes of political subjectivation. This implies that, although Lefort's theory of democracy links it to a specific political sensibility (which Laclau identifies with the horizon of liberalism), for Laclau populism is the horizon of all political forms as such. On this point, see Ernesto Laclau, *On Populist Reason* (London: Verso, 2005), 164–71.

16 Claude Lefort, "Politics and Human Rights," in Thompson, *Political Forms of Modern Society*, 239–72.

17 Claude Lefort, "Démocratie et avènement d'un 'lieu vide,'" in *Le temps présent*, 461–9.

18 Lefort, "Permanence of the Theologico-Political?" 228.

19 Lefort, "Question of Democracy," 18.

20 The following discussion is based primarily on the commentary Lefort makes of Marx's text in "Politics and Human Rights," 245–55.

21 For a discussion of the history of the term "liberalism" by Lefort himself, see his essay on "Libéralisme et démocratie," in *Le Temps Présent*, 745–59.

22 Habermas, *Between Facts and Norms*.

23 Rawls, *Political Liberalism*.

24 Claude Lefort, "La liberté à l'ère du relativisme," in *Le Temps Présent*, 631–43.

25 Claude Lefort, "Le relativisme déchaîne l'imbécillité," in *Le Temps Présent*, 683–7.

26 Claude Lefort, "La logique totalitaire," in *L'invention démocratique: les limites de la domination totalitaire* (Paris: Fayard, 1981), 85.

27 Ibid., 96.

28 Ibid., 100.

5 Cornelius Castoriadis: Auto-Institution and Radical Democracy

BRIAN C.J. SINGER

Introduction

In what sense can Cornelius Castoriadis (1922–97) be considered an important thinker of radical democracy? To be sure, he was an advocate of radical democracy, but advocacy by itself hardly makes one an important thinker. If Castoriadis deserves inclusion in this reader – and it is my belief that he does – it is because he tied democracy to a larger project, that of "autonomy" or "auto-institution." It is with this larger project – which resonates far beyond the pale of political theory – that the importance of his work lies. And it is in the light of this larger project that his more strictly political thinking must be judged.

The project of auto-institution has several parts. First, there is its pre-history, when, in the 1950s and the first half of the '60s, Castoriadis was the major figure, along with Claude Lefort, of *Socialisme ou Barbarie*, an important journal (and groupuscule) of post-Trotskyist leanings. During this period, beginning from a strictly Marxist position, Castoriadis began pulling hard on the thread of critique, tugging on an ever-wider array of forms of domination or heteronomy, to the point where, by 1966, his Marxism, the journal, and group had all unravelled. As this belongs to the pre-history, I do not discuss it here.[1]

The second, and more important, part for our purposes concerns the elaboration of the philosophical basis of his project. The key work here is the *Imaginary Institution of Society*,[2] particularly the second half, although one should also include many of the essays in the *Crossroads* series,[3] as well as one of the posthumously published series of lectures.[4] Here Castoriadis moves across a dizzying range of fields – philosophy, sociology, psychoanalysis, linguistics, and mathematics – to develop a general ontology of the "social-historical." And it is here that he introduces his most important concepts, such as institution, the radical imaginary, the identitarian-ensemblist or ensidic dimension, and the magma of imaginary social significations. I examine this dimension of his thought in the following section of this chapter.

A third part concerns his studies of ancient Greece – more precisely, ancient Athens. The latter gives his discussion a certain historical concreteness, as ancient Athens is deemed the first genuinely autonomous society – that is, the first society capable of questioning, in word and action, its own institutions and traditions. The creation of democracy is judged to be integral to such autonomy, as was the creation of tragic theatre, historical writing, and, more ambiguously, philosophy. In this discussion, a number of essays in the *Crossroads* series remain important,[5] but it is only with the series of recently published volumes of lectures that the richness of this component of Castoriadis's thinking becomes evident.[6] I consider his discussion of ancient Athens in the third section of this chapter.

The fourth part concerns Castoriadis's contemporary analysis. Here one must include his comments on contemporary events, his critique of the present state of society, and his advocacy of new, more democratic forms. This component again can be found throughout the *Crossroads* series, but one should also mention several books of interviews,[7] as well as a number of separate works precipitated by particular events.[8] As this aspect of his thinking is, in my view, the least developed, I leave it to the end.[9]

The Institution of the Socio-historical

To understand the turn to social ontology, one must consider the reversibility of the terms "liberation" and "domination," not just in an "actual" sense – as exemplified by the fate of Soviet Marxism – but above all in a conceptual sense, where reason, by the very ambiguity of its claims to the mastery of self and environment, proves less a tool of liberation than a force for new and more extensive forms of domination. This deadlock already appears in the work of Max Weber, where the increasing rationalization of the modern world, as exemplified by bureaucratization, results in the formation of an "iron cage" (or, more literally, a "shell as hard as steel")[10] – a thesis continued by the Frankfurt School with its vision of a "totally administered" or "one-dimensional" society. Castoriadis would provide a critical addendum: a totally bureaucratic, administered society is impossible, as demonstrated by his earlier analysis of the everyday functioning of both capitalist factories and Soviet totalitarianism. They simply cannot function outside the meaning, motivation, and individual initiative that exceeds, and even counters, their "rational enframing." With the "limits of reason" exposed in practice, Castoriadis sought to understand these limits in a more general theoretical sense. What, in its most basic sense, constitutes "reason"? – a question he posed by asking if there were not some minimal kernel of rationality without which social life would not be possible. Once this minimum was determined, he then could ask what else, outside "reason," was necessary for social existence? In effect, to pose the limits of reason at this most elemental level was to point to the existence of another, equally necessary dimension of social life, as it was evident that the latter can be neither totally rational and transparent nor totally irrational and opaque. Consider briefly each of the two dimensions that form his social ontology.

Reason is rooted in what Castoriadis terms the "identitarian-ensemblist" (or ensidic, for short) dimension of "institution" (the reason of philosophy being the interminable elaboration of this dimension). The latter provides the most basic operative schemas necessary for all social communication and social activity – what, following the Greek, he calls the *legein* and *teukhein*. The identitarian moment refers to the principle of identity, the first, most fundamental plank in any notion of reason.[11] Simply put, a social object (or person) must be given an identity – a relatively consistent, durable identity – that identifies it as this particular object (or person). The term "ensemble" can be translated as "set" (as in mathematics' "set theory"): the self-identical objects (or persons) can be placed in an ensemble (or ensembles), which can then be distinguished from other sets, which, in turn, permits the establishment of relations within and between different ensembles according to different criteria. To flesh out the analysis a little, consider briefly the ensidic dimension relative to the *legein*, or, what is central to it, to language. Castoriadis's analysis is not entirely foreign to the linguistic turn – and not least because he critiques the "philosophy of consciousness." Although he does not stop at this turn, his analysis of the ensidic dimension of the *teukheim*, though focused on techne, remains similar to that of the *legein* in many of its key aspects.

At the most basic level, language supposes the identification and designation of a set of discrete and distinct phonemes. Castoriadis speaks of these phonemes as material-abstract: material in the sense that they can be heard, and abstract in the sense that they bear a normative form that enables them to be recognized as a specific phoneme, despite all the concrete variations in tone, pitch, and dialect. These material-abstract phonemes can be combined into new and determinate ensembles – lexemes, morphemes, grammatical classes, syntactic types – whose individual units can be subjected to different operations, such as their separation, combination, or substitution (the latter including Saussure's paradigmatic or syntagmatic relations). And the sorts of operative schemas applicable to the signifiers can be expanded to the level of the signifieds, or to that of signs more generally, and even to the referent, once the latter is caught within a "signitive relation." For the signitive relation indicates that the "object" has been identified and classified, and thus, at a minimum, can be separated from, combined with, or substituted for other objects – all of which implies that the object has a social existence, that it exists in and for society. This is true of natural objects as well, for once subject to the ensidic operations proper to language, they lose their natural immediacy, and acquire another, properly social existence. As this rather simplified sketch suggests, Castoriadis holds that structuralist linguistics is particularly adept at describing the ensidic dimension of language – what he terms its "code." The latter is absolutely necessary for speaking (and for distinguishing, choosing, posing, assembling, and so on); it provides language with the necessary fixity, regularity, and determinacy without which communication would be impossible. But the code does not exhaust the character of language; the whole purpose of the exercise is, after all, to circumscribe the ensidic dimension of social institution. The question is: what does this dimension fail to grasp (here relative to the analysis of language)?

At this point, Castoriadis must introduce what he terms the "imaginary dimension of institution." To begin, at the level of the signifier, the ensidic dimension can identify the phonemes, but it cannot pose them. There is no "rational" reason, for example, that English has the sound "th" when most other languages do not. Phonemes are not given naturally; as material-abstract entities, they entail the creation of forms. A similar claim must be made relative to the signifieds and to signs more generally. Although the ensidic dimension stabilizes a term, such that it can be subjected to various "operative schemas," that dimension cannot account for the content of the sign, its meaning, or signification. Castoriadis is in agreement with Saussure when the latter speaks of the "arbitrariness of the sign," by which he means that there is no necessary reason a given signifier is attached to a given signified or set of signifieds. And Castoriadis underlines that the signitive relation that attaches the sign to the referent, and causes the latter to become a social object removed from its "natural" immediacy, is also "arbitrary." For it is not a logical relation, as it establishes relations between levels that are not equivalent; or a "real" relation, in that it is not reducible to anything that exists prior to it; or, finally, a "necessary" relation ultimately determined by what it signifies. The signitive relation, like the signifier and signified, is irreducibly a creation, one essential to any idea of institution.[12] How is one to explain the creation of social forms, whether that of the sign, the object, or the relation that holds them together? Castoriadis claims that it cannot be explained in rational, logical terms, that it escapes the terms of an ensidic logico-ontology, and notably those of cause and effect. Social forms are, in the last instance, created *ex nihilo*; they are formed by what he terms the radical imaginary.

Before I examine the radicality of the imaginary, consider the latter as a dimension of the actual functioning of language. However necessary the ensidic dimension (or code), it is the imaginary dimension, the *langue* in Castoriadis's parlance, that bears primacy at the level of the establishment of meaning or signification – hence he speaks of imaginary social significations. A purely ensidic language – one thinks of mathematics[13] – would be a pseudo-language, rigid in its application, impoverished in its contents, and closed in on itself. A signification, contrary to the semanticist dream of denotative transparency, does not constitute a universal form commensurate to that which it refers. Rather than being equivalent to its object, it is simply a reference point (*point de repérage*), adequate to the always specific uses to which it is put. This is to say, a signification always points beyond what it immediately states, to what is implied by other significations, objects, and referents, even as it opens itself to other uses. In opposition to the structuralist claim, these referrals are not constructed as a discrete set of determinate, diacritical relations, but as "an indefinite [cluster] of interminable referrals to *something other*."[14] Thus the imaginary social significations are seen as forming a "magma" with neither distinct elements nor determinate relations, where the ensidic dimension provides a minimal stability to what otherwise would appear an abyssal chaos. Still, the imaginary dimension constantly undermines this stability and organization, which is why language cannot be conceived as forming an airtight, synchronic pattern, with a change in one relation necessitating a change in them all. It is why language is inherently diachronic, always open to saying new things, the bearer of an indefinite creativity.

The linguistic turn has raised the stakes of any discussion concerning language. One thinks, for example, of Jürgen Habermas, whose turn to language also sought to limit, at the level of general theory, the rationalist or instrumentalist tendencies in the modern world (to counter, here explicitly, the earlier Frankfurt School's "pessimism"). But the differences with Castoriadis are enormous,[15] and I will limit myself to just one fundamental point. What interests Castoriadis about language is not its ability to promote an accord, and thereby "ontologize" a consensual, contractual, and "democratic" moment relative to social existence, but the imaginary dimension of language that enables the formation of new, unpredictable social significations. It is difficult to reach agreement, even about the sense of what one is arguing about, when new meanings are constantly being created. (In contrast to structuralists, however, for Castoriadis the flexible, open-ended character of the *langue* ensures some communicability between different universes of meaning.) By emphasizing the creativity of language and, by implication, history, Castoriadis ensures that "theory" is subordinated to "praxis," whereas Habermas's search for a rational consensus (or at least for the conditions that would allow for such) would seek the opposite. A free society for Castoriadis is less one that subordinates itself to an accord that everyone freely agrees on than one that is able to create new meanings and objects without being beholden to any principle of heteronomy, something that reason threatens to become.

As an imaginary creation, language is not dissimilar to any other social idea, thing, or person, or indeed to institution in general – that is, to the institution of the socio-historical. When Castoriadis speaks of imaginary institution, he does not mean that institution is unreal or false, but that it is irreducible to a "rational," "natural," or "real" substratum. Institution is *sui generis*; it institutes its own world, an always particular world of particular significations, which is to say that it institutes its own imaginary. As such institution entails the creation of new meanings, forms, and values: meaning can be grasped only if given form, and all forms have significance and value, either positive or negative, just as values too must find expression in form.[16] And as such, institution establishes what for a society is real and unreal, true and false, just and unjust, and so on in a manner specific to that society. In its imaginary dimension, institution implies an effect that exceeds any determinate cause, whether material or ideal. In this sense, institution implies a moment that refuses to fall under any law, whether natural, historical, social, economic, or providential. At the base of this creativity is the radical imaginary, the source of all representations and significations, including the first "originary" signification that institutes the very possibility of institution (as well as the representation of what is real or rational). The radical imaginary thus appears as a demiurgic concept, the idea of a cause beyond causality, an origin without an origin. Some, like Karl E. Smith, following J.P. Arnason, have rejected this idea of a creation *ex nihilo*, preferring to see institutional creation as a more "developmental" process.[17] To be sure, when one looks back, one can always find a trace of the past to explain the present, although when looking forward the future appears unknown. The question is whether the future appears unknown simply because of a (temporary?) limit on knowledge or because, between past, present, and future, there lie gaps, however infinitesimal, that mark the presence of the radical imaginary, opening up the possibility of genuinely new beginnings. By speaking of the "historical" relative to the socio-historical, Castoriadis is signalling the radically indeterminate temporality of institution. But the institution of the socio-historical, of necessity, will also seek to counter such radical indeterminacy, and not simply via the ensidic dimension. Heteronomous forms, in particular, will seek to fix institution within what has already been instituted. By contrast, autonomous forms will be more open to institution's instituting moment.

As the creation of original forms, institution escapes all teleology – and thus what can be termed the primacy of theory. It is not, or not generally, a matter of intentions and purposes realized by the will of a subject in a world of objects. The idea of institution is to be contrasted with that of constitution, which supposes a "sovereign" subject, either individual or collective, who would consciously reconstruct the world as an objectification of its ideas.[18] The existence of institution is prior to that of subjects, objects, and their relations, which cannot exist outside institution. As such, institution is also alterior to the subject, and places insuperable limits on its dreams of sovereign mastery. The alterity of institution is present in the indefinite and interminable referrals implicit within a given social imaginary, as well as in the mutability of the interaction between individuals; indeed, it is present in the very idea of the historical as alteration. Ultimately, however, alterity must be seen, at least at the collective level,[19] as residing in the abyssal, chaotic character of the radical imaginary, which, being without a ground (*le sans-fond*), is always able to throw up other new and unexpected materials in the construction of another world, possibly an autonomous one.[20]

In a sense, when speaking of auto-institution, Castoriadis is trying to recover Marx's critique of alienation, but outside the philosophy of consciousness and its subject-object dualism. An autonomous society is, literally, one that explicitly gives itself its own law (*nomos*). More generally, it is one that actively questions its order, opens itself to the figures of its alterity, and welcomes its creative, instituting dimension. To become autonomous, a society must place the law it gives itself under discussion, which is to say that its law can always be disputed and, possibly, changed. The opposite of autonomy is heteronomy, understood as the occlusion of society's existence as auto-institution. A heteronomous society represents its laws as bearing an "external" origin – for example, the laws of God, nature, reason, or history – that would guarantee their truth, justice, and/or necessity, and thereby place them beyond all possible dispute. In a heteronomous society, the world of significations is closed, in that any question that can be posed from within bears an immediate and final response, while questions from without simply cannot be posed. Heteronomy is manifested and, indeed, materialized in the concrete institution of a society, one example being the institutionalized forms of hatred of the Other presented by xenophobia, racism, sexism, and so on (based on the simple, solipsistic formula: we are good, the good is us; you are not us, and therefore you are bad). As almost all societies have been heteronomous, the question is: how should we understand this seemingly "natural" tendency to mask the auto-instituting character of society? The ensidic dimension, by seeking to fix a minimum of order in the magma of imaginary social significations, already would seem to imply a moment of closure. What is more, questioning cannot but be limited, as any question is always based on numerous unquestioned presuppositions, suggesting the existence of the instituted dimension behind all instituting. But such general explanations seem insufficient, for they also apply to an autonomous society. When speaking of a heteronomous society, one is not dealing with signification in general, but with a type of primary signification – that is, an imaginary signification around which a society coheres, and which establishes common conditions and orientations – one that claims that society's order and sense are given from elsewhere. And it does not suffice to explain this primary signification as symptomatic of class societies, for societies without classes have been heteronomous, while the few examples of autonomous societies have all been class societies. Ultimately, Castoriadis must place the roots of heteronomy in the individual psyche and its development. Having avoided the properly psychoanalytic dimension of his thought to this point, I will say only a few words here.

In a sense, Castoriadis posits the origins of heteronomy in the "closure" that characterizes the primordial psychic state of the infant as it emerges from the womb. Drawing on Freud's discussion of "primary narcissism," he posits a first, undifferentiated autistic state, where the self, because it is without an outside, is "represented" as being at one with the world, and where the "representation" of the self, because it is at one with desire, is a source of pleasure. Psychic and social development involves disrupting this state of complete psychic self-satisfaction and self-sufficiency by introducing levels of alterity within the psyche (the development of an unconscious, ego and superego) and without (the development of a reality principle that relays the demands of others) – a process that can only be painful, a source of much anger and ambivalence. Socialization continues this splitting (the social self always being at variance with the "pleasure-ego") even as it relays something of the satisfaction of the original, indivisible totality through its identificatory schemas. In this sense, identification with a group offers a partial substitute for the lost sense of absolute ontological security and omnipotence of the original psychic monad, while channelling destructive urges outwards to a designated Other. Thus closure at the institutional level appears a compensation for the loss of closure, and subsequent vulnerability, at the level of the individual self. Tolerance, the capacity to treat others as equal without being similar, thus represents a tremendous achievement at both a psychic and social level. It supposes a splitting within, which allows the self to recognize its own alterity and vulnerability, and renders possible a splitting without – that is, the distantiation of the self from the instituted, which permits the questioning of the closure of meaning.

To return to the more broadly institutional level, such closure can occur in the name of the supernatural, divine revelation, nature, reason, the laws of history, the invisible hand, or the being-thus of Being. The more "transcendental" principles are the more heteronomous, as they push the basis of institution further outside the realms of human action and comprehension. The more immanent principles, by contrast, promise human understanding, but seek to dictate the direction of human action. Ultimately, Castoriadis attributes the heteronomous tendencies specific to the modern world to the imaginary extension of the ensidic dimension in reason. Rationalization, variously understood, becomes our God, although, in contrast to the other principles of heteronomy, it bears no internal limit. Thus, even as it occludes the creative character of human history, rationalization subjects our world to uncontrollable dynamics. In seeking to circumscribe the ensidic dimension, Castoriadis seeks to provide the philosophical basis for questioning and, ultimately, limiting these dynamics.

At this level of abstraction, the discussion of auto-institution, however important, can be only a beginning. It does not address the question of the content of an autonomous society. It does not question the purpose of institution (institution for institution's sake, or creativity for creativity's sake hardly makes sense). Even less does it speak to the form of the political, economic, and cultural institutions of an autonomous society. Admittedly, these are questions that can never receive a definitive response; for they are questions that must remain questions, subject to continuous discussion and action, if an autonomous society is to remain autonomous. Yet one feels the need to say more. Should one not, relative to an autonomous society, give content to one's arguments, and argue for particular values and arrangements? By itself a negative social ontology can provide neither the arguments nor the concepts with which such arguments can be constructed. But the later, if not the earlier, Castoriadis does not really engage in such argumentation; instead we have a comprehensive discussion of ancient Athens and, more generally, classical Greece.

Ancient Greece and Democracy

Castoriadis is hardly the first to return to the ancients,[21] but his return is different, for he understands the extraordinary historical creativity of ancient Greece between the seventh and fourth centuries BC – which saw the rise of democracy and the invention of rhetoric, philosophy, history, and tragic theatre – as, precisely, a movement towards autonomy. This immediately contrasts his interpretation from those who, like Leo Strauss or Alasdair MacIntyre, seek in the ancients, or in their metaphysics, a return to "perennial truths" that would provide an "objective" basis for morality, law, politics, and/or the philosophical life. Castoriadis emphasizes a kinship between philosophy and democracy: both "participate in the same fundamental creation, that is, in the questioning of the given, whether of political institutions in the narrow sense or the global institution, the representation of the world."[22] As such, he criticizes the anti-democratic tradition associated with Plato, as it seeks, within the terms of philosophy, to provide a definitive response to "the question of the given," not least by treating political questions as a matter of *episteme* (limited to those schooled in the proper "science"), rather than as a matter for the general public to decide. At the same time, Castoriadis evinces little sympathy for the critique of metaphysics associated with Nietzsche or Heidegger. In contrast to Nietzsche, he does not see Socrates as introducing a principle of rationality (or in the case of Euripides, psychological rationality) contrary to the mores of the aristocratic city, which marks the decadence of the *polis* (and tragic theatre). As for Heidegger, Castoriadis rejects, among others things, the idea of an "ontological difference," an idea that he deems completely foreign to the Greeks, and "an avatar of that idea central to philosophy, which imposes an infinite distance between one thing, God, and everything else, i.e. the creatures."[23] Ultimately, Castoriadis's return to Greece is not – or not simply – a return to philosophy, as philosophy typically entails the subordination of the *vita activa* to a *vita contemplativa*, which itself seeks a principle of certitude. Thus he prefers to cite from Pericles' funeral oration (as narrated by Thucydides) a phrase he sees as epitomizing the character of the polis: "we love beauty without excess and philosophize without softness," which he interprets as meaning we act together after reflection, and we think and act boldly.[24]

In a sense, Castoriadis is closer to those who would revive the civic republican tradition in order to reintroduce a more robust notion of equality and participation, and to criticize the contemporary fixation on negative liberty. Still, for Castoriadis, equality and participation do not of themselves require the active questioning that characterizes an autonomous society – as evidenced by Sparta (which he disparages) and, to a lesser degree, republican Rome (which he largely ignores). Moreover, the Athenian political experience must be situated within a larger Greek ethos, which is why he also speaks of poets, tragedians, and historians, as well as philosophers. Perhaps the figure Castoriadis most resembles in his return to the ancients is Hannah Arendt. Yet he criticizes Arendt – as well as the ancients – for bringing a halt to the political realm (and, therefore, to political questioning) before the realms of work and labour (the domestic household, or *oikos*, but also what Arendt terms the "social"). Castoriadis is aware that, just as all instituting is based in the instituted and all questioning is based in what remains unquestioned, so political action must be grounded in pre-political activity. But there can be no *a priori* categorical response to the political question *par excellence*: the question of where exactly the line dividing the political and non-political should be drawn.[25] Arendt, if not the Athenians, tends to remove substantive content from the political realm, seeing in the latter the revelation in word and action of the self, as driven by a quest for "immortal" fame. But beyond the fact that such a quest is inherently "aristocratic" (as fame is meaningless if not reserved for the few), if the political realm were merely a place for self-expression or self-affirmation, there would be no "statesmen" pursuing an idea of the public good, only demagogues pursuing their personal projects *pereat mundus*.[26] The purpose of the *polis*, and of citizens' political action, concerns good governance, and beyond good governance the legislation of good laws – the laws being integral to the political realm, and not, as in Arendt, being like the city walls, circumscribing that realm without being of it. This is why political action for the Greeks entailed not just individual agonistics, but also *philia*, or friendship.

Considering now Castoriadis's substantive discussion of ancient democracy, it can be divided into two major topics: democratic (auto)institution and the (auto)limitation of that institution. Regarding the first topic, democracy, for Castoriadis, is not defined by a constitution, state form, or static set of institutions; rather, it is a process whereby a society institutionalizes itself in a way that allows for constant questioning of its established arrangements through public discussion – as opposed to (private) violence – thereby opening up the question of both individual and collective liberty. To quote Pericles again, democracy is *autonomos* (gives itself its own law), *autodikos* (judges itself), and *autotelès* (governs itself) – a division that implies an articulation, not a separation, of powers, with the citizen participating actively in all three branches.[27] As such, democracy requires *isègoria* (an equal right to free speech among citizens), *parrhèsia* (an obligation to speak frankly), and *paiedia* (the citizen's education, understood as a life-long achievement). The citizen participates not only in large public assemblies in the *agora*, but in many smaller assemblies and committees, to which he is appointed by lot.[28] Elections are limited to those positions that demand expertise – for example, the position of military commander, which demands specialized knowledge in military strategy. Elections must be limited because they are inherently aristocratic, there being necessarily only a few experts. And the reason for electing experts is that the best judge of their expertise is the citizen body that employs their services (and not other experts). The supposition here is that there can be no expertise relative to general, properly political matters because they concern everyone. The citizen both governs and is governed, but in turn – there being no positions of rule that would "represent" the citizen body, although there are leaders. With citizens so active, it is hard to speak of a "state," particularly a state separated from "civil society." There are administrative functions, but no "bureaucracy," and many of the administrative positions, having little status, are filled by slaves. Castoriadis notes that there were mechanisms for focusing attention on the general interest – for example, those in outlying areas could not vote on matters of war and peace, as they could not be expected to hold disinterested opinions, given that in times of war their farms probably would be pillaged. And there were mechanisms that served to create a distance between the citizen body and its decisions – what might be termed a space for second thoughts. Castoriadis mentions the *apatè tou dèmou* (which allowed one to be accused of having a decision passed on the basis of false information) and the *graphè paranomôn* (which allowed one to be accused of having a decision passed in the heat of momentary passions, which would not stand up to scrutiny on second reading). At this point we are beginning to discuss how Athenian democracy sought to limit itself relative to its own worst tendencies. The discussion of such auto-limitation, however, requires that we encompass more than political institutions narrowly considered.

The problem of auto-limitation is not restricted to a concern with limiting the threat of a separate oppressive power. What is equally important for the project of auto-institution is confronting the fragile and unpredictable character of human action – for the critique of heteronomy denies that there is any guarantee that justice will be served, the good realized, and the future bettered. For Castoriadis, Athenian democracy, and Greek culture more generally, demonstrated an awareness of the limits of the human condition in the "flesh" of its social significations and institutions. Thus he insists that Greek city-states did not have constitutions in the modern sense, formed from fundamental laws based on truths held to be self-evident.[29] Human laws (*nomoi*) were considered to be artificial "conventions" – human creations distinct from the "necessity" of natural laws (*phusis*). Thus, to repeat, political thinking appeared based on *doxa*, while political action was understood in terms of *phronesis*, which supposes an indefinite sphere of deliberation dependent on seizing the opportune moment. More generally, Castoriadis claims that Homer, Hesiod, Anaximander, Heraclitus, and probably many of the Sophists saw chaos as preceding cosmos and as coexisting with both the natural and human order. The cosmos, in effect, was deemed not to be entirely orderly, being subjected to processes of creation and destruction that exceed human understanding. Violence and, by implication, injustice were, therefore, seen as endemic, even fundamental.[30] The *polis* and its justice sought to overcome the chaos represented by violence, but both were understood as supposing violence, as the citizen must be willing to use force to defend the city and uphold justice. This is in contrast to Christianity, where violence appears at neither the beginning nor the end of the world, and where, therefore, one can imagine a future (and a past before the Fall) where the lion lies down with the lamb. In this regard Greek religion provided little solace: the gods' moral behaviour was no better than that of humans; and the afterlife was a mere shadow of present life.

It is, however, in the classic tragedies – which were far more public (and thus political) than our own theatrical productions – that the Greeks' awareness of the limits of human action was most evident. The tragedies present the chaos of human affairs due to the lack of correspondence between our desires, decisions, and the meaning of our acts. Hubris is to be understood, precisely, as a failure to understand one's limits, a failure that is always possible because one's knowledge (of oneself) is necessarily imperfect and incomplete – not least because it is impossible to define these limits according to some abstract rule valid for all occasions. Castoriadis spends considerable time analysing individual plays. For example, he highlights the line from the chorus in *Antigone* that speaks of "man as the most surprising and terrible of beings." and interprets it as claiming that, because humans create their own world – rather than simply finding themselves in the world, like gods or animals – they are necessarily a risk to themselves. The play itself is understood not in terms of an opposition between the law of the family and that of the city, or between individual conscience and *raison d'État*, as in Hegel, Lacan, or Judith Butler; rather, the core of the tragedy lies, according to Castoriadis, in the claim, on the part of both Antigone and Creon, to "*monos phronein*," to think not so much for themselves as *by* themselves, as if they were each the only person truly capable of thinking.[31] But the problem of hubris cannot be limited to the tragedies. Castoriadis understands Socrates as a hubristic hero: a good citizen who continuously questioned his fellow citizens in the search for truth, but who, even as he claimed to know only that he did not know, demonstrates that he knew more than his interlocutors without, however, offering a positive argument – thereby putting into question the democratic postulate of universal competence.[32] Above all, there is the tragedy of Athenian democracy itself, undermined by its imperial pretensions and the rash decisions taken during the Peloponnesian War. Still, the claim is that the question of limits can be properly posed only from within an autonomous society.

Contemporary Society and Democracy

Castoriadis sees a second project of auto-institution in modern Europe, beginning, at the earliest, in the thirteenth century and continuing, arguably, into the present. Because such a project is contrary to the general bent of human institution, and has appeared only twice in history, Castoriadis sometimes adopts a militantly pro-Western attitude that on occasion can grate. In his defence, he would argue that only an autonomous society is capable of questioning its own ethnocentrism, claiming that the Greeks were the first to adopt non-ethnocentric attitudes towards, in this case, the barbarians.[33] Admittedly, when pushed he does not deny that other cultures do not question their institutions, but adds that such questioning remains limited. Still, the West cannot, in any concrete sense, provide a model for other parts of the world, and he opposes all imperial projects, the attempt to impose autonomy by heteronomous means being, in principle, a contradiction in terms that can have only disastrous results when put into practice.[34] Still, despite his Eurocentric tendencies, he remains deeply ambivalent about this second project, for it includes not just the democratic project that questions traditional authorities and criticizes the sources of domination, but also the imaginary elaboration of the ensidic dimension that results in the autonomization of the techno-scientific and economic dimensions, with their dreams of limitless accumulation, the indefinite conquest of nature, and the boundless pursuit of private pleasures. Between the two poles – that of autonomy and that of limitless rational mastery – it is the second that is triumphing, to the point where he refuses to speak of Western countries as democracies, and decries a general cultural decline, the sign of an ever more general ebbing of imagination and creativity.

One would have thought that Castoriadis's "ontological labours" could have allowed for a more nuanced and mediated view of the present. It is not that there is no relation between autonomy and rationality; after all, reason struggles against all inherited claims, while refusing the strictly imaginary claim to a world already saturated with meaning. Moreover, he would claim that there can be auto-institution without some notion of reason – and even that reason can never be grounded in its own rationality, being always accompanied by an imaginary elaboration that extends far beyond filling a few foundational holes. One wonders therefore, if the avocation of autonomy – and not just the techno-scientific-economic imaginary – bears a relation to the fragmentation and disorientation of contemporary individuals that Castoriadis otherwise condemns? One might think that, with at least two interrelated, if mutable poles, Castoriadis would posit different spheres, analyse their articulations, and point to the resulting tensions, conflicts, and opportunities.[35] And even if one were to pose but one pole based on a single master signifier – on the grounds, suggested in some of his writings, that only such a primary signification can provide a minimal unity and coherence to society – does not his analysis suggest that this pole could never be exhaustive of societal institution? Again, do his investigations of the socio-historical not demonstrate the illusory character of both the determinism claimed by (at least certain versions of) technoscience, and a voluntarism seduced by the idea of mastery? And should not their illusory character suggest a more complicated, underlying reality, leading to a deeper, more sophisticated examination of the present horizon. One is left instead with a diagnosis reminiscent of the "one-dimensional" society of the Frankfurt School's first generation – although here it leans more towards simple denunciation than analysis. Castoriadis could reply that he is speaking only Cassandra-like of certain tendencies. The result, however, suggests a politics of radical rupture, where the appeal to the creativity of the radical imaginary threatens to become what Castoriadis denies the Greeks: an almost messianic faith in the capacity of the future to wipe clean the present.

These points are not without relevance to his discussion of radical democracy. Castoriadis, like several other thinkers, distinguishes between politics (*la politique*) and the political (*le politique*). He understands politics as focused on power and concerned with the decisions that have a binding character on the life of the community, while the political involves the conscious questioning of institution – that is, discussion around, and participation in, decision-making by the citizen body. Thus, while politics can be said to characterize all societies, the political for Castoriadis can only be democratic.[36] And the political can be truly democratic only if it is not representative, for he agrees with Rousseau that representation introduces a division between ruler and ruled, which allows us to be "free" only once every four years (and even then the choices are pre-packaged), and encourages a depoliticized and privatized life. We live, in his view, in a liberal oligarchy, not in a democracy. Not unlike Hannah Arendt, he holds up the model of the "council democracies" formed during the first heady days of the modern revolutions (for example, the "societies" of the French Revolution, town-hall democracy in the early American republic, the soviets before the Bolshevik seizure of power). To the argument that we cannot have direct democracy because modern societies are too large, Castoriadis notes that the idea of political representation first emerged in medieval cities that were much smaller than ancient Athens. The Athenians had elections; they did not, however, elect representatives, but those with a specialized knowledge in those limited areas where such knowledge was required. Moreover, the ancients employed lotteries as well as elections – and there is no reason to exclude either under modern conditions – indeed, modern technology should enable improvements in both. As to the claim, attributed to Benjamin Constant, that the moderns are not interested in the public pursuit of common affairs because they are more interested in the private pursuit of happiness, Castoriadis dismisses it as a variation of the much older argument that *hoi polloi* are too mired in their work to have the time, inclination, or the "culture" to participate directly in public life. It is thus no surprise that he has been accused of upholding a Rousseauist notion of popular sovereignty, with its idea of an indivisible, infallible general will.[37] In his reading of Greek democracy, however, such a will is not possible, let alone desirable.[38] This is not to say that he upholds Greek views in all matters; he criticizes the Greeks relative to slavery, the treatment of women, "foreign relations" between cities, the exclusivist definition of the citizen, and the failure to question the customary life rooted in the *oikos*. In an exchange with Chantal Mouffe, who defends representative democracy on the grounds that it promotes, beyond the question of rule, individual rights and the protection of minorities, Castoriadis replies that he is not against human rights, minority rights, or political factionalism. These, however, appear in his thought as no more than disconnected empirical preferences – that is, he fails to theorize any connection between modern representative democracy and the evolution of modern rights and pluralism, or the "overcoming" of those Greek traits he dislikes. In truth, he is not entirely comfortable with modern pluralism, and states that we do not have to treat modern complexity fatalistically. Ultimately it is up to us to decide what kind of society we wish to live in; the price of our freedom might well have to be paid in economic terms, but economic value need not be the sole value, and he personally would rather have a new friend than a new car. The appeal to the radical imaginary, however, was not originally a personal *cri de coeur*, and one should remember that the idea of imaginary institution was to be understood, in the last instance, as unmotivated, subconscious, and anonymous.[39]

Continuing with the disputes regarding the character of democracy, consideration must be given to the arguments with Claude Lefort,

Castoriadis's *frère ennemi* since the days of *Socialisme ou Barbarie*. Castoriadis claims that Lefort understands democracy in terms of indetermination, whereas he himself understands it in terms of creation, and that the former is essentially empty, while the latter implies positive content.[40] The criticism appears somewhat disingenuous, if only because creation, when related to the radical imaginary, supposes indeterminacy.[41] In truth, the differences go much deeper. When Lefort speaks of power, he understands it in terms of its "symbolic" function – that is, through power, society establishes a relation with itself whereby it is able to give itself an identity, a form, sense, and value. By contrast, when Castoriadis speaks of power, he refers less to its imaginary dimension (assuming, for the moment, the equivalence of the imaginary and the symbolic) than to its narrowly institutional functions (legislative, juridical, and governing)[42] or to its tactical or strategic usage in everyday politics. When Lefort speaks of power relative to the symbolic, he implies that society is divided, even as power is divided from society; for power, as a source of law at a distance from, and in excess of, society's "reality," renders society present to itself from "without." As such, power entails a figure of externality, and even of domination – one that is not reducible to class domination in society, although it secures and supplements the latter. Democracy, for Lefort, does not so much eliminate the "transcendence" of power as deny that transcendence its positivity, thereby rendering the place of power "empty," such that it can no longer be occupied fully by those who would claim to embody that positivity. Consequently, the societal order under democracy loses its apparent solidity, as that order can be questioned, power contested, and social conflict expressed, notably in the form of a division between those who would dominate and those who, in the name of liberty, would resist domination. In contrast, then, to Castoriadis, for Lefort the externality of power and, therefore, domination – and the conflict over domination – cannot be eliminated. The people cannot (and do not really want to) occupy the place of power directly, and in his mind any claim to such – with its promise to eliminate social divisions, and thus the division of power – would be a harbinger of totalitarian rule. From a political perspective, Lefort is therefore suspicious of all talk of auto-institution (and auto-gestion), while, from a more strictly philosophical perspective, he suspects such talk of reviving the philosophy of the subject and its antinomies. Instead of advocating, like Castoriadis, direct democracy, Lefort speaks (at least at one point) of *démocratie sauvage*, where one struggles not over power, but against the power holder for the indefinite extension of rights and liberties. Thus, as Antoine Chollet has pointed out, Lefort saw May 68 as a successful revolt, while Castoriadis viewed it as a failed revolution.[43]

Castoriadis argues that the social division is not a structural necessity. Different divisions (between classes, powers, spheres of activity, and institutions and their purported "foundations" in heteronymous societies) do not need to exist; their existence is, as it were, empirical, specific to certain societies. However, "there is in every society a multiple difference with regard to self (*un multiple écart de soi*) of an ontological character."[44] Such an *écart de soi* – which must be understood as referring not just to the individual psyche, but to institution more generally – rules out the formation of a transparent regime constituted from a single, unified, all-powerful sovereign will. In this sense, he would agree with Lefort. Where, presumably, he would claim Lefort goes a step too far is in the movement from "multiple difference" to the single division that posits the externality of power in its symbolic function. [45] For Castoriadis this multiple difference is manifest in the excess of the instituting over the instituted and, perhaps above all, in the chaos that traverses both institution and the psyche, even as it lies at both their source and limit. Chaos is without foundation (*sans-fond*), bubbling, as it were, from below – the ultimate figure of the subversion of all power. Lefort's notion of division, by contrast, serves the positing of a foundation above, which establishes power in its difference – even when, under democracy, the power is "empty" and the foundation uncertain – which thereby establishes the appearance of a society that, in its generality, bears a principle of order, sense, and value. But perhaps behind these differences lies the difference between ancient and modern democracy. Castoriadis, as the representative of the former, could point out that it makes little sense to speak of Athenian democracy in terms of totalitarianism. On the other hand, Lefort is far more sensitive to the specificity of modern democracies – not just their representative character, but their pluralism and individualism. Andreas Kalyvas has argued that Lefort presents a negative theology, ultimately rooted in a medieval imagination, where the absent place of power is a substitute for the presence of God, Christ, or the monarch; and then, quoting Nietzsche, Kalyvas contrasts Lefort's chasing the shadow of the deity to Castoriadis, who knows the deity to be truly dead.[46] The argument is not without truth, particularly if one holds that pagans are atheists. As moderns, however, we might want to argue that, with the symbolic mutation thematized by Lefort in his discussion of modern democracy, the continuity with a properly politico-theological era is broken, as power divides – and not just between its temporary occupants (the representative power holders) and its "origin" (the singular plural of the people, who cannot hold power directly). Power is also divided from law and knowledge, which, in turn, gives rise to a proliferation of other differences and a host of other (absent) gods. The Greeks, because of their greater alterity, will appear the more radical. But then the Greeks, perhaps because of their paganism, did not have to confront the problem of the Same and the Different in the same manner or with the same urgency; they were free to imagine another, different, and possibly simpler world. The question is: are we too free to imagine a different world?

NOTES

1 The writings of this period, along with introductions by Castoriadis, were collected in eight volumes by Éditions 10/18 between 1974 and 1979. For a good selection in English of Castoriadis's 1946–79 writings, see David Ames Curtis, ed., *Cornelius Castoriadis, Political and Social Writings*, 3 v. (Minneapolis: Minnesota University Press, 1988–93). See also the first part of Castoriadis, *Imaginary Institution of Society* (Cambridge, MA: MIT Press, 1987 [1975]), which was first published in *Socialisme ou Barbarie* in 1964–65.

2 Castoriadis, *Imaginary Institution of Society*. Recently, his previously unpublished earlier philosophical writings have been collected in idem, *Histoire et création: textes philosophiques inédits 1945–1967* (Paris: Seuil, 2009).

3 The six volumes are: 1. *Crossroads in the Labyrinth* (Cambridge, MA: MIT Press, 1984 [1978]); 2. *Domaines de l'homme* (Paris: Seuil, 1986); 3. *Le monde morcelé* (Paris: Seuil, 1990); 4. *La montée de l'insignifiance* (Paris: Seuil, 1996); 5. *Fait et à faire* (Paris: Seuil, 1997); and 6. *Figures of the Thinkable* (Stanford, CA: Stanford University Press, 2007 [1999]). Many of the essays in the volumes that were not translated into English can be found in *Philosophy, Politics, Autonomy: Essays in Political Philosophy*, ed. David Ames Curtis (Oxford: Oxford University Press, 1991); idem, *World in Fragments: Writings on Politics, Society, Psychoanalysis, and the Imagination* (Stanford, CA: Stanford University Press, 1997); and idem, *The Castoriadis Reader* (Cambridge, MA: Blackwell Publishers, 1997). Mention should be made, with caution, of the Agora International Web site (http://agorainternational.org/), which provides enormous bibliographical materials related to Castoriadis in several languages (including English) as well as hyperlinks to all materials that can be accessed on the Internet.

4 Cornelius Castoriadis, *Sujet et vérité dans le monde social-historique: séminaires 1986–87* (Paris: Seuil, 2002).

5 Notably, Cornelius Castoriadis, "The Greek *Polis* and the Creation of Autonomy," in Curtis, *Philosophy, Politics, Autonomy*; idem, "Greeks and the Modern Political Imaginary"; and idem, "Aeschylean Anthropogony and Sophoclean Self-Creation of *Anthrōpos*," in *Figures of the Thinkable*.

6 See Cornelius Castoriadis, *Ce qui fait la Grèce 1: d'Homère à Héraclite* (Paris: Seuil, 2004); idem, *Ce qui fait la Grèce 2: la cité et les lois* (Paris: Seuil, 2008); idem, *Ce qui fait la Grèce 3: Thucydide, la force et le droit* (Paris: Seuil, 2011); and idem, *On Plato's* Statesman, ed. and trans. David Ames Curtis (Stanford, CA: Stanford University Press, 2002).

7 In English: Cornelius Castoriadis, *A Society Adrift: Interviews and Debates, 1974–1997*, ed. Enrique Escobar, Myrto Gondicas, and Pascal Vernay; trans. Helen Arnold (New York: Fordham University Press, 2010). In French: Cornelius Castoriadis and Daniel Cohen-Bendit, *De l'écologie à l'autonomie* (Paris: Seuil, 1981); Cornelius Castoriadis and Daniel Mermet, *Post-scriptum sur l'insignificance* (Paris: Éditions de l'aube, 1998); and Cornelius Castoriadis and MAUSS, *Démocratie et relativisme* (Paris: Mille et une nuits, 2010).

8 See the work, written with Claude Lefort and Edgar Morin, published shortly after May 1968, and which was republished twenty years later with additional essays by each of the authors, as *Mai 68 la brèche: suivi de vingt ans après* (Paris: Complexe, 1988); as well as a work on the former Soviet Union that, arguably, has not aged well, *Devant la guerre* (Paris: Fayard, 1981).

9 There is another, more strictly psychoanalytic component of the project of auto-institution that should be mentioned, and that looks at the development of the autonomous individual. I am folding it here into the more strictly philosophical problematic, particularly as its most extensive discussion is to be found in *Imaginary Institution of Society*, chap. 6. Still, it should be realized that, in the latter part of his life, Castoriadis was a practising psychoanalyst associated with the "Quatrième groupe" (which split from Jacques Lacan's "École freudienne de Paris"), and beyond scattered essays in the *Crossroads* series, there are rumours of considerable unpublished and/or unfinished materials dedicated to the psyche and its problems. Should such works be published in the future, this dimension of his work will become more salient. Let me add, for purposes of bibliographical completeness, that Castoriadis's more important essays and interviews on aesthetics have been (re)published as *Fenêtre sur le chaos* (Paris: Seuil, 2007). In addition, for readers who wish to read more about Castoriadis's thought, there are now two excellent books: Suzi Adams, *Castoriadis's Ontology: Being and Creation* (New York: Fordham University

Press, 2011); and Nicolas Poirier, *L'ontologie politique de Castoriadis: création et institution* (Paris: Payot, 2011).

10 Max Weber, *The Protestant Ethic and the "Spirit" of Capitalism and Other Writings*, trans. Peter Baehr and Gordon Wells (New York: Penguin, 2002), 121.

11 Theodor Adorno takes a not-dissimilar ontological turn when he speaks of identity (which he almost presents as reason's original sin) and contrasts it to the non-identical. We shall see that, for Castoriadis, the non-identical (if we can equate it with the other, non-ensidic dimension) is less a "materialist" residue (what relative to the object identity fails to grasp) than identity's necessary accompaniment and, as such, fundamental to any notion of institution.

12 The signitive relation is thus more than "representation" in that it does not, or does not simply, re-present something already present (whether in the real world down here or the world of ideas up there); it posits a new form and a new signification.

13 Although following Frege, Castoriadis does not think that mathematics can ground itself ensidically.

14 Castoriadis, *Imaginary Institution of Society*, 243, emphasis in original.

15 Although, like Habermas, Castoriadis employs language – and institution more generally – to undermine the ontological primacy of the subject. For Habermas's appreciation of Castoriadis, see Jürgen Habermas, *The Philosophical Discourse of Modernity*, trans. Frederick Lawrence (Cambridge, MA: MIT Press, 1987), 327–35.

16 It also, of course, creates a world of things and persons in close conjunction with the creation of meanings, forms, and values.

17 Johann Arnason, "Culture and Imaginary Significations," *Thesis Eleven* 22 (January 1989): 25–45; and Karl Smith, "The Constitution of Modernity: A Critique of Castoriadis," *European Journal of Social Theory* 12, no. 4 (2009): 505–21.

18 The distinction between constitution and institution was first formulated by Maurice Merleau-Ponty, *Themes from the Lectures at the Collège de France, 1952–1960*, trans. John O'Neill (Evanston, IL: Northwestern University Press, 1940), 40; and idem, *Institution and Passivity. Course Notes from the Collège de France (1954–55)*, trans. Leonard Lawlor and Heath Massey (Evanston: Northwestern University Press, 2010).

19 At the individual level, alterity has to be related to the idea of the unconscious.

20 For Castoriadis, art is a form that opens onto this "Without Ground": "The work of art exists only by suppressing what is quotidian and functional,

and unveiling an Other Side [*Envers*] that drains our habitual situations of all their meaning/signification, creating a tear through which we can glimpse the Bottomless Abyss on which we constantly live." See Castoriadis, *Fenêtre sur le chaos*, 46.

21 Castoriadis's knowledge of the ancient Greek language and texts is exceptional, and recognized by Hellenists; see the introductory essay by Pierre Vidal-Naquet, "Castoriadis et la Grèce ancienne," which introduces *Ce qui fait la Grèce 1*.

22 Castoriadis, *Ce qui fait la Grèce 2*, 197.

23 Castoriadis, *Ce qui fait la Grèce 1*, 263.

24 Castoriadis, *Ce qui fait la Grèce 2*, 163–8; and idem, *Ce qui fait la Grèce 3*, séminaires 12, 13.

25 Similarly, both Arendt and the Greeks must be faulted for not sufficiently questioning who is and is not a member of the political community; *Ce qui fait la Grèce 2*, 158ff.

26 Which began to happen, Castoriadis admits, during the period of Athenian decline.

27 Castoriadis, *Ce qui fait la Grèce 2*, 75.

28 These are not unlike our contemporary juries, but concern non-judicial as well as judicial matters, and when judging the latter are not restricted to questions of fact.

29 "The greatness of democracy consists in recognizing this fundamental philosophical fact: the law is posed and spoken from nothing. Not in an empirical sense, to be sure – legislative acts are always enmeshed in an historical continuity … But nothing in the sense that laws cannot be deduced from anything else, whether a commentary of the Decalogue or as a consequence of Plato's theory of being." See Castoriadis, *Ce qui fait la Grèce 2*, 202–3.

30 This was generally how slavery was understood. According to Castoriadis, the Greeks sought to justify slavery only in terms of the existence of naturally slavish peoples (even as there is evidence that some of the Sophists argued against the institution). For most Greeks, the difference between the slave and the freeman was to be understood as largely a contingent, pre-political matter – and not, as Arendt argues, the consequence of a "political" decision by the formerly free man that life was worth more than freedom in the face of military defeat. It was because slavery was seen as contingent that slaves could be found in positions of skill and responsibility.

31 Castoriadis, *Ce qui fait la Grèce 2*, 141–7.

32 Castoriadis claims that Socrates' accusers were also guilty of hubris.

33 Thus he notes that for Homer the Trojans were not inferior to the Greeks, for Herodotus the barbarians were peoples in their own right, with their own histories and accomplishments, and that for Aeschylus the Persians, in the play of the same name, appear as fully human.
34 Castoriadis and MAUSS, *Démocratie et relativisme*, 44–6.
35 Both Arnason and Smith, in the essays cited earlier, seek in this manner to employ Castoriadis against Castoriadis.
36 This immediately distinguishes Castoriadis from Claude Lefort or Pierre Rosanvallon, who understand the political as the presentation of society's foundation, which allows the collectivity's claim to unity, coherence, and identity to come into view. From this perspective, the political exists in all societies, and the significance of power appears symbolic (as the presentation and representation of the order within which decisions are made, and alone make sense) before appearing "political."
37 Jean Cohen, "The Self-Institution of Society and Representative Government: Can the Circle Be Squared?" *Thesis Eleven* 80 (February 2005): 9–37.
38 Claude Lefort claims that, in contrast to the moderns, who maintain the place of power empty, the ancients filled it with the citizen body. Again such a characterization appears too Rousseauist, as the ancients did not conceive of power as a body, or even, arguably, as a place apart.
39 This exchange with Chantal Mouffe is in Castoriadis, *Démocratie et relativisme*, 109–31.
40 Ibid., 41, 54.
41 In truth, the claim echoes earlier disputes in which Lefort was suspicious of all parties and party platforms, lest they deny "working-class experience," while Castoriadis insisted that one had to state explicitly what one stood for.
42 Castoriadis rejects the executive function, as the latter concerns less the "execution" of the law than what does not directly concern the law – for example, declaring war or determining the budget. Behind the rejection of the executive function, one can detect a suspicion of the division of powers.
43 Cited in Poirier, *L'ontologie politique de Castoriadis*, 365.
44 Castoriadis, *Sujet et vérité dans le monde social-historique*, 240–2.
45 Remember that, when he speaks, relative to Athenian democracy, of the establishment of a "reflexive distance," he speaks only of the distance between the citizen body and its decisions, and then as a strictly temporal distance, situating today's decisions in light of tomorrow.
46 Andreas Kalyvas, "The Institution of the Social: Lefort and Castoriadis" (paper delivered at "Claude Lefort: An Intellectual and Political Memorial," New York, 30 October 2010).

6 Guy Debord and the Politics of Play

DEVIN PENNER

It might seem odd to include Guy Debord in a book about rethinking democratic politics. After all, Debord was the de facto leader of the Situationist International (SI), a highly exclusionary avant-garde organization, for its entire fifteen-year existence. During its short incursion onto the French political scene (from 1957 to 1972), the SI expelled at least forty-five members, which is particularly remarkable because the organization had a combined total of only around seventy members.[1] Furthermore, Debord's crucial concept of the "spectacle" emerges directly out of the Marxist tradition, a body of theory that historically has downplayed questions about the nature of "politics" or "democracy."

Despite these obvious difficulties, in this chapter I make the case that the democratic impulse of Debord's political thought should not be dismissed so easily. Focusing on Debord's concept of the "situation," I draw out the aspects of his work that point towards a radical notion of politics as an inherently conflictual and divisive process. The situation, like all of Debord's films, is premised on confronting its audience, spurring them into action, and ultimately forcing them to reconsider or at least reveal their position. Although this concept is not democratic in and of itself, I argue that, when considered in tandem with Situationist[2] notions of "play" and "poetry," as well as their advocacy of workers' councils, the situation helps us to understand the practice associated with a radical democratic politics of division.

Before proceeding, I should note that I do not address fully the many criticisms of Debord's work. My primary aim is simply to extract what Debord can positively contribute to a radical democratic politics. To make this argument, I begin by laying out Debord's best-known concept, the spectacle, showing how it leads to its antithesis, the concept of the situation. In the second part, I further develop the concept of the situation by presenting "play" as its political ethos; in the third part, I move on to the Situationist tactic of *détournement* and other more concrete examples of situations. I conclude by putting Debord's key concepts in relation to some of the key themes in radical democracy. Looking at the themes of conflict/division, representation, leadership, and the capacity of the many, I assert that Debord's thought exhibits some of the central tensions in radical democratic theory, but, in a concrete and practice-oriented fashion, it also points to some ways of moving beyond these tensions.

From the Spectacle to the Situation

Written in the context of post-war France, Guy Debord's major work, *The Society of the Spectacle*, responds above all to the spread of Fordist processes of mass production and mass consumption. Assembly-line techniques vastly improved industrial productivity, while increased union power – in part, a result of mass-production techniques – allowed workers to obtain a share of this prosperity. Indeed, the combination of rising wages and cheapening commodities led to a dramatic step forward in the standard of living of workers: the United States and other industrialized Western countries moved beyond the stage of scarcity to enter what John Kenneth Galbraith famously called "the affluent society."[3]

As Anselm Jappe rightly recognizes, Debord's originality lies in the fact that he was "the first to interpret [this new] situation in the light of the Marxian theory of value."[4] Debord understood that unprecedented economic growth in the 1950s and early 1960s led not to the demise, but to the consolidation of capitalism. Economic crises seemingly had become a thing of the past. Through coordination, compromise, and state intervention, it appeared that capitalism could smoothly and indefinitely make both capitalists *and* workers much richer. What Debord needed to show, then, was that the transition to a society of "economic abundance" was of no use if this merely meant an "abundance of commodities." His concept of the spectacle attempts to explain how workers remained alienated and impoverished in their everyday life,[5] despite finally having leisure time and being "treated like grown-ups ... in their new role as consumers."[6]

A second, simultaneous historical trend is crucial to the development of Debord's theory: the rise of the electronic mass media in general and advertising in particular. Put briefly, his argument goes something like this. Advances in communications technology – especially television, which became widespread in the 1950s – mean that "spectacular representations" mediate more and more social interactions.[7] The result is the increasing *separation* of individual workers, an argument that is merely an extension of Marx's notion of "commodity fetishism." For Marx, individuals are isolated in capitalist society, with their key moment of social contact occurring through commodities in the market. We enter the supermarket and "interact" with, for example, one of millions of identical boxes of Frosted Flakes, along with the slightly different knock-off versions. The only real marker we see is the quantitative category of price, so it is not clear if the Frosted Flakes we consume were produced via a fifteen-hour working day, through draconian labour practices, or by destroying the environment.[8]

Similarly, in the society of the spectacle, we know nothing about the conditions of the production of images and information. We simply ingest an endless stream of images and words, all of which is, to quote Debord, "immune from human activity, inaccessible to any projected review or correction."[9] Instead of commonly consuming Frosted Flakes, we commonly witness the spectacle of Michael Jackson's 2005 child molestation trial, or the emotive reporting of CNN's Anderson Cooper from the middle of post-Katrina New Orleans. And, in time, we come to live our own lives *passively* through such spectacular representations; we follow the false on-camera lives of "media stars" – distractions that, according to Debord, lead to the "crumbling of directly experienced diversifications of productive activity."[10]

Against the alienated, inauthentic way of life that is pushed forward by capitalist imperatives, Debord proposes the category of "the situation." It should be clear by now that Debord defines *the* spectacle in very specific terms as a stage of capitalism. But, if we remove the definite article to think in more general terms of *a* spectacle – a public event that is memorable for its impressive appearance – a "situation" is actually a spectacle. Aside from the reference to capitalism, the key difference is that actors and audiences/spectators are separated in Debord's category of *the* spectacle; in the concept of the situation, by contrast, spectators are actors at the same time. As Debord summarizes in what can be considered the founding text of the Situationist International, the situation seeks to "draw [the spectator] into activity by provoking their capacities to revolutionize their own lives. The situation is thus designed to be lived by its constructors. The role played by a passive or merely bit-part playing 'public' must constantly diminish, while that played by those who cannot be called actors, but rather, in a new sense of the term, 'livers,' must steadily increase."[11]

A number of important elements of this passage are worth elaborating on before I turn to a more explicit discussion of how the situation helps us to think about the practice of a politics of division. In the first place, a "situation" is above all *an atmosphere* that characterizes a certain time and space – situations are "collective ambiances" or "ensembles of impressions," as Debord puts it, that are developed in spaces temporarily liberated from their usual functions.[12] The idea is to remove individuals from their everyday lives – from the inertia of normal routines and conventional ideas – by introducing them to very different and provocative surroundings.

This means that, second, situations are premised above all on their emotional effects: what matters is how an atmosphere makes people feel. Consequently Debord advocates "psychogeography," the "study of the precise laws and specific effects of the geographical environment ... on the emotions and behaviour of individuals."[13] The idea is to figure out a configuration of ideas, objects, and people whose combined effect will emotionally overtake their normal individual meanings, thereby instigating a shift from passive spectators to active "livers" of the event. The importance of emotions and affect is also clear in the intended result of the situation: the event is to give its "livers" a chance to exist outside the world of the spectacle and the desires it monologically promotes, allowing them to clarify their "simple basic desires" and leading to the playful development of new ones.[14]

Third, situations are ephemeral and unrepeatable: an atmosphere is total – it is a "single space-time construction"[15] – and therefore cannot be recreated. In fact, Debord argues that it would not be desirable to recreate situations even if it were possible. It is the "fleeting effect" of the situation that matters because the aim is "immediate participation in the passionate abundance of life." Only traditional, bourgeois aesthetics seeks an eternal construction because its aim is contemplation, not participation.[16] Participation involves being completely open to one's continually changing surroundings, as is also apparent in the Situationist concept of *dérive* (literally, drifting), a technique of wandering through different zones of a city to experience the various impressions they leave. According to Debord, the key to *dérive* lies in the ability to react and make spontaneous, emotionally driven decisions, which is why, like a situation, a *dérive* neither could nor should be reproduced.[17]

Lastly, the entire concept of the situation is premised on agency: situations must be constructed *by some group of people.* It is possible for a situation to occur spontaneously, as atomized individuals collectively react to, for example, a natural disaster. But Debord is clearly emphasizing an artificially constructed atmosphere, one that a group like the Situationist International would design. He explains this in greater detail in the first volume of *International Situationniste,* distinguishing three main roles in the construction of situations: "directors" coordinate the event, "direct agents" are collaborators who practically assist in running it, but the key group is the "few passive spectators" who are unaware of the overall plan and are supposed to be "reduced to action" during the event.[18] Given the transformative goal of situations – to awaken passive spectators – it is clear that their constructors should be at a "higher" level of consciousness, so it is not surprising that an editorial in the 1963 issue of *Internationale Situationniste* claims that "the first ventures in constructing situations must be the work ... of the revolutionary avant-garde."[19]

The Situation and "Play"

This basic definition of the situation no doubt leaves some questions, especially the last aspect, which brings to mind the Leninist conception of the revolutionary vanguard and consciousness "from without."[20] There are some clear differences vis-à-vis Leninism, however, specifically with regards to the limited role and political goals the Situationists saw for their organization. In this regard, Vincent Kaufmann rightly points out that the SI had no designs on political power and did not want to govern. Contrary to Leninism, they understood that "real revolutionaries know how to make themselves forgotten … [or] disappear."[21] Their task was only to spur the working classes into critical thinking – to encourage the workers to "become dialecticians," as Debord puts it[22] – after which point the organization would "realize itself" by dissolving.

There is another, indirect way in which charges of Leninism might be addressed, and one that is more interesting in that it points towards a radically democratic interpretation of the SI. The basic idea is that the Situationist concept of "play" should be understood as the underlying political ethos of the situation. "Play" can be seen as the ethos *within* the situation, while the situation is also designed to bring about, to quote Debord, the "future reign of freedom and play."[23] But despite many textual references to the concept of play, it is usually underplayed in secondary literature on Debord and the Situationists. Their understanding of the concept is shaped most directly by Johan Huizinga's 1938 work, *Homo Ludens*, yet this book receives only one mention – and in a footnote – in three of the most significant English-language works on the Situationists.[24]

What is unique about Huizinga's work is, first of all, its general contention that "playing" is as much a defining feature of human nature as reasoning (*homo sapian*) or working (*homo faber*) – in his words, "civilization arises and unfolds in and as play."[25] Of more specific interest is the way Huizinga defines play. Using historical evidence from a number of societies, he argues that play is not opposed to seriousness. Instead, play has four fundamental characteristics: 1) a free or voluntary basis, independent of physical needs; 2) an extraordinary or exceptional nature; 3) a limited spatial and temporal existence; and 4) a specific set of rules to provide order.[26] All four of these characteristics are quite clear when considering the example of children playing the game of tag. The game is played for "fun," rather than for biological necessity, and the players recognize that the "fun" will end at some point as they have to return to "reality" to, for example, find food or sleep. While the game is going on, however, the players agree to a certain set of rules that specify boundaries and how one becomes "it," while cheating likely leads to rule changes or ostracism. As the idea of ostracism suggests, play might be fun, but it is serious at the same time. Indeed, the seriousness of play results from what *Homo Ludens* stresses as its agonistic nature. And, for Huizinga, play's value lies precisely in the *intrinsic* merits of the struggle or conflict that occurs within a certain, rules-bound context.[27]

At first glance, the metaphor of children playing tag might seem to have little to do with radical politics. Huizinga does not extend his definition of play into the realm of politics, nor is his concept of play overly radical. In fact, Debord's key criticism of *Homo Ludens* is that Huizinga's rules of play are "arbitrary conventions" that must be given a "moral foundation."[28] Debord does not elaborate on this point, but a work by Raoul Vaneigem, Debord's Situationist collaborator for a time, makes it easier to see how the concept of play could become the basis for a radical democratic politics. While recognizing that play always requires rules, organisation, and discipline, Vaneigem asserts that "play comes to an end as soon as authority crystallises, becomes absolute and assumes a magical aura." Consequently, a radical notion of play always undermines "hierarchical society," and points towards "a new type of society based on real participation," affirming "transparent social relationships," "self-realisation," and equality.[29]

As Vaneigem rightly recognizes, the essence of play is the continual ability to change the rules of the game by all those who are subject to them. Debord hints at the same conclusion in thesis 178 of *Society of the Spectacle*:

> The proletarian revolution is that critique of human geography whereby individuals and communities must construct places and events commensurate with the appropriation, no longer just of their labor, but of their total history. By virtue of the resulting *mobile space of play*, and by virtue of *freely chosen variations in the rules of the game*, the independence of places will be rediscovered without any new exclusive tie to the soil, and thus too the authentic journey will be restored to us, along with the authentic life understood as a journey containing its whole meaning within itself.[30]

This and Vaneigem's definitions both suggest that the essence of play is not creativity per se, but rather what Cornelius Castoriadis calls "self-institution." Above all, the players recognize that they are the "instituting society," instead of deferring to the inertia of the current structures of the "instituted society."[31]

Although the basic rules of a children's game such as tag are inherited from previous generations, it is the prerogative of any group of children to playfully adapt these rules or to use them as the inspiration for imagining an entirely new game. Consequently, Castoriadis would consider play to be an example of "autonomy" rather than "heteronomy." The latter indicates that a particular society's laws and norms – its *nomos* – emerge from a source outside itself, such as tradition, religion, nature, a monarch, or a despot; autonomy, on the other hand, is defined as the "unlimited self-questioning about the law and its foundations as well as the capacity, in light of this interrogation, *to make, to do* and *to institute*."[32] Just as playing children feel free to question and change the nature of the game, an autonomous society recognizes the precarious and limited nature of *all* its laws, including its constitution, and thus the need for continual and collective debate, affirmation, or alteration of them.

At the opposite pole to "play," Debord's "society of the spectacle" clearly falls into the category of heteronomy. Indeed, the Situationists' main concern was the way individuals are fixed into specific "roles" that are defined *for them* by the spectacle.[33] This basic point makes it easier to see the centrality of play to the concept of the situation. The task of a situation is to interrupt the spectacle's fixed roles: to promote "play," what has to be accentuated is the idea that the rules establishing various "roles" – including the basic role of "spectator" – are constructed and thus collectively changeable. In Vaneigem's words, the absolute and "magical aura" of authority under capitalism needs to be removed. As I explain in the next section, Situationist practice attempted to undermine these roles by confronting the spectator in two main ways: one was by playing with media form itself, to show that a specific medium might have alternative, participatory implications; the other was to *détourn* familiar content, undermining its old meaning by placing it in a radically new context.

Howls for Sade and *Détournement*: Confronting Spectators, Instituting Play

Debord's first film, *Howls for Sade,* is a clear example of the first tactic, playing with the medium. One of his earliest ventures in constructing a situation, *Howls for Sade* is only a "movie" in the loosest sense of the term. It is comprised of five expressionless voices speaking unrelated (and often appropriated) phrases against the background of a white screen. The "conversation" is occasionally interrupted by periods of dark-screened silence, including a twenty-four minute period for the film's finale.[34]

Obviously Debord's aim was not to write a counternarrative to mainstream movies; rather, he aimed to challenge the entire cinematic *form,* and particularly the passive position of the spectator in it. As Vincent Kaufmann puts it, his films sought "above all to divide, to exclude, and to establish a relationship of intransigent confrontation with the viewer."[35] To counter the one-way forms of communication characteristic of the spectacle, his films focused on provoking an emotional reaction from the audience. *Howls for Sade* did this in the most direct sense, by trying to force the audience to adopt an "active" stance by offending and irritating them with prolonged periods of silence.

Howls for Sade is no doubt an extreme example, which was indeed effective in irritating the audience but not necessarily in "drawing them into activity."[36] When "activity" is defined according to the concept of "play," Debord's mistake is quite clear. For the fundamental issue indicated by the concept of play is not one-way communication per se, but rather how messages are received – that is, whether one tends passively to accept hegemonic meanings or actively and self-reflectively to interpret received messages. Jacques Rancière makes a similar point in the *Emancipated Spectator*. The one-way separation of the screen from its audience, Rancière argues, does not necessarily mean the audience is passive. In fact, he goes on to claim that it is wrong to reduce spectators to ignorant, passive recipients, neglecting the active work of observation and interpretation that is "peculiar to the spectator."[37]

This is not to say, however, that the tactic of playing with the medium is completely futile. A better, less irksome example is a lecture Debord delivered at a conference on the theme of everyday life organized by Henri Lefebvre. Challenging the traditional lecture format, Debord's talk was deliberately delivered through a tape recording rather than in person. Debord made clear the aim of this shift in the lecture itself: he wanted "to break with the appearance of pseudocollaboration, of artificial dialogue, between the 'in person' lecturer and his spectators." By implementing a "slight discomforting break" with the traditional format, he hoped to "bring directly into the field of questioning ... the very practice of lecturing, as well as any number of other forms ... that are considered 'normal' and not even noticed, [but] which ultimately condition us."[38]

Here the problematic assumption that spectators are necessarily passive under "normal" circumstances remains, but Debord certainly gets nearer to the heart of the issue. There are no doubt hegemonic or dominant meanings that are transmitted regularly though one-way media such as television, as Debord's concept of the spectacle emphasizes; however, as Rancière's response suggests, these hegemonic codes are always to some extent appropriated and reappropriated by their audience, changing or "pluralizing" these meanings in the process.[39] Instead of opposing mediation entirely, then, Debord's situation could be reframed as an attempt to increase the audience's self-reflective awareness of their position as spectators, thereby shifting the opposition of hegemonic versus plural meanings towards the latter.

Still, given the problems that Debord's arguments regarding the media form raise, a second crucial Situationist tactic is perhaps better suited to encouraging audience creativity and reflexivity: *détournement*. The direct translation of this French term is "diversion," but, following Ken Knabb, I use the original term because the English word is confused by additional connotations of "idle entertainment."[40] Indeed, far from promoting idleness, Situationist *détournement* involves the purposeful and political diversion of something from its original meaning, and in this sense Sadie Plant is right to suggest that the appropriate translation of the term "lies somewhere between 'diversion' and 'subversion.'"[41] It is important that both moments of diversion and subversion are acknowledged, for this is how Debord distinguishes the Situationists from two of their influences, the Dadaist and Surrealist avant-garde movements of the early twentieth century. Both movements suffered from a "fatal one-sidedness," according to Debord, although for opposite reasons: Dada was premised entirely upon the negative destruction of the existing cultural order, while Surrealism just positively validated dreams and previously suppressed desires.[42] Situationist *détournement* worked to bridge this gap, emphasizing a positive moment of building anew from the remnants of the old – it was both a "negation and prelude," as the title of a 1959 editorial put it.[43]

This basic method, a critical form of pastiche or hodgepodge, dominates the remainder of Debord's films. The film version of *Society of the Spectacle*, for example, comprises select theses from the book read against the background of *détourned* images, from the aerial bombardment of Vietnam to a clip from the 1950s movie *Johnny Guitar*.[44] Along a similar line, Naomi Klein cites *détournement* as the root of the contemporary practice of "culture-jamming," the deliberate subversion of advertisements to promote anti-consumerist messages.[45]

Although the practice of culture-jamming and related media such as *Adbusters* have popularized *détournement* to some extent, the theoretical logic of the concept is best illustrated through the Situationists' discussion of language. In an article entitled "All the King's Men," they cite "power's stranglehold over language" as central to its domination of the social totality. But while power constantly attempts to "co-opt" words, giving "falsified, official" meanings that suit its purposes, the fundamental ambiguity of words always makes possible the practice of "poetry." Akin to play, what "poetry" does is re-root language in the people, rather than having it controlled by a *separate*, spectacular force. Therefore, the article concludes, the "point is not to put poetry at the service of revolution, but to put revolution at the service of poetry."[46]

"Poetry" occurs only through the *détourning* of words – that is, there must be both negative and positive moments of destabilizing official meanings and creating new ones. To this end, a 1966 *Internationale Situationniste* article suggests that a Situationist dictionary would be a "bilingual dictionary" that both deconstructs imposed meanings and attempts to "give [these concepts] a new content." Consistent with the notion of play, however, the "new content" would be provisional, corresponding only to the "present historical phase." It is necessary, in the

Situationist view, to challenge the idea of fixed or universal definitions, and consequently a Situationist dictionary ultimately would involve *détourning* the entire concept of dictionary.[47]

It is precisely these interruptive, playful dimensions of *détournement* that help it to move beyond earlier (Marxist) notions of the cultural struggle for hegemony. The concept is an effort to think through the practices central to this struggle, especially in terms of the context-based, emotional effects of images and events. As Tom Ward aptly puts it, *détournement* is above all about using familiar images to interrupt a "perfectly closed circle" of expectations, where people ignore what is outside their daily routine because "they *think* they already know what to expect – and want no part of it."[48] The task, in other words, is to confront the spectator visually, creating a situation that enjoins them to recognize the inherent instability of words, concepts, and norms, and, in particular, their creative potential to playfully reconstruct them.

Actual Situationist practice did not always yield the best examples of playful interruption, as it was often too offensive to promote spectator engagement; however, this does not undermine the value of some of their basic ideas, as a number of recent writings on the relationship of play and new social movements attest. Benjamin Shepard, for instance, points to the Situationists as forebears of a "new theatrical mode of protest," adopted and developed by contemporary community-based activist groups such as Reclaiming the Streets, ACT UP, and Billionaires for Bush. What these groups have in common, he argues, is a playful and creative spirit that promotes dialogue by showing that all ideas are open to ridicule.[49]

While recognizing that playful tactics are by no means a panacea, Shepard rightly explains how "play" addresses some of the deficiencies of purely rationalist approaches to organizing. Premised on self-interest and unambiguous policy proposals, rationalist approaches miss the affective motivations and satisfactions that draw people into social movements and bind them together as self-sustaining progressive organizations in the face of "the insurmountable," a phrase that is reminiscent of the enormous power Debord earlier attributed to the spectacle.[50] As Shepard argues, it is the playful form of confrontation embodied in actions such as Reclaiming the Streets' popular street carnivals that best break down the spectator/actor divide, developing the necessary foundation for an alternative vision of politics in the process.[51] With their emphasis on style, performance, pranks, atmospheres, and play, the Situationists clearly recognized the importance of emotional reactions. And their concepts of the situation and play pointed towards a radically democratic notion of politics, as I explain in the next section.

Conclusion: Debord and Radical Democratic Politics

If the situation's principal aim is to interrupt habits and accepted ideas, it does not appear that far from, for example, Rancière's democratic politics of division. Indeed, Rancière similarly claims that his own works seek to question "common sense" concepts for the purpose of reconstructing emancipatory ones – that is, ones that do not assign individuals to places and functions.[52] To be sure, I have downplayed the Marxist dimension of Debord's thought so far in order to highlight the radical democratic potential of his concepts. In fact, Debord's advocacy of workers' councils and his insistence that "workers become dialecticians" has led even sympathetic commentators like Steven Best and Douglas Kellner to criticize him for an "old-fashioned workerism" that "privilege[s] the working class as the revolutionary subject of history" over more decentralized social movements.[53]

To be fair, Best and Kellner's argument is considerably overstated. Debord's definition of the "proletariat" is much broader than now-outmoded notions of the industrial working class, going so far as to include all of those "who have lost all power over the use of their own lives."[54] This very broad and negative definition, premised on the inauthenticity of life under capitalism, leaves considerable room for people in a variety of class positions to identify themselves subjectively with the "proletariat," rather than treating it as a rigid, objective category. But Debord's notion is still a long way from much more open-ended theories of identify formation and subjectification put forward by more explicit proponents of radical democracy.[55]

Nevertheless Debord can still help us to think through four key issues in radical democratic theory: the place of division and conflict in politics, the critique of representation, the question of leadership, and the political capacity of the many. With regard to each of these issues, Debord's efforts are particularly interesting when the situation is viewed through the prism of "play." Two different approaches to the issue of division and conflict, for instance, can be teased out of Debord's works: one approach tends towards a cruder, more dogmatic Marxism; the other is informed by the concept of play. The former approach is associated with the strict reform/revolution opposition outlined by the Situationists in documents such as "Minimum Definitions of Revolutionary

Organizations," which was adopted at their seventh conference in 1966.[56] The document reduces radical politics to an either/or choice between the side of the working class or that of the spectacle and the capitalist class, and promotes confrontations to force those in the middle to decide. The result is that the political is turned into an antagonistic terrain of "us/them" similar to what Chantal Mouffe's "agonistic pluralism" advocates in a tamed, "adversarial" form (although the frontiers of the distinction are no doubt more class based for Debord than Mouffe would be willing to allow).[57]

As Andrew Schaap argues, the problem with such "with us or against us" divisions is that they preclude the emergence of other, new perspectives, and therefore offer an overly simple and constricted vision of political reality.[58] The concepts of the situation and play, in contrast, lead to a more open-ended approach to the issue of division. For what is a situation if not a number of different individuals concretely experiencing the same event from their own peculiar vantage point and then actively responding to it, ultimately by either forming a bond for collective action or dissipating as a result of irresolvable disagreements? The basic trajectory is similar to Hannah Arendt's movement from the "human condition of plurality" – which implies contingency and unpredictability, just like the situation – to "power," the ability to "act in concert."[59] The concept of play further emphasizes the necessity of conflict because of its focus on the endless process of self-institution. It implies that decisions are made freely by the players themselves, without the force of entrenched hierarchy and in a way that considers, but is never beholden to, past customs and traditions. Because all players are different, there no doubt will be conflicts and divisions during the "game" of politics, as well as over what the "rules of the game" should be. But, as Huizinga suggests, the value of play lies precisely in the intrinsic merits of this conflict: the struggle itself is what makes the players active, inciting their creative energies in the process.

In the context of modern liberal democracy, there is one obvious objection to the analogy between the "game" of politics and play in the sense of children's games such as tag – the former is now largely meditated by representatives, while the latter is immediate, with players directly adopting and adapting the rules that govern their activity. The question, then, is: can Debord's views of representation be rendered consistent with the notion of play? The answer is yes, with a qualification: Debord offers a strong critique of forms of representation that are inconsistent with play, but the alternative notion of representation he and the Situationists put forward is relatively limited.

Debord's concept of the spectacle can be summarized as a critique of representation, of the way images and appearances have come to dominate interactions in a consumerist society. As he asserts in the very first thesis of *Society of the Spectacle*, modern capitalist society "presents itself as an immense accumulation of spectacles. All that once was directly lived has become *mere representation*."[60] Although it seems in many instances that Debord wants to replace everything that is mediated and indirectly experienced with that which is immediate and directly experienced, the qualifier "mere" suggests that his target is not representation per se. Indeed, he later clarifies that the rule of the spectacle is confined to "wherever representation takes on an independent existence,"[61] leaving space for an alternative relationship between the directly lived and its representation.

If the problem with spectacular representation is the total disjuncture between essence – that is, reality, lived experience – and appearance, to the point where the latter is autonomous of and replaces the former, the solution for Debord is obviously to re-establish a bottom-up essence-to-appearance relationship. Therefore it is not surprising that the Situationists adopted direct democracy for their own organization, albeit a federal form with some caveats about delegation, and they endorsed a similar model for workers' councils. Within the SI, decisions were to be made through majority vote, with the general assembly of all members considered their highest decision-making body. A system of delegates was also set up insofar as not all members were able to attend all general meetings, but delegates were always revocable if they failed to carry out their mandate. The SI was organized through a federal principle to ensure considerable autonomy to groups operating in different states, although each national section had to employ democratic decision-making procedures and follow the guidelines adopted by the SI as a whole through the general assembly. Finally, there were explicit provisions so that serious disputes within a section led to the constitution of a "*tendency*," a dissident group of members who were to "draft texts to clarify and sustain their point of view" until the general assembly could meet to resolve the issue.[62]

Workers' councils, the organizational form that Debord claimed could bring about the "realization of that active direct communication that marks the end of all specialization, all hierarchy, and all separation,"[63] were also to operate through a federal model of democracy in which individual councils were to a large extent autonomous. Unlike the SI, however, democracy would be more delegative than direct in workers' councils.[64] As a result, it was even more important to ensure that delegates were accountable and easily revocable. As Vaneigem argues in a 1969 article on self-management, the general assembly of all members must be the highest body of a councilist organization. Acknowledging the importance of the divisions and conflicts between the members to the democratic vitality of the organization, he writes that, "through its representatives, the whole assembly with all its tendencies must be present at the moment of decision." It was necessary, in other words, for delegates to be in constant dialogue with their base. "The abundance of telecommunications technologies," Vaneigem continues, will make this possible, allowing the "immediate confirmation, correction or repudiation of [the delegates'] decision at all levels." Given that Vaneigem cites "telex," a technology superseded first by fax and then by email, as an example of technological advance, the idea of constant delegate-base dialogue is no doubt more plausible now than in the period in which he suggested it.[65] But the limit to Vaneigem's and Situationists' efforts to develop alternative notions about representation was not the speed of 1960s technology, but their narrow focus on improving the delegate model. This narrow focus prevented them from looking at other forms of representation that are equally well suited to the ethos of play and the requirements of radical democracy – specifically, ones based on the lottery system. Interestingly, a major critique of Huizinga's notion of play is that it neglects games based on chance.[66] Along a similar line, a return to the chance-based practice of sortition (the drawing of lots), which was so integral to ancient Athenian democracy, arguably have helped the Situationists move beyond their simplistic delegate model of representation.[67]

As the above discussion of workers' councils attests, Debord repeatedly confronted longer-term matters such as organization, institutions, and collective mobilization, contrary to the anti-institutional views of radical democracy promoted by figures such as Rancière and Sheldon Wolin, for whom democracy is merely a spontaneous, interruptive impulse that can never be embodied.[68] In doing so, Debord's aim was always to develop a notion of leadership that would not detract from the high regard he held for the capacity of the masses. He poses the situation, for example, as an agonistic moment of play that is to bring about an ongoing regime of play. In other words, the situation is intended as an *initial* moment of epiphany – of refusing to accept what is given – that is to lead to institutions (such as workers' councils) based on this new political ethos. What this means is that the situation can involve leadership so long as it does not congeal into an absolute authority. As the Situationists put it in an editorial, leadership in constructing situations, specifically the role of "director," must be a matter of "temporary subordination" instead of "permanent specialization."[69] Along a similar line, they asserted that a revolutionary avant-garde organization "must explicitly aim to dissolve itself as a separate organization at its moment of victory."[70] Ultimately the Situationist International dissolved itself in 1972 because of its inefficacy after the May 1968 uprising, but it had hoped that it would be forced to dissolve itself for a different reason: to make way for a truly democratic society.

It is worth noting the consistency of this notion of temporary leadership with Huizinga's notion of play. In the later chapters of *Homo Ludens*, Huizinga laments the decline of the play-element in Western culture over the past two centuries. The cause of this decline, according to Huizinga, is the increasingly technical and professional organization of modern life. He points, for example, to the distinction between amateurs and professionals in organized sports, which "means that the play-group marks out those for whom playing is no longer play, ranking them inferior to the true players in standing but superior in capacity."[71] The "spontaneity" of play also disappears, as paid professionals display their talents in the context of top-down, tightly controlled league organizations.

Huizinga's basic point is reflected in a common criticism of today's professional athletes: they are in it for the money, rather than for their love of the game. Although there is no necessary reason the best athletes in a particular sport should not compete against each other regularly, the problem with professionalization becomes clearer if we turn to a different sphere of society: politics. Much like sports, modern politics is thoroughly professionalized. Politics is largely considered a career choice – a way to network and make a name for oneself – rather than a civic duty. Major North American political parties, no matter what their ideological orientation, employ public relations specialists to help ensure that the "right" message is getting out, and there are various mechanisms party leaders can use to punish those who veer too far from party lines. The result is that public debate is much more controlled and stale than playful, creative, and agonistic.

Huizinga's argument has some obvious weaknesses, particularly in his broad generalizations about tendencies in modern civilization. It seems, however, that some of Debord's ideas would strengthen Huizinga's critique significantly. After all, one of Debord's chief concerns is the specialized nature of modern society, where individuals engage in narrow tasks in a way that is separated from other individuals as well as from a more holistic view of the overarching structure of society. His concept of "the spectacle" is designed precisely to mark a new and higher phase in the development of capitalist specialization: rapid post-war economic growth and technological advances mean that each "role" in the spectacular system – from those of academic disciplines to public relations specialists to the tasks of the ordinary worker – becomes even more refined, and therefore each individual becomes even further removed from questioning the entire system of roles.[72] In this regard, Debord adds a material foundation to Huizinga's argument, rooting the phenomenon of professionalization in, above all, the political economy of post-war capitalism.

Not surprisingly, Debord and a number of Situationist editorials responded to professionalization and bureaucratization by calling for the end of the "miserly reign of specialists" and for the need to "go beyond the failures of previous specialized politics" of parties and other radical groups.[73] It is precisely in this rejection of specialization and the reign of "experts" that Debord and the Situationists showed their confidence in the capacity of the masses collectively to make the most important decisions for a radically democratic society. But while the Situationists clearly believed that the masses would be able to realize fully their potential in the absence of the spectacle's hierarchies and roles, it was less clear that they succeeded in advancing this cause. At times it seems that the Situationists sought to preserve theory as their domain, ruthlessly criticizing all theories except their own as ideological. For instance, Debord claims in his 1966 report to the seventh Situationist conference that "our task first and foremost is to create an overall critical theory and ... to *communicate* it to every sector already objectively involved in a negation which remains subjectively piecemeal."[74] The resulting two-pronged model, with avant-garde Situationist theory on one side and proletarian mass practice, embodied in workers' councils, on the other, meant that their "situations" were not necessarily *radically democratic* in the sense that they were not attached to the root of democratic power, the people. Still, in their ideas about the interruptive nature of the situation and how its playful ethos might be sustained, Debord and the Situationists provided what Castoriadis calls a "germ of new creation."[75] Although their ideas remain problematic and incomplete, they help us to think about the practice associated with radical and agonistic democracy – that is, about politics beyond the anti-political impulse of the Marxist critique of political economy, as well as the tame, circumscribed debates of modern liberal democracies.

NOTES

1 Jean-Jacques Raspaud and Jean-Pierre Voyer, *L'Internationale Situationniste: chronologie, bibliographie, protagonistes* (Paris: Champ Libre, 1972), 11–14; "Members of the Situationist International," *Not Bored!* 24 June 2010, available online at http://www.notbored.org/members.html. Debord was certainly at the forefront of these expulsions. For example, he wrote a letter reproaching original SI member Walter Olmo for "having accepted … several ideas that are stupid" shortly before Olmo's expulsion in January 1958. See Guy Debord, *Correspondence: The Foundation of the Situationist International (June 1957–August 1960)*, trans. Stuart Kendall and John McHale (Los Angeles: Semiotext(e), 2009), 58.

2 I treat Debord as essentially synonymous with the Situationist International in this chapter, using editorial notes in *Internationale Situationniste* as if they were written by Debord and works by other Situationists to expand on his claims. Although this is an oversimplification, it is not overly problematic: Debord had an enormous impact on the development of the journal's articles, and the point here is to look at how Debord and the Situationists can help us to think about radical politics, not to quibble about issues of authorship.

3 John Kenneth Galbraith, *The Affluent Society*, 4th ed. (New York: New American Library, 1985), 1. On the key features of the Fordist state, see David Harvey, *The Condition of Postmodernity: An Enquiry into the Origins of Cultural Change* (Oxford, UK: Blackwell, 1989), 125–40.

4 Anselm Jappe, *Guy Debord*, trans. Donald Nicholson-Smith (Berkeley: University of California Press, 1999), 17–18.

5 Like other members of the Situationist International, Debord draws the term "everyday life" from Henri Lefebvre. Following Lefebvre's usage, the term indicates the distinctly human activities that are left after all "highly specialized occupations" are removed, including philosophy, as well as "dreams, the imaginary, art, play, ethics, [and] political life." See Henri Lefebvre, *Critique of Everyday Life*, vol. 1, trans. John Moore (London: Verso, 1991), 85–6.

6 Guy Debord, *The Society of the Spectacle*, trans. Donald Nicholson-Smith (New York: Zone Books, 1994), §§ 50, 43.

7 Ibid., § 60.

8 See Karl Marx, *Capital*, vol. 1, trans. Ben Fowkes (New York: Penguin Books, 1981), 145, 165–7.

9 Debord, *Society of the Spectacle*, §§ 18, 24.

10 Ibid., §§ 60–1.

11 Guy Debord, "Report on the Construction of Situations and on the International Situationist Tendency's Conditions of Organization and Action," in *Situationist International Anthology*, rev. ed., ed. Ken Knabb, trans. Ken Knabb (Berkeley, CA: Bureau of Public Secrets, 2006), 41.
12 Ibid., 40.
13 Guy Debord, "Introduction to a Critique of Urban Geography," in Knabb, *Situationist International Anthology*, 8.
14 Debord, "Report on the Construction of Situations," 39; Situationist International, "Preliminary Problems in Constructing a Situation," in Knabb, *Situationist International Anthology*, 49.
15 Guy Debord, "One More Try if You Want to Be Situationists (The SI in and against Decomposition)," in *Guy Debord and the Situationist International: Texts and Documents*, ed. Tom McDonough, trans. John Shepley (Cambridge, MA: MIT Press, 2003), 55.
16 Guy Debord, "Theses on Cultural Revolution," in Knabb, *Situationist International Anthology*, 53.
17 Guy Debord, "The Theory of Dérive," in Knabb, *Situationist International Anthology*, 62.
18 Situationist International, "Preliminary Problems in Constructing a Situation," 50.
19 Situationist International, "The Avant-Garde of Presence," in Knabb, *Situationist International Anthology*, 143.
20 Vladimir Lenin, "What Is to Be Done?" in *Selected Works in Three Volumes*, vol. 1 (New York: International Publishers, 1967), 122.
21 Vincent Kaufmann, *Guy Debord: Revolution in the Service of Poetry*, trans. Robert Bononno (Minneapolis: University of Minnesota Press, 2006), 202.
22 Debord, *Society of the Spectacle*, § 123.
23 Debord, "Report on the Construction of Situations," 39; Situationist International, "Questionnaire," in Knabb, *Situationist International Anthology*, 178.
24 The works in question are Jappe, *Guy Debord*; Sadie Plant, *Most Radical Gesture: The Situationist International in a Postmodern Age* (London: Routledge, 1992); and Greil Marcus, *Lipstick Traces: A Secret History of the Twentieth Century* (Cambridge, MA: Harvard University Press, 1989). One of the few writers to stress this fact is Libero Andreotti, in "Play-Tactics of the Internationale Situationniste," *October* 91 (Winter 2000): 36–58.
25 Johan Huizinga, *Homo Ludens: A Study of the Play-Element in Culture* (Boston: Beacon Press, 1960), ix.
26 Ibid., 7–13.
27 On the agonistic element of play, see especially ibid., 31, 48–50, 71–5.

28 Guy Debord, "L'architecture et le jeu," *Œuvres* (Paris: Gallimard, 2006), 191; my translation.
29 Raoul Vaneigem, *The Revolution of Everyday Life*, trans. Donald Nicholson-Smith (London: Rebel Press, 2006), 258.
30 Debord, *Society of the Spectacle*, § 178, emphasis added.
31 Cornelius Castoriadis, "Power, Politics, Autonomy," in Curtis, *Philosophy, Politics, Autonomy*, 150–3.
32 Ibid., 162–4, emphasis in original.
33 On the concept of "roles," see Debord, *Society of the Spectacle*, §§ 59–61; Vaneigem, *Revolution of Everyday Life*, 131–50.
34 Guy Debord, "Howls for Sade," in *Complete Cinematic Works: Scripts, Stills, Documents*, ed. Ken Knabb, trans. Ken Knabb (Oakland, CA: AK Press, 2003), 1–12.
35 Kaufmann, *Guy Debord*, 235, 226.
36 On the reception of the film, see Len Bracken, *Guy Debord: Revolutionary* (Venice, CA: Feral House, 1997), 19–21.
37 Jacques Rancière, *The Emancipated Spectator*, trans. Gregory Elliott (London: Verso, 2009), 10–17.
38 Guy Debord, "Perspectives for Conscious Changes in Everyday Life," in Knabb, *Situationist International Anthology*, 90, 481 fn. 90.
39 This point is made forcefully by Michel de Certeau with regards to the practice of reading. As he puts it, "a text has a meaning only through its readers; it changes along with them; it is ordered in accord with codes of perception that it does not control." See Michel de Certeau, *The Practice of Everyday Life*, trans. Steven Rendall (Berkeley: University of California Press, 1984), chap. 12.
40 Knabb, *Situationist International Anthology*, 480 fn. 14.
41 Plant, *Most Radical Gesture*, 86.
42 Debord, *Society of the Spectacle*, § 191.
43 Situationist International, "Détournement as Negation and Prelude," in Knabb, *Situationist International Anthology*, 67.
44 Guy Debord, "The Society of the Spectacle," in Knabb, *Complete Cinematic Works*, 43–110.
45 Naomi Klein, *No Logo: Taking Aim at the Brand Bullies* (Toronto: Vintage Canada, 2000), 282.
46 Situationist International, "All the King's Men," in Knabb, *Situationist International Anthology*, 149–51.
47 Mustapha Khayati, "Captive Words: Preface to a Situationist Dictionary," in Knabb, *Situationist International Anthology*, 222–3, 226–8.

48 Tom Ward, "The Situationists Reconsidered," in *Cultures in Contention*, ed. Douglas Khan and Diane Neumaier (Seattle, WA: Real Comet Press, 1985), 150.

49 Benjamin Shepard, "If I Can't Dance: Play, Creativity, and Social Movements" (PhD diss., City University of New York, 2006), 2, 35–43.

50 Benjamin Shepard, L.M. Bogad, and Stephen Duncombe, "Performing vs. the Insurmountable: Theatrics, Activism, and Social Movements," *Liminalities: A Journal of Performance Studies* 4, no. 3 (2008): 10–11, 5–6.

51 Benjamin Shepard, "Play, Creativity, and the New Community Organizing," *Journal of Progressive Human Services* 16, no. 2 (2005): 55–6; Shepard, Bogad, and Duncombe, "Performing vs. the Insurmountable," 3.

52 Jacques Rancière, "Democracy, Dissensus and the Aesthetics of Class Struggle: An Exchange with Jacques Rancière," *Historical Materialism* 13, no. 4 (2005): 299–300.

53 Steven Best and Douglas Kellner, *The Postmodern Turn* (New York: Guilford Press, 1997), 117.

54 Debord, *Society of the Spectacle*, § 114.

55 See, for example, Jacques Rancière, *Disagreement: Politics and Philosophy*, trans. Julie Rose (Minneapolis: University of Minnesota Press, 1999), 35–8.

56 Situationist International, "Minimum Definition of Revolutionary Organizations," in Knabb, *Situationist International Anthology*, 285–6.

57 Mouffe, *Democratic Paradox*, 101–5, 110.

58 Andrew Schaap, "Political Theory and the Agony of Politics," *Political Studies Review* 5, no. 1 (2007): 70. To be more precise, Schaap's critique of Mouffe's agonistic pluralism is that it is not able to escape the Schmittian friend/enemy distinction on which it is based. Arendt's agonism, on the other hand, does not suffer from this defect.

59 Arendt, *Human Condition*, 7, 179.

60 Debord, *Society of the Spectacle*, § 1, emphasis added.

61 Ibid., § 18.

62 Situationist International, "Provisional Statutes of the SI," in Knabb, *Situationist International Anthology*, 461–3, emphasis in original. The thrust of the statutes is that the general assembly was to act as final arbiter in all disputes; however, what the text actually says is that the issues raised by tendencies were to be resolved "by rediscovered unanimity, by break or by a practical supersession of the divergence."

63 Debord, *Society of the Spectacle*, § 116.

64 Ibid.

65 Raoul Vaneigem, "Notice to the Civilized Concerning Generalized Self-Management," in Knabb, *Situationist International Anthology*, 368–9. Vaneigem recognizes the contradictory nature of technology, which may lead to either democratic or anti-democratic outcomes. Although it could be used to enhance communication between delegates and their base, alternatively it might be used "as a pretext for the continuation or return of specialists."

66 Roger Caillois, *Man, Play, and Games*, trans. Meyer Barash (New York: Free Press of Glencoe, 1961), 5.

67 On the role of rotation and sortition in Athenian democracy, see Castoriadis, "The Greek *Polis* and the Creation of Autonomy," 106–8, 117.

68 On Rancière, see Chapter 7 in this volume; on Wolin's anti-institutional view, see Sheldon Wolin, "Fugitive Democracy," *Constellations* 1, no. 1 (1994): 19.

69 Situationist International, "Preliminary Problems in Constructing a Situation," 50. As the Situationists used it, "temporary" referred to a moment, not a stage of development. Although technically Lenin's "dictatorship of the proletariat" would be a temporary stage on the road to socialism, the Situationists considered this idea to be an example of "permanent specialization."

70 Situationist International, "Minimum Definition of Revolutionary Organizations," 286.

71 Huizinga, *Homo Ludens*, 195–8.

72 Debord, *Society of the Spectacle*, §§ 25, 42, 57.

73 Situationist International, "Ideologies, Classes, and the Domination of Nature," in Knabb, *Situationist International Anthology*, 135; idem, "Response to a Questionnaire from the Centre for Socio-Experimental Art," in Knabb, *Situationist International Anthology*, 186; Debord, *Society of the Spectacle*, §§ 115–16.

74 Guy Debord, "Report to the Seventh SI Conference in Paris," in *The Real Split in the International*, trans. John McHale (London: Pluto Press, 2003), 133, emphasis in original.

75 Cornelius Castoriadis, "The Crisis of Culture and the State," in Curtis, *Philosophy, Politics, Autonomy*, 240–1.

Part III

New Directions and Possibilities in Radical Democratic Thought

7 A Politics in Writing: Jacques Rancière and the Equality of Intelligences

RACHEL MAGNUSSON

In recent years Jacques Rancière's writings have caused a flurry of excitement in certain academic circles. What has particularly captured his readers' imaginations are his interventions on aesthetics and politics. In relation to politics, it is claims such as democracy is the rule of those whose only qualification is that they have no qualification to rule,[1] or politics "exists when the natural order of domination is interrupted by the institution of a part of those who have no part,"[2] or "politics is the manifestation of dissensus, as the presence of two worlds in one"[3] – as well as his analyses of political subjectification, processes of equality, and the partition (or distribution) of the sensible – that have most intrigued his readers. It is this combination of provocative assertions and analyses about politics that spurs the temptation to want to pin down and evaluate what appears to be the new and interesting theory of politics in Rancière's work.[4] In this chapter I argue, however, that it is important to resist this temptation.

One reason is that, if we were to approach Rancière's work as if it offers a straightforward theory of politics, we would tend to overlook the indeterminacy that is at the heart of his understanding of our relations with one other, with words, and with the world. In fact, part of the aim of this chapter is to show how indeterminacy is at work in Rancière's accounts of politics – both in the "content" of his understanding of politics and in the "form" of his writing. It is the recognition and mobilization of this indeterminacy in his writings that, I argue, opens up a new terrain for seeing, thinking, and enacting politics.

Many of Rancière's interpreters note this indeterminacy in one way or another. For example, Peter Hallward argues that Rancière affirms a "fundamental inconsistency or 'unclassifiability,' an essential instability of experience." Davide Panagia similarly describes how "[i]mpropriety hovers throughout Rancière's oeuvre without landing with specificity at any one point. Given his own *style indirect libre* vis-à-vis the treatment of words, images, and things, his manner of impropriety makes appearances throughout."[5] Where disputes arise, however, is over what this indeterminacy means and what the consequences are for Rancière's thought. For many of Rancière's interpreters, this indeterminacy is attributed, for better or for worse, to his anarchist sympathies: in essence, he insists on indeterminacy because of his love for freedom and disruptiveness.[6] Alongside interpreters such as Sam Chambers, I argue that this characterization is misleading.[7] I contend that the importance of indeterminacy is not its association with freedom or disruptiveness, but the mobilizations of *equality* that indeterminacy allows. In other words, it is indeterminacy that makes democracy possible for Rancière: the political institution of a dispute over who has the capacity to speak and think. In fact, I argue that Rancière's most original contribution to our thinking of radical democracy is his insistence that politics always capitalizes on indeterminacy to demonstrate, albeit most often indirectly, our equal capacity as humans – or, as he sometimes puts it, the equality of intelligences.[8]

To explore the role of indeterminacy in Rancière's rethinking of politics and in his method, I first attempt, quite ironically, a summary of his account of politics, I then turn to a discussion of his method, and finally to a brief exploration of his preoccupation with the "equality of intelligences" and the challenge it seems to pose.

An Account of Politics

Unlike most thinkers of politics, including many in this volume, Rancière argues that politics must be strictly distinguished from what we normally consider it to be: an activity of ruling or governing. According to Rancière, the activity of ruling and governing suppresses politics; in his terms, it involves policing, not politics. Under policing he includes all those practices of government and society at large that attempt to make institutions work, to make people get along, to make all parts of society function smoothly. These practices of policing – whether they are enabling or oppressive – work because they draw upon the authority of a particular ordering of places and capabilities, a particular representation of society to itself, or, in his words, a particular "partition of the sensible."[9] Rancière claims that all societies rely on a count, logic, or distribution that allots everyone a place in society – although some people are so low in this hierarchy that their place is one of exclusion, the "part with no part."[10] A person or group's place is then associated with certain jobs, ways of living, forms of speech, modes of interacting, and capacities for thought and action.[11] Thus, in any society, there is an overall order of appearances that links people to places and places to ways of being. This overall order is what Rancière means by "the police." The police is the logic that governs who can be seen, what can be heard, what seems possible, and so on. As he describes it, it is "an order of the visible and the sayable that sees that a particular activity is visible and another is not, that this speech is understood as discourse and another is noise."[12]

Rancière claims that, for a society to run smoothly, the police's distribution of places and capabilities must appear to be all that exists. So whatever the partition of the sensible is – whether it be a highly stratified society of monarchical rule or a modern society of competing group interests – its own image of community must be reinforced. At times this might involve oppressive tactics, but most often the police is legitimized through the discourses, images, and appeals that highlight some things and mask others. What this means is that the police should not be thought of as simply a system of oppression. It is certainly a coercive force in some ways at some times, but it is also the logic that enables all those organizational institutions and practices of rule that are necessary for any society to function.[13] To sum up, the police is the expression of a society to itself. It is the distribution of ways of being, doing, and saying upon which all the mechanisms that make societies work rely.

In contrast, politics is an activity that disrupts, questions, or challenges the police and its authoritative partition of the sensible. Politics disturbs the police: the order of appearances, the image the community has of itself, the logic of places and capabilities. Politics is, in Rancière's words, "first and foremost an intervention upon the visible and the sayable."[14] More specifically, for Rancière it is a process that interrupts the day-to-day functioning of police practices with a declaration and demonstration of equality. Indeed, for Rancière, politics always confronts the police with the problem of equality. Any police order – in fact, any community at all – will have divisions that mark some people, in some ways, to be better than others. And yet, he argues, for this hierarchical distribution to work, people must be clever enough to know their place.[15] As such, a kind of equality – which Rancière sometimes refers to as an "empty equality" – sustains and supports the inequality of a police order.[16]

This "empty equality" is also another name for indeterminacy: the fundamental arbitrariness of any social and political order. Interestingly, Rancière argues that Hobbes saw this too. However, rather than seeing political potential in this "empty equality," Hobbes saw the danger of "the war of all against all."[17] Society's order rests upon people's recognizing and obeying this order, but this ability to recognize and obey implies a shared capacity for understanding that can be mobilized to undermine the legitimacy of the order. This is what worried Hobbes about the upstart preachers of his day who valued only their own opinions: their assertion of their equal capacity threatened the stability of his world.[18] If everyone were to reclaim their equal capacity, this would dissolve all order and create a state of anarchy, a state of man against man.[19] In contrast, Rancière sees promise in this "empty equality." It is not anarchy that attracts Rancière, however, but the ability of people to transform a recognition of their equal capacity to understand, speak, and think into a specific challenge to the police order. In fact, this is what he thinks politics does: it targets an inequality of the police by mobilizing the "empty equality" that exists within any police order.

Moreover, Rancière argues that what distinguishes politics is the specific way it targets an inequality of the police. The specificity of politics lies in the "disagreement" it sets up with the police. Take, for instance, the claim made a few decades ago that women are not inferior creatures meant to be kept in the home, but are human beings capable of work, thought, and action. According to Rancière's understanding of politics, such a declaration latches onto a specific contradiction of the police – a "wrong" – in order both to denounce this contradiction and to demonstrate the possibility of another alternative.[20] For example, how could a mother be the best judge in the home and for her children, but be incapable of good judgment outside the home? Could this not be seen as a contradiction? Would it not be more rational to argue either that women are not capable of good judgment anywhere or that they are capable of good judgment everywhere? Rancière describes this form of argumentation as exhibiting a "rationality of disagreement."[21] He claims that politics employs a rationality that takes seriously certain claims of the police order that it should not (women are capable of good judgment), then uses these claims to argue against an inequality that exists within the police order (women can exercise good judgment only in the home, whereas men can exercise good judgment anywhere). In so doing, politics opens up a space for dispute, conflict, and disagreement. Where at first there was only the logic of the police – women and men have different natures, and women's nature is tied to the home – politics exposes an indeterminacy or gap in the logic of the police and exploits this to create a venue to argue about men and women's natures, their capacities for judgment, their equality or inequality. In other words, it manifests a division and makes visible the fundamental contingency of any social and political order.

Politics does not simply open up a situation, however, where a conflict with the police can be seen and heard. Politics also manifests a new relation of equality. For instance, the declaration that women are not inferior creatures meant to be kept in the home is what also demonstrates women's equality with men. In making such a claim, in setting up a dispute with the police, women show themselves to be creatures capable of rationality, public speech, dispute, and so on. Within the conflict that develops with the police, women act *as if* they are the equals of men, and in so doing they establish a relation of equality that did not previously exist. They perform, show, and live a new relation of equality. In fact it is also this enactment of equality that helps to demonstrate the "wrong" of the police. It is not only that politics calls attention to a contradiction or inconsistency of the police through argument, it also calls attention to this contradiction by showing another kind of reality to exist. As Rancière writes, "the *demonstration* proper to politics is always both argument and opening up the world where argument can be received and have an impact – argument about the very existence of such a world."[22] Thus, politics establishes a stage on which a dispute can be played out with the police, and this requires an enactment of an equality that simultaneously creates an equality that did not previously exist and helps to demonstrate that the police does not fully represent all that exists.

It is important to note, however, that politics does not reveal some true relation of equality lying beneath the inequalities and injustices of the police. Before the women's movement, for example, women were no doubt intelligent and capable – and a few were even acknowledged as such – but they were not the equals of men because this equality was not seen, heard, or recognized. The relation of equality that many women and men now live out was not lying dormant under the false displays of the police; it was created and enacted through women's political action. Their action gave a particular form to the "empty equality" that was implicit in the police order. Their political action transformed this "empty equality" into a relation of equality between women and men that could be seen, tested, and debated. In this sense, then, politics is fundamentally creative.

In fact this creative side of politics explains why Rancière does not speak of political subjects, but of political subjectivization. Just as politics does not reveal some true relation of equality, but enacts a new relation of equality, so there are also no political subjects in advance of politics. The activity of politics itself – the staging of a disagreement and the performance of an equality – is what creates political subjects. To continue with our example, as women became involved in challenging the naturalized gender relations of the police, they also underwent a process of political subjectivization. Through their engagement in politics, there arose a new idea of what it meant to be a woman, of what it meant to be a human, of what it meant to be a feminist – a new "we." In this sense politics produces its own subject. This subject, however, is not pure, but rather conflictual and heterogeneous – political subjectivization removes people from their previously established place in the police order, challenges this concept of place, and suggests a new configuration that defies an easy mapping onto the existing organization of bodies and identities. The new political subjects – woman, feminist – for instance, are not only internally contested (what really counts as being a woman? a feminist?), but are also part of the conflict with the police (how can women be only wives and mothers, if we are women and are neither?) and affirm a new identity, a new relation of equality (a woman is a human being, a feminist is a person who resists patriarchy). Rancière sometimes refers to this creation of a new subjective identity more properly as a "disidentification,"[23] an "in-between" subject, [24] or "the relation of a self to an other."[25] He wants to stress, in other words, that political subjects are not fixed or static identities that pre-exist politics; rather, what distinguishes politics, and thus political subjectification, is that it challenges our normal identities and categorizations at the same time as affirming some new identity or relationship. One way to understand this is that the political subject is a part of the drama of politics itself: political subjects are sites where the conflicts and manifestations of politics play out.

Politics exists, therefore, because there is always more than what the police represents; or, put differently, the police's own contingency is what makes politics possible. There will always be something missing, something masked, something that does not line up in the order of the police, and politics can capitalize on this inconsistency to suggest another arrangement, another possible way to see the world. Put otherwise, politics exploits indeterminacy. This is also why Rancière argues that the gap between words and things "defines the space of political rationality."[26] It is not that paying attention to "things" can help us correct our "words," but that the inevitable distance that exists between things and words can be mobilized to create both new words and new things. Rancière sometimes refers to this as our poetic, or literary, virtue.[27] As he explains,

> humans are political animals because they are literary animals: not only in the Aristotelian sense of using language in order to discuss questions of justice, but also because we are confounded by the excess of words in relation to things. Humans are political animals, then, for two reasons: first, because we have the power to put into circulation more words, "useless" and unnecessary words, words that exceed the function of rigid designation; secondly, because this fundamental ability to proliferate words is unceasingly contested by those who claim to "speak correctly" – that is, by the masters of designation and classification who, by virtue of wanting to retain their status and power, flat-out deny this capacity to speak.[28]

Politics is possible, therefore, because of this human ability to play with words, to play with the gap between words and things in such a way that something new emerges. In other words, indeterminacy both makes room for the demonstration of our common capacity and is itself evidence of our common capacity to *use* language.

There are a few other important things to stress about Rancière's account of politics before we move on. First, he explains that, because of the way politics comes about – exploiting a "wrong" in the logic of the police – it is always historically bound. As he writes, "[p]olitics does not come out of the blue. It is articulated with a certain form of the police order, which means a certain balance of the possibilities and impossibilities that this order defines."[29]

Second, he also insists that politics is rare:[30] because of its local and historical nature, sometimes what might have been politics becomes too particularist;[31] because of its engagement with the police, sometimes what might have been politics fails to disrupt the order of appearances, and thus falls within the categories of the police and becomes a part of everyday struggles for power or goods;[32] because of its literary bent, sometimes what might have been politics remains individualistic and withdrawn from any conflict with the police;[33] and because of its critique of the police, sometimes what might have been politics forgets any demonstration of equality.[34] Put otherwise, there seem for Rancière to be many examples of politics-in-some-form, or politics-by-other-means, but politics in its full form – a drama of disagreement that interrupts the police order and enacts a new relation of equality – is something rare.

Third, Rancière treats politics and democracy as almost interchangeable terms. Democracy is not, for Rancière, a particular kind of regime that expresses the will of the people.[35] Instead, through a rereading of Plato, he argues that democracy was originally the name for what he calls politics.[36] Democracy "is the institution of politics itself, the system of forms of subjectification through which any order of distribution of bodies into functions corresponding to their 'nature' and places corresponding to their functions is undermined, thrown back on its contingency."[37] Rancière argues that what Plato describes as democracy was not rule by the people, but the rule of chance, the rule of those who have no title, no qualification to govern. So the reason Plato and others since have hated democracy is not that they hated "the people," but that they hated the disorder that democracy can cause. Democracy, or politics, shows us the contingency of our way of seeing and organizing the world – it points to this contingency to suggest another possibility, but in so doing can cause all our secure categorizations to crumble. As Rancière writes, "democratic action is the form of action which carries out the disruption of any ultimate legitimacy of power, or, if you turn it on its positive side, the affirmation of the equal capacity of anybody."[38]

It is clear, then, that for Rancière indeterminacy plays a central role in his understanding of politics: its presence suggests that an "empty equality" – an equal capacity to speak, think, and understand – might underpin all social orders, and its existence creates a space for politics, a space for a demonstration of equality to be made. But this raises another important question: why does Rancière insist that politics is always concerned with equality? Why exactly are democracy and politics nearly always synonymous in Rancière's schemata? For it would seem that Rancière's account of the structure of politics – the disruption of the logic of the police with the manifestation of a new arrangement or view of things – could be disconnected from any dispute about equality. Perhaps one might want to grant that all politics stems from some recognition of common capacity because this is what enables the institution of a political dispute, but why does this necessitate that equality be the content of what is disputed with the police?

Take, for example, the environmental movement in North America, which, according to Rancière's definition, could be interpreted as engaging in politics. Over the past forty years, it has challenged the logic of the police by creating a political stage on which environmental concerns now appear and can be argued about. However, the disputes that the environmental movement has set up with the police are not primarily focused on issues of equality. No doubt some environmental concerns call into question hierarchies of our police order, but in general environmental concerns do not hinge on a conflict over the equal capacities of human beings.[39] Therefore, even though one could argue that the environmental movement manifests many of the key features of politics as it is described by Rancière, it nonetheless also seems to fall outside his categorization of politics. Given this, should we discount the North American environmental movement as political? Or should we discount Rancière's theory of politics because it fails to account for a movement that seems so obviously political? Or, instead, does this problem suggest that we must reconsider what Rancière is doing in his delivery of a "theory" politics? I suggest the last of these options.

An Exploration of Method

Rancière's commitment to, or perhaps even obsession with, equality can be seen as a signal to his readers that he is not offering a straightforward theory of politics. In various places Rancière comments on the purpose of his own writings. For instance, in a strange article in *Parallax* where he refers to himself in the third person, Rancière states, "[h]e never intended to produce a theory of politics, aesthetics, literature, cinema or anything else. He thinks that there is already a good deal of them and he loves trees enough to avoid destroying them to add one more theory to all those available on the market."[40] Instead, he says, his works were intended, in part, as "polemical interventions."[41] *Disagreement* reveals this quite clearly: his definitions of politics take shape in discussions of what politics is not – the art of rule, a practice of consensus, a humanitarian order – and against influential thinkers of the political – Plato, Aristotle, Marx, Habermas. His own "theory" of politics is thus situated against customary discourses on the political. In this sense, it is not hard to see how many of his writings could be classified as critical interventions intended to disrupt dominant conceptions.

Through their displacement of dominant conceptions, however, his writings are also constructions that suggest a new way of thinking about politics, art, literature, and so on. Rancière uses various metaphors to explain these constructions: the tracing of a line to draw a new picture,[42] the disentangling of a knot,[43] a translation into a new idiom,[44] the restaging of a scene,[45] or the drawing of a moving map.[46] In a sense, then, he is constructing a theory of politics, but not one that is meant to correspond exactly to a reality "out there." As he insists, the "categories by means of which I tried to think politics, art and their relationships are not ontological determinations."[47] Instead, his constructions are meant to shift our understanding of the reality that exists in such a way that it becomes possible to see another reality; they make certain things visible that could not previously be seen, connections where none previously existed, open up space where previously everything was closed, give a name to something that was previously nameless. "Construction," however, is also a somewhat misleading term because it implies that Rancière is building a fixed framework that allows us to see our world differently. But Rancière always insists that he is not offering a new framework, but rather a new path, voyage, or adventure.[48] As he writes, "[w]hat he does himself is to construct a moving map of a moving landscape, a map that is ceaselessly modified by the movement itself. This is why, indeed, his 'concepts' are instable: police and politics, distribution of the sensible, aesthetics, literature, etc. don't mean the same thing from the beginning of the travel to the end; first because the travel is a fight too, a multi-waged fight where the emphasis can be put on different aspects; second because the travel – or the fight – continuously discovers new landscapes, paths or obstacles which oblige to reframe the conceptual net used to think where we are."[49] Thus, if one follows Rancière's own characterization of his method, his "theories" of politics, art, literature, and so on are always in process. They are an ever-shifting characterization that challenges the normal way of presenting the world both to highlight previously obscured features and to demonstrate the openness that exists in the here and now.[50]

What is interesting about Rancière's account of his method is that it is reminiscent of his accounts of politics. His writings are intended to intervene and disrupt the dominant partition of the sensible and to offer a reconfiguration of this partition. Indeed, it seems that Rancière imagines himself to be engaging in a form of political activity: he is undoing and remaking the connection between words and things with particular aims in mind. Having said this, because his writings are individualistic and not a demonstration of common capacity – French philosophers are generally already recognized as capable of thought in our police order – he is not engaging in politics proper, according to his own categorizations. Nor would he ever claim to be participating in politics in the full sense through his writing. Nevertheless, I think it would be fair to say that in his writings Rancière is consciously practising politics-in-some-form.

In fact, his discussions of writing in general point to the ways in which he thinks it is possible for writing and politics to overlap. He remarks: "As [Plato] conceived it, writing meant the wrong circuit on which words are launched as orphans, available to anybody, without being guided by the voice of the master who knows how they have to be related to things and also who is entitled or not entitled to make an appropriate use of them. In my terms, writing – and its other side, reading – is a redistribution of the sensible. Writing frees words from a given relation between signs and bodies. By so doing it blurs the distinction between gold and iron and it makes this mix-up available to anybody."[51] Thus, just like politics, writing can reconfigure the police order. It "contributes to the reframing of forms of experience."[52] Moreover, his comment on writing also points to another connection with politics: because of writing's detachment from its author's presence, it gives space for others' interpretations and interventions. Writing might provoke others to pursue their own reconfiguration of the partition of the sensible; it might provoke them to think and act themselves. In other words, it might encourage emancipation.

Interestingly, on this note, "emancipation" was one of Rancière's first objects of study after he broke with his mentor Louis Althusser. In his early works, *The Nights of Labour* and *The Ignorant Schoolmaster*, he pursued the question of how people came to challenge the order of society and their place in it. What he found in his historical investigations was that writing, circumstances, or other people could not lead people to emancipation through insight or instruction, but they could encourage people to *assume* their equality. And, in fact, that was what emancipation really was – not enlightenment, not critical insight, not the freedom to vote, but the decision to enact one's equality. To be emancipated was to assume, demonstrate, and perform one's equal capacity – to act *as if* one was already an equal. Significantly it is this reflection on emancipation that Rancière claims lies "at the ground of the rethinking of politics he pursued, from *On the Shores of Politics* to *Disagreement*."[53] It is this reflection on emancipation, therefore, that influences his understanding of what writing about politics could and could not do.

Given this, it seems likely that, with his own writings, Rancière hoped to encourage emancipation, but not by informing his readers about the true nature of politics. Instead, one can infer that Rancière designed his discussions of politics in such a way that they might trigger "new passions" that might spark others to write against an inequality of the police, to express their equality, or even to establish a new form of political conflict.[54] In fact, I argue that, in his writings, Rancière seems to want to further the openness and detachment that writing possesses in general, by refusing to offer any systematic theories and by crafting his own texts polemically and ambiguously. His writings are indeterminate, in other words, because he hopes that others might take up where he left off.

It is possible, therefore, to see Rancière as engaging in politics-in-some-form in two senses: first, insofar as his writings aim, like politics, to exploit the indeterminacy of words and things in order to intervene and call attention to a problem in the police's partition of the sensible; and second, insofar as his writings aim to exhibit indeterminacy in order to encourage emancipation. If one recognizes this double political aim of his writings, this in turn helps to explain Rancière's insistence on equality. Indeed, Rancière's insistence that politics always involves a dispute over equality is not a claim about the-final-truth-about-politics, but an aspect of what is politically directed about Rancière's description of politics.

To support this political interpretation of what Rancière is doing in his writings, one can point to his own name for his method: "the method of equality." His method is one of "equality" because his account of politics draws our attention to problems of equality. In societies where questions of equality are often overlooked because "equality" is thought to be guaranteed by a constitution, to be a passé political concern, or considered to be the cause of self-centred individualism, Rancière's focus on equality is surprising. It shakes up our easy assumptions, and forces us to think about problems of equality anew, and it makes equality appear, in various ways, to be more possible. In this way, then, his is also a method of equality because it aims at emancipation. His writings present equality as something his readers could assume. He not only makes his readers *see* equality differently, he presents various forms or practices of equality that seem possible to emulate or reinstitute in a different way. His writings might not trigger a process that culminates in a new manifestation of politics in the full sense, but they might open up the world in such a way that readers become emancipated and encourage the emancipation of others.

Thus, it is possible to see Rancière's insistence that politics must involve equality as part of what is political about his writing. He wants issues of equality to be seen again, and he wants to encourage others to assume their equality. Seen in this light, the problem that the environmental movement seemed to pose for Rancière's theory of politics is not a serious one. Since Rancière was not offering a definitive theory of politics, there is no need to dismiss either the environmental movement as not politics or his theory of politics. Rather, his theory of politics can be expanded and adapted as his readers see fit, and this is presumably something Rancière would encourage. Rancière himself might want to argue for equality's centrality in politics, but this is because of his own political preoccupations. It does not mean that other manifestations of politics should not be seen as such because they do not fall within that to which he wants to draw our attention.

A Politics of the Equality of Intelligences

If one interprets Rancière's insistence that politics must concern equality in this political light, however, this should not lead one to downplay his interest in equality in favour of some more "neutral" interpretation of his theory of politics. Instead, I argue that it is his very obsession with equality – and more particularly with the equality of intelligences or, in other terms, our common capacity to speak and think – that makes his writings on politics so insightful and provocative. For what his concern with the equality of intelligences provokes is a consideration of its centrality in any democratic politics, as well as a re-evaluation of our tendency to reinforce a hierarchy of intelligence even as we pursue a more just world. To be sure, it is not that Rancière's preoccupation with the equality of intelligence results in a direct argument for a politics of equality of intelligences in his writings that readers must contend with; rather, it is a preoccupation that resurfaces in most of his writings and it is a possibility that is integrated, as we have seen, into his rethinking of politics and his "method of equality." Given this, Rancière's presentation of the potential of the equality of intelligences seems to demand further consideration.

But first, where can one see evidence of this preoccupation with the equality of intelligence? If one is alert to it, one can find it in all his works. For instance, in a discussion in *On the Shores of Politics* about how democratic practice – or "*vita democratica*," as he names it – approaches division differently than most traditions in philosophy and social science, Rancière notes that at the heart of this approach lies "the notion of equality of intelligences as the common prerequisite of both intelligibility and community, as a presupposition which everyone must strive to validate on their own account."[55] Much later, in *Hatred of Democracy*, in the context of a brief commentary on the debates surrounding the role of the state in politics, Rancière claims that the French strikes of 1995 were democratic because they "revolved around the fundamental political question: that of the competence of the 'incompetent,' of the capacity of anybody at all to judge the relations between individuals and the collectivity, present and future."[56] Again, in setting up his analysis in *The Emancipated Spectator*, Rancière argues that many artists today repeat the division between activity/passivity that in turn reinforces a general division between those who are capable and those who are not; and, moreover, that this hierarchical categorization repeats itself until one realizes that those who are passive, those who are spectators, are also exercising equal intelligence: "She observes, selects, compares, interprets."[57] And, finally, in a recent article commenting on his method, Rancière writes:

> If "division" is at the heart of his texts on politics, this has nothing to do with any vision of politics, based on the distinction between friends and enemies. "Disagreement" and "dissensus" do not imply that politics is a struggle between camps; they imply that it is a struggle about what politics is, a struggle that is waged about such original issues as: "where are we?," "who are we?," "What makes us a we," "What do we see and what can we say about it that makes us a we, having a world in common?" Those paradoxical, unthinkable objects of thinking mark for him the places where the question "How is this thinkable at all?" points to the question: "Who is qualified for thinking at all?" This question, he thinks, is ultimately what is at stake in the war of discourses which is the field of "theoretical" practice.[58]

Thus the question or possibility of the equality of intelligences inserts itself into all Rancière's reflections, no matter what his intended object for discussion.

What might be already evident is that this preoccupation with the equality of intelligences stems from Rancière's sustained interest in, and early investigations of, emancipation. As he notes, what nagged at him was the question: "how can those whose business is not thinking assume the authority to think and thereby constitute themselves as thinking subjects?"[59] However, Rancière explores the declaration of the equality of intelligences most directly in his examination in *The Ignorant Schoolmaster* of the eccentric nineteenth-century pedagogue, Joseph Jacotot. For example, in *The Ignorant Schoolmaster*, Rancière highlights how Jacotot's practice of universal education mobilizes the empty equality that the contingency of the social order reveals, by positing the intellectual equality of students with their teacher, of the son with his father, of the peasant with the intellectual. More specifically, he relates how Jacotot decided, after an experience of teaching Flemish students French without being able to explain anything to them, that it is possible that students do not need superior minds to teach them, that their minds are equal to those of their teachers, and that they can teach themselves anything. Jacotot capitalized on the impossibility of measuring once and for all the intellectual capacity of a mind; the impossibility of knowing whether the hierarchical divisions between teacher and student or expert and ignorant are based on real intellectual superiority or simply arbitrary convention. This inability to measure the capacity of a mind – this fundamental indeterminacy – allows Jacotot to assert that it is possible to believe, or more precisely to act on the assumption, that all intelligences are equal. From this assumption of equality, Jacotot then proposes to see what is possible: what kind of learning will happen if we assume all intelligences are equal? What kind of independent thinking will develop once the myth of the inequality of intelligences that schools and society promotes is seen as a myth? What kind of emancipation will occur? In other words, what kind of world can be opened up if we assume that all intelligences are the same?[60]

Thus Rancière finds in his explorations of Jacotot an example of an emancipatory practice centred on a form of politics of the equality of intelligences. To be sure, it is not politics in the full sense, because, as Rancière reminds us, Jacotot did not think the equality of intelligences could be expressed in institutions or in the social order, but only between individuals.[61] Rancière's presentation of Jacotot, however, leaves this politics of the equality of intelligences open as a possibility to his readers. He does not ask us to dismiss the pedagogue's practice as naive or out of date, but demands that we think about Jacotot's declaration of the equality of intelligences. What might a politics of the equality of intelligences look like? What consequences would it have? Is such a fully formed politics even possible? And how is this political dispute already present, in one way or another, in other democratic struggles? Is it, as Rancière suggests, the "fundamental conflict" of all politics, even if it is never conducted as such?[62]

Unfortunately, most readers of Rancière have not taken up these questions with much seriousness. This is partly because some readers interpret his theory of politics as a conventional one, and thus they do not pay attention to the political character of his preoccupations.[63] But often, it seems that his readers simply would like to avoid the politics of the equality of intelligences and all of its implications. In fact, even though many of Rancière's readers acknowledge his preoccupation with the equality of intelligences, they interpret his interest in it in such a way that saps it of its political potential. I will close this chapter with a brief example of how such reinterpretations of the equality of intelligences take place.

Todd May, in his article "Rancière in South Carolina," a shorter version of his book *The Political Thought of Jacques Rancière: Creating Equality*, wants to use Rancière's political thought to help him explore an incident in Clemson, South Carolina, that ignited racial tensions in the city. In particular, May focuses on Rancière's distinction between politics and policing, his claim that politics is rare, his concept of the part with no part, and his idea that politics "is about the presupposition of equality."[64] It is in relation to this last and most important idea for May that we see the declaration of the equality of intelligences get rewritten. For, as I have done in this chapter, May traces this idea that politics is about the presupposition of equality to Rancière's exploration of Jacotot and, in particular, Jacotot's declaration that all intelligences are equal. May clearly wants to distance himself, however, from a literal interpretation of this declaration: he does not want readers to think he actually believes that all intelligences are equal. For instance, he makes sure to underscore, albeit correctly, that Rancière never argues that people *are* equally intelligent; he simply suggests that it is a possible presupposition from which to work.

Even more important, however, May reinterprets what is meant by the equality of intelligences in the first place. He writes: "What does it mean to presuppose that people are equally intelligent? This has nothing to do with standardized tests or with the ability to do advanced math or physics. Instead, it has to do with the ability of people to shape their lives. Everyone, we might say, unless they are damaged in some way, is capable of creating a meaningful life ... Each of us is capable of meeting the challenges life puts before us, without appeal to an authority that must guide us through our own ignorance."[65] What we see in this passage is an effort by May to interpret the declaration of the equality of intelligences as simply another declaration of the fundamental liberal tenet that we are all the best governors of our own lives. May wants the equality of intelligences to mean that we are all equally capable of "meeting the challenges life puts before us." This is not, however, what Jacotot or Rancière meant by the equality of intelligences.

For them the declaration of the equality of intelligences was meant as a *literal* presupposition: what if we operated in teaching and in the world *as if* we were all, really and truly, equally intelligent – in other words, if we operated precisely on the assumption that we are all equally capable of learning any subject matter, including "advanced math or physics"? What if we believed that there were not people who were "just smarter" – and thus might deserve more riches, power, voice, and so on – but that in fact anyone was capable of learning anything? What would this assumption of the equality of intelligences set in motion?

In fact it is this literal version of the declaration of the equality of intelligences that makes it political disruptive. In *The Nights of Labor*, for instance, Rancière emphasizes that the radical move of workers such as Gabriel Gauny was to assume that they too could be artists, poets, philosophers. It was precisely their not keeping to their proper place as workers – beings capable only of creating through the toil of their bodies – by asserting their equality as intellectual beings that challenged the social order. Otherwise, if the equality of intelligences is taken only to mean that people are equally capable of leading their own lives, there is no suggestion that workers can ever be anything more than workers. To be sure, they can be free to lead their lives as they see fit *as workers*, and perhaps even demand better conditions *as workers*, but they cannot be artists or intellectuals. Thus, if we follow May's interpretation, in today's liberal societies, at least, there is no fundamental challenge to the categorization of people in the social order into those who are capable of thought and those who are not. And this is the particular political challenge that interests Rancière, and one that I argue is pertinent today. If by the equality of intelligences we mean *literally* that all minds are equally capable of learning anything, then that presents a challenge to the social order, and thus there is *politics*: workers are no longer "just workers"; they can be, and be seen as, thinking, speaking, and understanding beings.

May's attempt to distance himself from any literal interpretation of the equality of intelligences therefore suggests that he wants to avoid any accusation that he is ridiculous enough to believe that all intelligences are equal. This feeling that the presupposition of the equality of intelligences if taken literally is ridiculous can be interpreted as testifying to two different phenomena: on the one hand, that, despite all sorts of egalitarian sympathies, intellectuals are deeply invested in the hierarchy of intelligences; on the other, that Rancière's suggestion of the equality of intelligences is a powerful and disruptive political declaration that provokes even seeming allies to want to distance themselves from its consequences. If we follow Todd May's interpretation of the equality of intelligences, not only does something fascinating about Rancière's rethinking of politics democracy get covered over, but the challenge posed by a politics of the equality of intelligences disappears from view. I suggest that we resist this impulse to dismiss the equality of intelligences, and instead take up its challenge more seriously. This will be possible, however, only if Rancière's own writings on politics are not seen as advocating a straightforward theory of politics, but as opening up certain terrains, or offering up certain operations, for further thought and action.

NOTES

1 Jacques Rancière, "Ten Theses on Politics," trans. Rachel Bowlby and Davide Panagia, *Theory & Event* 5, no. 3 (2001), Thesis 3.
2 Rancière, *Disagreement*, 12.
3 Rancière, "Ten Theses on Politics," Thesis 8.
4 Most of us will want to evaluate his writings as if they were offering a "theory" of politics out of habit. However, there are interpreters of Rancière, such as his peer and friend Alain Badiou, who insist on evaluating his writings in this manner because of a fundamental disagreement over the relation between philosophy and politics. See, for example, Alain Badiou, *Metapolitics*, trans. Jason Barker (London: Verso, 2005), 116–18.
5 For example, Peter Hallward, "Jacques Rancière and the Subversion of Mastery," *Paragraph* 28, no. 1 (2005): 27; and Davide Panagia, "The Improper Event: On Jacques Rancière's Mannerism," *Citizenship Studies* 13, no. 3 (2009): 298.
6 See, for example, Badiou, *Metapolitics*, 109, 121–3; Bruno Bosteels, "Rancière's Leftism, Or, Politics and Its Discontents," in *Jacques Rancière: History, Politics, Aesthetics*, eds. Gabriel Rockhill and Philip Watts (Durham, NC: Duke University Press, 2009), 158–75; Jodi Dean, "Politics without Politics," *Parallax* 15, no. 3 (2009): 20–36; Peter Hallward, "Staging Equality: Rancière's Theatrocracy and the Limits of Anarchic Equality," in Rockhill and Watts, *Jacques Rancière*, 140–57; Nick Hewlett, *Badiou, Balibar and Rancière: Rethinking Emancipation* (New York: Continuum Books, 2007); Todd May, *The Political Thought of Jacques Rancière: Creating Equality* (University Park: Pennsylvania State University Press, 2008); Nina Power, "Which Equality? Badiou and Rancière in Light of Ludwig Feuerbach,"

Parallax 15, no. 3 (2009): 63–80; Gabriel Rockhill, "The Politics of Aesthetics: Political History and the Hermeneutics of Art," in Rockhill and Watts, *Jacques Rancière*, 195–215; and Slavoj Žižek, *The Ticklish Subject: The Absent Centre of Political Ontology* (London: Verso, 1999), 172.

7 Chambers insists that the "impurity" of politics means that, despite Rancière's polemical juxtaposition of the term against what he calls "the police," politics is not *purely* disruptive and anarchic. Rather, "the line between politics and police cannot be understood as impenetrable. The divide must be porous; it must allow a certain type of movement over and back. Politics can never be purely other to police for the simple reason that politics itself cannot be pure." One consequence of this, according to Chambers, is that attempts by Todd May and others to pull Rancière into anarchism are problematic. See Samuel Chambers, *The Lessons of Rancière* (Oxford: Oxford University Press, 2013), 84–5.

8 As we shall see, politics and democracy are for the most part interchangeable terms for Rancière.

9 Rancière, "Ten Theses on Politics," Thesis 7.

10 Rancière, *Disagreement*, 14.

11 Ibid., 28.

12 Ibid., 29.

13 Ibid.

14 Rancière, "Ten Theses on Politics," Thesis 7.

15 Rancière, *Disagreement*, 16–17.

16 Ibid., 34.

17 Ibid., 17.

18 Hobbes, *Leviathan*, 93.

19 Ibid., 183–6.

20 Rancière, *Disagreement*, 13.

21 Ibid., xii.

22 Ibid., 56.

23 Ibid., 36.

24 Jacques Rancière, "Politics, Identification and Subjectivization," in *Identity in Question*, ed. John Rajchman (New York: Routledge, 1995), 68.

25 Ibid., 66.

26 Jacques Rancière, *On the Shores of Politics*, trans. Liz Heron (London: Verso, 1995), 94.

27 Ibid., 51.

28 Jacques Rancière and Davide Panagia, "Dissenting Words: A Conversation with Jacques Rancière," *Diacritics* 30, no. 2 (2000): 115.

29 Jacques Rancière, "Afterword/The Method of Equality: An Answer to Some Questions," in Rockhill and Watts, *Jacques Rancière: History, Politics, Aesthetics*, 287.
30 Rancière, *On the Shores of Politics*, 88.
31 Jacques Rancière, *Hatred of Democracy*, trans. Steve Corcoran (London: Verso, 2006), 84.
32 Rancière, *Ten Theses on Politics*, Thesis 8.
33 Jacques Rancière, "A Few Remarks on the Method of Jacques Rancière," *Parallax* 15, no. 3 (2009): 121.
34 Rancière, *Disagreement*, 87.
35 Ibid., 99.
36 Rancière, *Hatred of Democracy*, 36.
37 Rancière, *Disagreement*, 101.
38 Rancière, "A Few Remarks on the Method of Jacques Rancière," 120.
39 To be sure, there is much discussion and debate within environmentalism of anthropocentrism and the equality of humans, animals, and other forms of life. For better or worse, Rancière has been quite dismissive of this question. As Jane Bennett reports: "When asked in public whether he thought than an animal or a plant or a drug or a nonlinguistic sound could disrupt the police order, Rancière said no: he did not want to extend the concept of the political that far; non humans do not qualify as participants in a demos; the disruption effect must be accompanied by the desire to engage in reasoned discourse." See Jane Bennett, *Vibrant Matter: A Political Ecology of Things* (Durham, NC: Duke University Press, 2010), 106.
40 Ibid., 114.
41 Ibid., 116.
42 Jacques Rancière, *The Philosopher and His Poor*, trans. John Drury, Corinne Oster, and Andrew Parker (Durham, NC: Duke University Press, 2003), xxvii.
43 Rancière, *On the Shores of Politics*, 4.
44 Rancière, "Politics, Identification and Subjectivization," 63.
45 Rancière, "A Few Remarks on the Method of Jacques Rancière," 117.
46 Rancière, "Afterword/The Method of Equality," 288.
47 Ibid., 287.
48 Rancière, "A Few Remarks on the Method of Jacques Rancière," 114; and idem, *Short Voyages to the Land of the People*, trans. James B. Swenson (Stanford, CA: Stanford University Press, 2003), 4.
49 Rancière, "A Few Remarks on the Method of Jacques Rancière," 120.
50 Ibid., 114.
51 Rancière, "Afterword/The Method of Equality," 278.

52 Rancière, "A Few Remarks on the Method of Jacques Rancière," 121.
53 Ibid., 115.
54 Rancière, "Afterword/The Method of Equality," 272.
55 Rancière, *On the Shores of Politics*, 51.
56 Rancière, *Hatred of Democracy*, 83.
57 Rancière, *Emancipated Spectator*, 13.
58 Rancière, "A Few Remarks on the Method of Jacques Rancière," 114.
59 Rancière, *Philosopher and His Poor*, xxv.
60 See Jacques Rancière, *The Ignorant Schoolmaster: Five Lessons in Intellectual Emancipation*, trans. Kristin Ross (Stanford, CA: Stanford University Press, 1991), chap. 1.
61 Rancière, *Disagreement*, 34.
62 Ibid., 22.
63 See, for example, Dean, "Politics without Politics," 20–36; and Hallward, "Staging Equality."
64 Todd May, "Rancière in South Carolina," in Rockhill and Watts, *Jacques Rancière*, 108.
65 Ibid., 111.

8 Democracy and Its Conditions: Étienne Balibar and the Contribution of Marxism to Radical Democracy

JAMES D. INGRAM

It is well known among students of recent European political ideas that Étienne Balibar's philosophical reputation received an early impetus, at the tender age of twenty-three, with his contributions to *Reading Capital,* edited with Louis Althusser in 1965 and containing essays by them and other members of Althusser's illustrious circle at the École normale supérieure, including Jacques Rancière and Pierre Macherey.[1] Less familiar may be the fact that Balibar maintained close ties to the Parti communiste français (PCF) as one of its most prominent theorists, and to *le maître* Althusser himself, for many years after this auspicious debut – in the latter case, after Althusser's descent into madness and hospitalization until his death in 1990.[2] The significance of these historical facts emerges when we consider that, at least since 1956, in France as perhaps nowhere else – not even among the generation of ex-Trotskyists who went on to form the core of Cold War liberalism and ultimately neoconservatism in the United States – a conventional litmus test of political lucidity has been the question of when one left Marxism and/or the Communist Party. As in the American case, the earlier the better – this balanced against a sort of residual aura of authenticity attaching to the author who can point to a youthful commitment to the far left, provided it has long since been safely abandoned. Balibar's unusual standing in this milieu is not only that he never "renounced" Marxism, but that he never technically *left* the Party. Instead, he was kicked out.

The circumstances are revealing of Balibar's political-intellectual journey beyond the limits of Marxism or communism as conventionally understood. In March 1981, in the wake of anti-immigrant actions by local Communist officials, Balibar published a fierce critique of the Party's growing racism, the roots of which he located in its failure to follow up its qualified support of the Algerian independence movement with active intervention in the struggles of North Africans and their descendants for equality and inclusion in France.[3] The consequence was immediate expulsion. Ever since, Balibar's central political and theoretical interests have read like a catalogue of traditional Marxist blind spots: political institutions, especially the nation-state, and the questions of nationalism, citizenship, and exclusion; race and political identity; the relation between political struggle and institutions; and the by no means merely ideological stakes of the great "bourgeois" contributions to political emancipation, democracy, and human rights. Along the way, he became one of the leading theorists trying to re-imagine democracy beyond its statist, capitalist, representative-bureaucratic frame – a project he joins others in associating with radical democracy, or the "democratization of democracy."[4] And yet, I argue, much as Balibar criticized the PCF in the name of what he regarded as its own democratic, egalitarian, and emancipatory values, his contributions concerning all these questions have come at least in part by pursuing Marx-inspired preoccupations and strategies of analysis that characterized his work from the beginning.

I underline Balibar's Marxist heritage as a way of drawing attention to the specificity of his contribution to contemporary democratic theory. Radical democracy, on its standard self-conception, emerges out of the critique and rejection of Marxism – its "determinism," its "economism," and, perhaps above all, its "anti-politicism." Confirmation of this narrative can be found in the texts and careers of figures such as Hannah Arendt, Claude Lefort, and Jacques Rancière, all of whom arrived at their mature accounts of politics and democracy through an extended critique of Marx and/or Marxism.[5] What, then, can we learn from a thinker who arrives at radical democracy not *against* Marxism, as an alternative to or replacement for it, but rather *through* Marxism, as its logical successor or fulfilment? What stands out in this context, I suggest, is Balibar's unflagging attention to the *difficulty* of "democratizing democracy," to the obstacles to thinking and realizing it. For if he joins these thinkers in proposing more and deeper democracy as a response to the key political challenges of our day, for him it is an answer that never stops giving rise to new questions. And although Balibar seldom pushes this point on a critical register, preferring to highlight his debts to and points of agreement with writers associated with radical democracy, his thinking of democracy in terms of its social, political, ideological, and institutional *conditions* constitutes his most distinctive and important contribution – and corrective – to this literature.

Unlike other notable "post-Marxist" thinkers, Balibar did not undertake a radical critique (Castoriadis, Lefort, Mouffe and Laclau, Rancière) or self-consciously transformative rereading (Badiou, Negri) of Marx that defined his subsequent trajectory. From the beginning, he has worked not so much to develop a "position" or to discern one in Marx as to elaborate problems and tensions drawn in part from a deep engagement with Marx's work. It is not my intention here to reduce Balibar's work to its Marxist inheritance; his intellectual trajectory is better read as a gradually expanding engagement with many thinkers – from Spinoza to Hegel to Freud, from Foucault to Arendt to Schmitt, to name just a few – and patient investigation of an evolving set of questions. It is characteristic of this oeuvre to return repeatedly to the same texts and questions, each time in a new light, depending on the theoretical and political problems at issue. In one important respect, however, Balibar has remained a faithful disciple of Marx. As he writes in his important 1993 study, *The Philosophy of Marx*, which declines to attribute a systematic "philosophy" to its subject, instead following him through a series of brilliant but divergent approaches to a set of political-philosophical problems (practice, ideology, history): "More than other writers, Marx *wrote in the conjuncture*. Such an option did not exclude either the 'patience of the concept' of which Hegel spoke, or the rigorous weighing of logical consequences. But it was certainly incompatible with stable conclusions: Marx is the philosopher of eternal new beginnings … This is why, in studying him, one cannot abstractly reconstruct his system. One has to retrace his development, with its breaks and bifurcations."[6] I suggest that this characterization of a philosophy that is constantly in motion, responsive both to the movement of ideas and that of politics and history, not only defines Balibar's reading of Marx; it can be applied to his own body of work as well.

Balibar's oeuvre, as I reconstruct it here, is likewise characterized by an open evolution, shaped by a shifting political-philosophical landscape. If it reveals more continuities than "breaks and bifurcations," this is because, unlike Marx but like more proximate influences (Althusser, Foucault, Derrida), Balibar has never aspired to theoretical totality, preferring to dwell on difficulties, tensions, and "points of heresy" in the texts and political conjunctures he considers.[7] To show how he has come to make a decisive contribution to radical democratic theory while troubling some of its basic assumptions, I proceed in four steps. First, I establish some distinctive features of his early thinking by taking its "untimeliest" moment: his 1976 defence of the idea of the dictatorship of the proletariat. I then explore his relation to radical democratic theory by focusing on his treatment of one of its central motifs: the "autonomy of the political." Following a schema he sets out in a 1996 essay (which can be read as establishing a sort of program for much of his subsequent work), I explore how, rather than dismissing the idea of autonomous politics, Balibar supplements it by insisting not only, with the whole of the Marxist tradition, on the "heteronomy of politics," but also, more originally, on what he calls the "heteronomy of heteronomy," or the politics of civility.[8] Balibar proposes these theoretical moments not as a succession, with each resolving the last, but as a set of overlapping perspectives, each illuminating a necessary yet insufficient aspect of political life. In the present context, what is most striking about his development of these three perspectives is how they complicate and enrich the idea of democracy, which, rather than appearing as the solution to the challenges of politics, society, or history, comes to seem both partial and endlessly problematic. Far from overthrowing the ideas of politics and democracy, however, Balibar's persistent troubling of them restores to them their specificity, their essential variability, ambiguity, and vulnerability, and their importance.

From the Dictatorship of the Proletariat to the Critique of Neo-racism

To measure the depth of Balibar's debt to Marxism, I begin not with the magisterial, proto-post-structuralist studies of *Capital* and the concept of class struggle that made his original and very early reputation, but with a project that might now seem much more antiquated: his 1976 defence of the concept of the dictatorship of the proletariat.[9] The book bearing this title was Balibar's contribution to a public debate within the PCF. At issue was the Party's ideological "modernization" – in particular, the question of whether it should drop the phrase "dictatorship of the proletariat" from its platform to facilitate a *Union de la gauche* with François Mitterrand's Socialists and thus a chance at state power. From a public relations perspective, the question was simple: a party seeking votes in an established liberal democracy should not be seen to favour dictatorship. And yet, Balibar insisted, deeper issues were at stake. As he wrote in a summary of his argument delivered to the 1976 Party Congress, "To imagine that we can fight for 'real' democracy, for democracy for the masses of the people, *without* passing through the dictatorship of the proletariat is to *ignore the existence of the dictatorship of the bourgeoisie*, to ignore the role of the State apparatus as an instrument of exploitation."[10] Without denying the authoritarian implications of the dictatorship of the proletariat in the Soviet Union and elsewhere, where he affirmed that it had quickly become "a dictatorship *over* the proletariat,"[11] Balibar argued that the idea was invented by Marx and Engels and developed by Lenin for good reason: the institutions of the modern state, even the constitutional-democratic state, entrench class power in ways that systematically frustrate the aims of the working class. Lenin, then, was right to insist on the need to struggle against these forms, even if there was an urgent need to rethink the authoritarian implications of his solution.[12]

Three aspects of Balibar's contribution to this now nearly forgotten debate are worth noting. First, his insistence on the depth of bourgeois domination and the difficulty of revolution is based on a conviction that *political institutions* can be neither neglected nor taken at face value – tendencies he then associated with "bourgeois legal formalism," but today we can extend to any excessively abstract analysis, from legal positivism to more or less the whole of normative political theory, especially in its liberal forms. Instead, according to Balibar, institutions, especially the state, must be seen in the light of the social relations that underlie them and that they in turn reinforce. Second, this analysis extends beyond the economic and even "the political," strictly speaking, to focus on the role of *ideology*, not taken in "idealist" terms as a matter of ideas, but, on the model of Althusser's "Ideological State Apparatuses,"[13] as reaching into the material domain of identities and institutions. It is precisely the ability of power relations to mould interests and identities that hinders the transition to more popular or "proletarian" democracy. Third, partly as a result of this depth of analytical focus, for Balibar the question of transformation is, as for the Marxist tradition from its origins, an eminently *practical* one. Democratic institutions cannot remain an "empty ought," mere ideals or desiderata, nor can they be thought of only as the negation of what is. They must be considered as the results of a possible practice, subject to inertia and resistance. Although Balibar assuredly would not write today, as he did in 1976, "I am for my part completely convinced that the transition to socialism … is 'on the agenda' for French society,"[14] this acute sensitivity to power relations – to the fact that political and legal forms can never be considered in the abstract and that ideology is not simply a matter of "ideas," but takes concrete, institutional and subjective forms – has continued to underlie Balibar's "post-Marxist" work.

We see this in his first writings to attract widespread attention outside Marxist circles: an exchange from the mid-1980s with American political sociologist Immanuel Wallerstein on the themes of racism and nationalism.[15] With Wallerstein, Balibar was quick to see how the "neo-racism" then (as now) on the rise in Europe, far from being simply an atavistic return of "prejudice" or "xenophobia," was new and specific to contemporary tensions within global capitalism and the post-colonial nation-state. Rather than explaining these tensions in Marxist fashion, however, with recourse to underlying economic dynamics (a role that fell to Wallerstein), Balibar focuses on political and especially ideological factors. On Balibar's account, the "ethnicization" of minorities (as well as majorities) stems from the state's effort to create a national community by means of "ideological state apparatuses" (citizenship, education, the military) and to convince the members of the resulting "imagined community" of the benefits they receive. The new racism thus grew out of what Balibar terms the "nation-form" – a particular mode of political organization that constructs new identities, softening some antagonisms (between national classes via the "class compromise" of the welfare state) while creating new ones (between those included in this compromise and those excluded from it). A "differentialist" or "culturalist" racism – a "racism without races," in the sense that it does not depend on the biological schemas of earlier European racisms[16] – grew out of the political contradictions of the capitalist welfare state as its capacities were undermined by economic, cultural, and demographic globalization.

Balibar's analysis illustrates some central features of his gradual and, in important ways, incomplete migration from Marxism to radical democracy. To be sure, all three of the preoccupations I have highlighted in his 1976 work are strongly in evidence: the significance of particular kinds of institutions (the "content of the form" of the modern nation-state), the interplay of ideology and identity with social and political institutions, and the difficulty of transforming social and political structures all play a central role in his analysis of nationalism and neo-racism. At the same time, clearly evident in this development is Balibar's determination to theorize in direct response to a specific political conjuncture, taking problems from the world around him, in the light of ongoing struggles for emancipation (in this case with reference to precisely the knot of problems that had precipitated his own estrangement from the PCF). Indeed, for all its erudition, patience, and abstraction, Balibar's work has always been rooted in the pressing questions of

French, European, and global politics. One could easily imagine how these tendencies – writing in the conjuncture as well as a shift from the proletariat to other sites of social struggle (anti-racism and "new social movements" more generally) – as well as his openness to the "autonomy of politics," the relative independence of political and ideological factors from the economy, might herald a transition from Marxism to radical democracy.[17] In fact, as I will explain, his trajectory is more subtle, complicated, and ambiguous than this formulation would suggest, amounting more to an opening towards democratic themes in response to, but also in fundamental continuity with, Marxist problematics, rather than any simple transition from one to the other.

The Autonomy of Politics and the Politics of Equaliberty

If there is one strand of Balibar's work that accounts for his standing within contemporary democratic theory, it is his decades-long effort to rethink emancipatory politics in terms of what he variously calls the politics of human rights, the expansion of citizenship, or the politics of "equaliberty" (*égaliberté*).[18] The latter term, his own coinage based on the Roman *aequa libertas*, refers to a form of politics, born in the French Revolution and coextensive with modernity, that aims simultaneously to realize equality *and* liberty, thus bringing the whole of modern emancipatory politics under a single heading. By replacing the category of "class struggle" with a reference to human rights – famously dismissed by Marx in "On the Jewish Question" as well as by successive Marxists from Lenin to Badiou and Žižek as empty and deceptive bourgeois ideology[19] – and by further insisting on their normative status and universality, it might appear that Balibar moves decisively beyond Marxism to a democratic, even liberal-democratic, conception of politics based on the "autonomy of the political" and the permanent validity of its normative categories.

As I have suggested, things are not so simple. On the one hand, Balibar had long seen Marxism as part of the history of modern revolutionary politics, the legatee and radicalized successor of the great "bourgeois" revolutions.[20] Emancipatory and transformative politics, liberation from arbitrary forms of authority and the pursuit of a more equitable distribution of social power and resources, thus form for him a single, complex, and internally divided political tradition. On the other hand, his elaboration of the politics of human rights, or equaliberty, remains far from conventional liberal understandings, especially by incorporating elements of the old idea of class struggle. The politics of human rights, as Balibar depicts it, cannot be reduced to the constitutional state or the rule of law, in the style of Anglo-American liberalism or the later Habermas. To the contrary, equalibertarian politics is by definition waged *against* the state and existing juridical categories, and bears an essential relation to "negativity," even "insurrection."[21] Far from offering an alternative to radical or revolutionary politics, for Balibar the politics of human rights is one of its most important expressions.

To be sure, part of the impetus for this sustained attention to human rights came from the political and theoretical limitations of Marxism. At a time when the proletariat and its traditional political agent, the Communist Party, were in steep decline, Balibar was not alone in seeking a new basis on which to theorize radical politics. Indeed, as a biographical matter, his work on nationalism and the nation-form, along with his activism on behalf of immigrants and minorities in France, converged in an interest in citizenship, which certainly has been seen as a bourgeois-liberal rather than a radical-revolutionary concern.[22] Moreover, his growing appreciation of ideas and identities as independent political factors, both in his work with Wallerstein and in his 1985 study of Spinoza, whom he read as proposing a communication-centred form of materialism,[23] could be interpreted in crudely Marxist terms as a shift from base to superstructure, all the more so since his investigations increasingly led him to consider not only the "negative" side of ideational politics (racism, nationalism), but also its "positive" side – namely, how ideas can inspire emancipatory political struggles. These concerns can then be said to have coalesced when, on the bicentennial of the French Revolution and the *Declaration of the Rights of Man and Citizen*, Balibar turned to address the enduring significance of the document and the rights it proclaimed.[24]

The immediate context of his 1989 essay was a discussion in France in which rights were promoted as a way of transcending political and ideological differences. As the basis of a liberal-democratic, anti-authoritarian consensus, it was hoped, human rights could "put an end to the revolution" once and for all.[25] But when he carefully studied the *Declaration*, arguably the founding statement of human rights, Balibar found that neither liberal nor radical readings, on which pre-given, extra-political rights limit the scope of democratic politics (a good thing for liberals, a bad one for radicals), gave an adequate account of the text and its historical effectivity. For one thing, upon closer examination, he found that the two figures juxtaposed in the document's title

– "man" and "citizen" – are not distinguished (so that, for example, the "natural" rights of "man" might form a basis for the "political" rights of "the citizen"). Instead, these two subjects and sets of rights are treated as identical, extending the rights of citizens to all. Moreover, the *Declaration* makes no distinction between "civil," "political," or "social" rights, which conventionally mark out the frontiers between liberal, republican, and socialist politics, and, further still, indicates no distinctions or trade-offs between "freedom" and "equality." On the face of it, the *Declaration* declares *all* denials of *anyone's* freedom *or* equality illegitimate.[26]

On the basis of this reading, Balibar concludes that the "rights of man" should not be understood as principles located above and beyond politics; rather, they imply a radical politics whose implications he – following, he would claim, the course of modern emancipatory politics itself – has been working out ever since. Taking a cue from Lefort, Balibar argues that rights claims in principle burst the bounds of every given, constituted political order, including and especially one that enshrines them.[27] Because human rights are intrinsically underdetermined, they invite their own universalization – both "extensively," in Balibar's terms, by including more people, and "intensively," by extending equaliberty into new domains, from the workplace to the school to the household.[28] Since it would contradict the very ideas of freedom and equality to free people "from above," equaliberty implies – in an insight Balibar associates with Rancière as well as with Marx – that emancipation can be the work only of those whose rights are at issue.[29] Equalibertarian claims thus come from disenfranchised groups that find in rights ways of fighting a system that oppresses, subordinates, or excludes them. And this means that what Arendt calls a "right to have rights" is not a right to *status* within a political community (as her formula is commonly interpreted) but what Balibar calls "a right to politics" itself – a right to participate in political processes that aim, among other things, at the invention of new rights, new forms of inclusion and empowerment.[30]

Ever since his initial theorization of "equaliberty" in the late 1980s, Balibar has associated it with the "autonomy of politics," as well as with the classical ideal of "emancipation." The two go together, as Balibar sees it, because autonomous politics "expresses the principle ... that the community ... cannot exist as such, nor govern itself, so long as it is based on the subjection of its members to a natural or transcendent authority, and on the establishment of constraint and discrimination."[31] Freeing politics from external (metaphysical, theological, "natural") bases or limits – typically understood as the basic idea of an autonomous conception of politics – implies freeing individuals from constraints that maintain them in a condition of unfreedom or inequality. A similar logic of implication explains the inseparability, even identity, of freedom and equality. The equivalence of the two terms is not, according to Balibar, a philosophical axiom but a practical truth, discovered and rediscovered through political experience. The fact that the *Declaration* posits this equivalence reflects the struggle out of which it emerged, which confronted two enemies at once: "*absolutism*, which appears as the negation of freedom ..., and *privileges*, which appear as the negation of equality."[32] The unity the *Declaration* posits is thus the historical result of a bourgeois-popular alliance. But the underlying truth it points to is that "(a) there are *no* practical, historical circumstances or situations in which *liberty* (and also determinate liberties) could be *suppressed*, without equality being destroyed at the same time; and (b) conversely, there are no situations in which equality could be attacked without liberty being threatened."[33] Since domination and subordination always go together, any struggle against unfreedom must also be a struggle against inequality and vice versa.[34]

Although this vision of equalibertarian politics offers a powerful articulation of the underlying unity of the modern emancipatory tradition that ties together its liberal, democratic, socialist, anti-imperialist, anti-sexist, anti-racist, and other forms and might seem to present a succinct and compelling articulation of the core values of radical democracy, Balibar never imagined that it was the whole of politics. Moreover, just as he calls on us to resist the philosophical temptation to base equaliberty on transcendent principles as well as the statist temptation to identify it with particular institutions, he is no less immune to the anarchist temptation to reduce it to mere opposition to the existing order. If the demand for equaliberty is "universal," it is universal only *qua* demand, as the negation of specific forms of domination and subordination. Beyond this negative moment, as soon as it becomes a matter of concretely transforming the community, the hyperbolic, radically indeterminate idea of equaliberty must be stabilized, and such a stabilization or concretization can be achieved only by means of a mediation, a third term. On Balibar's account, two such terms emerged historically, each of them in two opposed forms: freedom and equality could be mediated by *property* (either individual, as *liberalism*, or collective, as *socialism*) or by *community* ("fraternity" or "solidarity," based on either an ethnic or historical community, as *nationalism*, or a class, as *communism*) – an ideological matrix whose different combinations cover virtually the whole of modern politics.

With this last step, which relativizes and historicizes the idea of equaliberty by making its outcomes dependent on political practice, Balibar effectively takes his leave not only of liberal but also of radical democratic theory – even, he says more surprisingly, of Marxism. Liberalism, I have suggested, forecloses the radical, insurrectionary side of demands for equaliberty by trying to give them an extra-political foundation (natural rights) or to confine them within certain institutions (the constitutional state). Radical democracy, on the other hand, tends to make the opposite mistake: by reducing politics to this hyperbolic demand, it loses sight of the fact that this demand needs to be institutionalized if rights are to have any social and political reality. Balibar extends this criticism to Marxism, which he reproaches for succumbing to this second, anarchist temptation by imagining that the forces of democratization (the revolutionary proletariat) can be simply opposed to, and ultimately do away with, the state.[35] Instead, he argues, we must see the negative moment of emancipation as immediately confronted with – indeed, as always already entangled in – the positive moment of structures and institutions.

The Heteronomy of Politics and the Politics of Transformation

If Balibar comes closest to a position we might associate with radical democracy when he theorizes emancipation under the sign of "the autonomy of politics," he has always distinguished this from "the autonomy of *the political*." The latter thesis – whether we associate it with the philosophical-anthropological works of Carl Schmitt and Leo Strauss or with more democratic thinkers such as Arendt and Lefort – claims that politics constitutes a permanent domain of human affairs, inherent in human nature or sociality. This domain might be defined by cooperation or coercion, freedom or violence, but whatever its form it is understood as freestanding and amenable to independent philosophical analysis.[36] The perennial Marxist objection to the notion of "the political" – taken up by feminist and other radical critics as well as by comparative, cultural-historical students of politics – is that what counts as "political" changes. The sphere of politics shifts; its parameters depend on social, cultural, and other historically given background conditions. At any given moment the parameters of "the political" reflect past and present efforts to politicize and depoliticize different subjects, issues, and domains.[37]

Balibar has always taken this critical point. Indeed, it is at the heart of his earlier work on Marx and his objections to the PCF's strategic embrace of "formal democracy" in the 1970s. At the same time, he has refused to hew to the conventional Marxist model by giving socio-economic background conditions the last word – even, as Althusser did, "in the last instance." Balibar's approach to the autonomy and/or heteronomy of politics is unusually nuanced: rather than categorically affirming or denying autonomous politics, he treats it as a particular, limited perspective. That perspective, as we have seen, is that of emancipatory politics, which strives to assert full citizenship or democratic autonomy (equaliberty) where it is lacking. Since such a politics can claim equaliberty only against particular denials of freedom and equality, however, it follows, first, that such claims can be only partial and specific – the negations of particular negations of freedom and equality – and second, that such a politics is always determined largely by the conditions in which it finds itself. Balibar often makes this point via Marx's famous sentence at the beginning of the *Eighteenth Brumaire*: "Men make their own history, but they do not make it as they please; they do not make it under self-selected circumstances, but under circumstances existing already, given and transmitted from the past."[38] As Marx argued against the radical democrats of his day, the fact that we always act within certain structures means that equal citizenship, though important, is not enough. To be effective, equalibertarian politics must transform its background conditions – and with them, the nature of "the political" itself.

To take account of this need for politics to go beyond its given domain, Balibar introduces a second moment alongside the politics of emancipation: the politics of transformation. Its logic and essential relation to the "heteronomy" of politics can be grasped most readily through the structure of Marx's approach, which Balibar summarizes as follows: "To transgress the limits of the recognized – and artificially *separated* – political sphere, which are only ever the limits of the established order, politics has to get back to the non-political conditions of that institution (conditions which are ultimately, *eminently* political). It has, in other words, to get back to the economic contradictions, and gain a purchase on these from the inside."[39] That politics at any given time appears as a distinct sphere of society is itself only ever a contingent historical result, the effect of specific political, economic, cultural, and other conditions. For those who want to effect social transformation by political means, the political sphere itself therefore must be the target of another, deeper kind of politics – for Marx, class struggle as against parliamentarism or other forms of contesting law and state power. Here we see the complex interplay between the two perspectives in Balibar's work. On his reading of Marx, although the politics of transformation is distinct from the politics of emancipation, the two are not in contradiction. Rather, each implies the other: politics has to act on and transform its (ostensibly) non-political conditions to achieve its own autonomy. The heteronomy of politics, which focuses on the conditions of political practice, gives emancipatory politics its matter, while the autonomy of politics, which focuses on the demand for emancipation, gives transformative politics its point.

Balibar refuses, however, to resolve the two moments into a neat dialectic, insisting at once on their mutual irreducibility and on the permanent tension between them. He theorizes this tension as a permanent oscillation within democratic or emancipatory politics. Just as we cannot think of emancipatory politics exclusively in terms of its normative content (the demand for equaliberty), neither can we think of it only in terms of its institutional conditions. Politics shifts between the two perspectives, through an interplay of what Balibar calls "insurrection" and "constitution," the constituting power and the constituted power, or "revolution" and "institution."[40] Citizenship, for example, is at once the object of open-ended struggle for inclusion and equaliberty *and* a means of exclusion and normalization; it is the goal of some emancipatory struggles, but the site of others. The universality of equaliberty disappears as soon as a universal acquires a positive, instituted form, for then it inevitably becomes part of a system of norms that seeks to shape and order subjects, to include some by subordinating and excluding others. As Balibar puts it, "[n]othing is more clearly particularistic than institutional claims of universality."[41] Yet such institutionalization is as necessary to societies, which cannot exist in a state of permanent revolution, as it is to individuals, who cannot live entirely "without qualities." Balibar accordingly characterizes the relation between these moments not only, following Althusser, as "over-" or "underdetermined" and "conjunctural" (dependent on a specific historical constellation of forces and conditions), but as "ambiguous," "ambivalent," or – reflecting Derrida's influence – "aporetic."[42]

Balibar's analysis of the heteronomy of politics goes further than Marx and his successors in another respect as well. For Marx, at least on conventional readings, "the political" is determined by, and ultimately can be traced back to, "the economic." Likewise, for Marxism, up to and including Balibar's early work, the extra-political conditions that establish the political sphere are in principle determinate, even if they are so "overdetermined" that no final reckoning can be made of them.[43] This sort of position still can be seen in critics of the autonomy of the political who reproach political philosophies that overlook the extra-political determinants of the political sphere – what social philosopher Franck Fischbach, for example, calls a "denial of the social."[44] Balibar, however, generalizes the Marxian strategy of turning to the background conditions to the point of turning it against Marxism itself. Whereas Marx "urged revolutionaries ... to turn away from the 'apparent scene' of politics, structured by discourses and ideas/ideals, and *unveil* the 'real scene' of economic processes," Balibar explains, "I have a certain tendency to *invert this pattern* – not to return to the idea that 'ideas drive history,' but to emphasize the fact that 'material' processes are themselves (over- and under-) determined by the processes of the imaginary, which have their own very effective materiality and need to be unveiled."[45] Material *and* ideational factors, economics *and* ideology, constantly but covertly determine each other. The only certainty – Balibar goes so far as to pronounce it a "structural law of causality in history"[46] – is that there is *always* "another scene," an "infrastructure of the infrastructure," so that, consequently, there can never be a "last instance."

If Marxism in this sense failed to pursue the heteronomy of politics far enough (by ultimately appealing to a last instance), the perspective Balibar identifies with the heteronomy of politics contains another, still deeper aporia that leads him to seek an alternative. This emerges when he considers the politics of transformation more generally, taking Marx and Foucault as contrasting approaches to understanding politics in terms of its conditions. On Balibar's reading, whereas Marx seeks to address this "other scene" by showing how politics could arise from within processes of structural social-economic change, Foucault does it by studying society as an unbroken web of power relations, so that politics appears as the effect of power *on* power.[47] The difficulty both of these approaches run into, Balibar claims, is that neither can adequately account for or critically discriminate between different modalities of change. To be sure, Marx tries to describe possible processes of change in what could be called an "external" way, in terms of a "transformation of the world," whereby society acts on itself, whereas Foucault does so in an "internal," subjective way, as a "work of self upon self."[48] But in both cases we are presented with a protagonist (society, the subject) that is both subject and object of a process, both determined and determining. The vision of the politics of transformation that emerges thus oscillates between determination and liberation, determinism and voluntarism. This aporia is "real" and can even be productive, and is therefore not to be escaped or transcended. For Balibar, however, it exposes a constitutive limitation of the perspective of the politics of transformation, and thus the need for another vantage point.

The Problem of Violence and the Politics of Civility

We have seen that, for Balibar, the concept of politics typically associated with radical democracy, the politics of emancipation, is incomplete if it does not take into account the background conditions against and through which "equaliberty" must be realized, and, further, that this perspective in turn falls into an insurmountable problem of its own when it comes to understanding and discriminating among different kinds of political transformation. This problem of the modalities of change, and the need for a way of thinking about politics beyond emancipation and transformation, began to emerge in Balibar's work in "Violence and Politics: Some Questions," a paper for a 1992 colloquium on the work of Jacques Derrida.[49] Taking as his epigraph a formula from Derrida – "non-violence is in a sense the worst violence" – Balibar observes that politics always aims at ending or containing violence, yet it seems that it can accomplish this only by means of counterviolence. The questions he raises in this essay concerning violence, identity, and the limits of politics opened up a whole field of investigation he has subsequently gathered under the heading "civility" – a set of issues that is as alien to the Marxist tradition as it is to the radical-democratic, and that on first sight would seem, if anything, to bring him closest to a certain kind of liberalism.[50]

Balibar begins examining the problem of violence in relation to Marx, and it is here that his critique of Marxism is most thoroughly elaborated. For Balibar, what I referred to above as Marxism's "anarchist" element – the idea that the forces of emancipation can insulate themselves from and eventually abolish the existing order – betrays its inability to think the problem of violence. Marxism, he argues, has dealt adequately neither with the violence unleashed by revolutionary struggles, which has often undermined or even destroyed "successful" revolutions,[51] nor with extreme violence per se, be it "subjective" (war and civil war, terror, ethnic cleansing) or "objective" (famine, disease, "natural disasters" that are never without social and political enabling conditions). Balibar traces what he calls this "constitutive limitation" of Marxist theory to three philosophemes that lie at the very core of Marx's work: the "absolute privilege" Marxism grants to the systemic violence of exploitation, leading it to neglect all other forms of violence; the "anthropological optimism inscribed in the heart of its conception of 'progress'"; and a "metaphysics of history," of Hegelian and ultimately Christian inspiration, premised on the "conversion of violence into justice."[52] In these three ways, he argues, Marxism's politics are decisively stamped by its aim of abolishing violence. But Marxism imagines accomplishing this in a way that blinds it to the violence that necessarily intervenes between the present and what Balibar has taken to referring to as its "apocalyptic," "messianic," or "eschatological" horizon.[53] The issues these critical reflections raise go beyond Marxism, since most of the dominant ideologies of modern politics (liberalism, democracy) likewise lack a systematic reflection on violence in its many guises. How, Balibar therefore asks, can we think politically about forms of violence, obviously connected to politics yet apparently inassimilable to it, that threaten to derail politics, even to make it impossible?

According to Balibar, the problem of "extreme violence" or "cruelty" lies beyond the reach of both autonomous and heteronomous conceptions of politics. Emancipatory politics presupposes a minimal common ground between oppressor and oppressed or exploiter and exploited on which claims may be made and relations challenged; transformative politics presupposes a system of common relations that can be reversed or transformed. Neither approach can survive the elimination or radical exclusion of one of the parties; neither can explain how such extreme situations come about or what can be done against them. Both conceptions, in other words, are at a loss when faced with what Balibar calls "ultra-subjective" or "ultra-objective" violence – monstrous, gratuitous destruction, be it intensely personal (frenzied, irrational hatred) or completely impersonal (extreme systemic violence, such as that accompanying capitalism or colonialism), that serves no systemic or political end and cannot be dialectically converted back into justice or progress.[54] Both kinds of politics must be prepared to countenance violence, if only to counteract the violence they oppose, yet neither has any internal way of regulating this violence or even of conceiving of it as irreducible. In these ways, Balibar claims, violence, especially in its most extreme forms, poses the problem of the "heteronomy of the heteronomy" of politics – the fact that any politics, even a politics of transformation that aims to act on the conditions that determine the political realm, is itself subject to a set of conditions that arises from the nature and limits of political action itself.[55] Balibar's third perspective thus marks the outer limits of the other two. It aims to take into account what could be called, keeping with the language I have used here, the "conditions of the conditions" of politics – the conditions, that is, for there to be any politics at all.

Balibar has pursued this question principally in terms of institutions on the one hand, and identities on the other. In both cases, the tensions and ambivalences I highlighted in my discussion of the politics of transformation – between insurgency and constitution, revolution and institution – re-emerge, but in a new light. Whereas the contrast between emancipation and transformation allows us to see the fundamental ambiguity of institutions and identities, which can be regarded as means of emancipation *and* as vectors of oppression, the question of violence leads Balibar to different insights. Now institutions and identities mark out a space beyond whose limits politics (and even human life as such) becomes impossible: on the one hand, a total institution or a completely univocal identity, which would represent a sort of totalitarian stasis, and, on the other, the complete absence of any ordering principles at all, complete chaos. As he elaborates, "[t]he role of institutions is precisely to reduce – without suppressing – the multiplicity, complexity and conflictuality of identifications and sense of belonging, if necessary by applying a preventive violence or a 'symbolic' and material – corporeal – organized counter-violence ... But institutions are not a politics. At most they can be the instruments or the products of a politics."[56] If some amount of conflict or violence is inevitable, he concludes, it must be kept within certain bounds for politics and even life itself to be possible. "Civility" is Balibar's name for a politics that navigates between these limits, keeping the violence involved within such limits as continue to make politics possible.

Here, however, we might ask: does this third concept of politics as "civility" not run the risk of reinstating a philosophical "concept of the political" rooted in human nature or the nature of sociality or politics itself? If so, would this concept of the political, meant to tame the vacillations and contingencies of politics, not be politically liberal and temperamentally conservative?[57] It is true that the "heteronomy of heteronomy" is primarily concerned with limits, but Balibar is above all interested in limits that enable – rather than, as is typically the case with conceptions of the political, suppress – the insurrectionary politics of equaliberty and the revolutionary politics of transformation. Although it is true that the idea of civility is premised on warding off the worst, in contrast to theorists who focus on the "realistic" lessons of political violence and opt to preserve some version of the status quo – a distinguished company that includes not just Machiavelli and Hobbes, but Max Weber, Raymond Aron, and Judith Shklar – Balibar retains the Marxian (and Foucaultian) insight that the status quo itself is always violent, and that sustaining institutions and states of affairs is not invariably less harmful than seeking to transform or overthrow them. The aim of a politics of civility is accordingly not to supersede or replace revolutionary politics, but rather to "civilize" it, whether by considering how the "civilizing process" can proceed from the bottom up, as popular politics tames the state and elites, rather than from the top down, as liberal or "realist" conceptions of politics have done by defining a political realm to be policed by the state; or by considering Gandhi as a supplement and alternative to Lenin, and "anti-violence" as a supplement and alternative to violence.[58]

In the end, Balibar denies that civility offers a perspective that would trump or set boundaries for emancipation and transformation. Instead he proposes it as another necessary but insufficient perspective, albeit one that has been neglected within the tradition of radical politics. As he concludes in "Three Concepts of Politics," "there is no sense trying to turn these complex presuppositions into a system … If we do that, we shall obtain only another political philosophy, a schema for the transformation of political problems into a representation of *the political*."[59] Any definitive representation of the political, Balibar suggests, any attempt to determine or prescribe it once and for all, would fall afoul of the central insight of the politics of transformation – namely, that what is considered "political" changes, and that such change is always among the central tasks of radical politics. Moreover, any *a priori* philosophical delimitation of "the political" would betray the methodological principle, developed in his earlier work with Althusser, that political philosophy can be thought only in its particular conjuncture, a necessarily conflictual and contradictory situation that nonetheless can provide certain resources for transformation. If for Balibar this involves a constant search for openings for a radical-democratic politics of emancipation, it also means an endless investigation of the conditions this politics is up against and must work to transform, as well as, increasingly, a tragic awareness of the dangers, dilemmas, double binds, and reversals to which both these forms of politics are necessarily subject.

To return to the point of departure for these reflections, then, we can find the trifocal perspective Balibar advocates applied in his retrospective assessment of the role of his long-time political home, the Parti communiste français. The PCF, he now says, played a "tribunate" function in post-war France. Like the Tribunes who spoke for the plebes in the Roman Republic (as theorized by Machiavelli in his *Discourses on Titus Livy*), the PCF, by enabling radical popular claims to be made within official politics, held the more oligarchic, anti-democratic tendencies of the elites in check.[60] The implication of this analysis, of course, is that the deterioration of democracy today and its inability to confront conditions that are increasingly hostile to both justice and meaningful politics can be attributed in part to the absence of such a counterweight, both domestically with the wholesale conversion of the Western centre-left to a post-ideological "Third Way" and ultimately to an increasingly neoliberal status quo, and internationally with the disappearance of a competing social-political model like that once offered, however imperfectly, by the Soviet bloc. The inclusion of a "revolutionary" force within constitutional politics, Balibar suggests, not only expanded the space for equalibertarian claims; it also civilized the politics of the Fourth and early Fifth French Republics. Communism, and the existence of a radical-transformative alternative, was essential to the health of bourgeois-liberal democracy.

In this analysis, we see how a trifocal view of politics takes into account all three of the dimensions reconstructed above: the freedom and equality realized within ostensibly democratic institutions and the equalibertarian claims made against them; the structural obstacles to such claims within a given institutional order and the prospects for their transformation; and the balance of violence and civility such a dynamic requires and enables. Such a complex view, though never synoptic or conclusive, enables us to take into account the conditions of democracy as it is, as well as the possibility that it could become different, perhaps "more democratic." It allows us to see not only, as many liberal democrats would readily concede, that democracy is not and never can be "complete," but, against and beyond radical democrats, that the emancipatory-egalitarian demand for "more" democracy, though irreducible, is essentially incomplete. Without careful attention to social and institutional conditions – not only those now in existence, but also those that might accompany any "democratization of democracy" – as well as to the modalities of change between them, the mere call for "more democracy" risks being both empty and blind. This is by no means to disqualify "radical democracy," a rubric under which Balibar is happy to include himself. In a theoretical landscape in which this commitment is too often taken to be somehow self-sufficient, however, it is to relativize and complicate it in ways from which the politics of democracy in all its senses can only profit.

NOTES

This chapter began as a presentation at the 2009 Evian Philosophy Colloquium and was developed through a panel on "the political" at the 2010 Western Political Science Association meeting in San Francisco. I would like to thank the participants on both occasions, as well as Robin Celikates, Çigdem Çidam, Ayten Gündoğdu, Andy Schaap, Antonio Vázquez-Arroyo, and the editors of this volume.

1 Althusser and Balibar, *Reading Capital.*

2 Balibar offers a sort of obituary-*cum*-milieu study of Althusser and his circle at the École normale supérieure in "Althusser and the Rue d'Ulm," trans. David Fernbach, *New Left Review* 58 (July–August 2009): 91–107.

3 Étienne Balibar, "De Charonne à Vitry," *Le Nouvel Observateur* (9–15 March 1981), reprinted in *Les Frontières de la Démocratie* (Paris: Découverte, 1992), 19–34. For an overview of Balibar's political work that draws many insightful biographical connections, see Don Reid, "Étienne Balibar: Algeria, Althusser, and *Altereuropéenisation*," *South Central Review* 25, no. 3 (2008): 68–85.

4 Balibar credits this slogan to Boaventura de Sousa Santos, ed., *Democratizing Democracy: Beyond the Liberal Democratic Canon* (London: Verso, 2005).

5 Examples could be multiplied: Cornelius Castoriadis, Chantal Mouffe, Ernesto Laclau ... Probably the most explicit thematization of this progression came in the debate conducted in the pages of the *New Left Review* in response to Laclau and Mouffe's *Hegemony and Socialist Strategy*; see Stuart Sim, *Post-Marxism: An Intellectual History* (London: Routledge, 2000), chaps. 2, 3. Conversely, theorists who "missed" this stage (Antonio Negri, Alain Badiou, Slavoj Žižek) are notorious for their, at best, lukewarm commitment to "democracy," at least in its constitutional-representative forms.

6 Étienne Balibar, *The Philosophy of Marx*, trans. Chris Turner (London: Verso, 1995), 6.

7 Balibar takes this term from Foucault's *Order of Things*, where it refers to the incompatible alternatives made possible by assumptions that establish the framework of a particular *episteme*, or encompassing system of thought.

8 Étienne Balibar, "Three Concepts of Politics," trans. Chris Turner, in *Politics and the Other Scene* (London: Verso, 2002).
9 Étienne Balibar, *On the Dictatorship of the Proletariat*, trans. Grahame Lock (London: New Left Books, 1977).
10 Étienne Balibar, "On the Dictatorship of the Proletariat" (contribution to the 22nd Congress of the French Communist Party, orig. pub. in *L'Humanité*, 22 October 1976), in Balibar, *On the Dictatorship of the Proletariat*, 170.
11 Ibid.
12 If this recognition of the potentially authoritarian tendency of Leninist "democratic centralism" distances Balibar from the superficially similar suspicion of "democracy" expressed by Žižek and Badiou today, there is a deeper and more important difference between his position and theirs: whereas for them "democracy" is now the "real enemy," the principal ideological and structural obstacle radical politics must overcome to achieve real social transformation, Balibar (in this respect like Poulantzas, one of his principal interlocutors during the 1970s) regards democracy in terms closer to Marx himself, as one of the key "battlefields" of class struggle, rather than as an obstacle to be overcome.
13 Louis Althusser, "Ideology and Ideological State Apparatuses," in *"Lenin and Philosophy" and Other Essays*, trans. Ben Brewster (London: New Left Books, 1971).
14 Balibar, "On the Dictatorship of the Proletariat," 174.
15 Étienne Balibar and Immanuel Wallerstein, *Race, Nation, Class: Ambiguous Identities*, trans. Chris Turner (London: Verso, 1991).
16 Étienne Balibar, "Is There a 'Neo-Racism'?" in Balibar and Wallerstein, *Race, Nation, Class*, 21.
17 Such a narrative is common among those who include Balibar in a more general narrative of the French philosophical left's turn from Marxism to human rights. See, for example, Hewlett, *Badiou, Balibar, Rancière*; and Philippe Raynaud, *L'extrême gauche plurielle* (Paris: Perrin, 2010).
18 Exemplarily, Antoine Artous, *Démocratie, citoyenneté, émancipation* (Paris: Syllepse, 2010).
19 See, for example, Alain Badiou, *Ethics: An Essay on the Understanding of Evil*, trans. Peter Hallward (London: Verso, 2002); Slavoj Žižek, "Against Human Rights," *New Left Review* 34 (2005): 115–31.
20 See Étienne Balibar, *Cinq études de materialisme historique* (Paris: F. Maspero, 1974), 19–45 and passim; Balibar, *Philosophy of Marx*, 6–10; Étienne Balibar, "Un jacobin nommé Marx? Liberté, égalité, fraternité: à chacun de ces trois mots de la devise républicaine se rattache un moment de la pensée de Marx," *Magazine Littéraire* 258 (October 1988): 66–9.

21 Étienne Balibar, "Ambiguous Universality," in *Politics and the Other Scene*, 165.

22 It could be argued that Balibar broached this theme in the course of reflecting on the relations of North Africans and their descendants to the French polity. See "Sujets ou citoyens? (pour l'égalité)," *Les Temps Modernes* 452–4 (March–May 1984): 1726–53.

23 Étienne Balibar, *Spinoza and Politics*, trans. Peter Snowdon (London: Verso, 1998).

24 See Étienne Balibar, "'Rights of Man' and 'Rights of the Citizen': The Modern Dialectic of Freedom and Equality," in *Masses, Classes, Ideas: Studies on Politics and Philosophy Before and After Marx*, trans. James Swenson, 39–59 (New York: Routledge, 1994). A longer French version, based on a 1989 lecture, was published in *Les frontières de la démocratie* (Paris: Découverte, 1992) and is finally available in English in *Equaliberty: Political Essays, 1989–2009*, trans. James Ingram (Durham, NC: Duke University Press, 2014).

25 See Michael Scott Christofferson, *French Intellectuals Against the Left: The Antitotalitarian Moment of the 1970s* (New York: Berghahn Books, 2004).

26 Balibar, "'Rights of Man' and 'Rights of the Citizen,'" 44–50.

27 Lefort, "Politics and Human Rights."

28 Balibar, "Ambiguous Universality," 165–6.

29 Rancière went on to elaborate this conception of politics in *Disagreement*.

30 I have tried to elaborate this version of human rights politics in James Ingram, "What Is a 'Right to Have Rights'? Three Visions of the Politics of Human Rights," *American Political Science Review* 102, no. 4 (2008): esp. 408–13.

31 Balibar, "Three Concepts of Politics," 2.

32 Balibar, "'Rights of Man' and 'Rights of the Citizen,'" 47.

33 Ibid.

34 Ibid., 50–4. By insisting that liberty must always go along with equality, Balibar avoids reducing emancipatory politics to the egalitarian pole – a tendency that arguably can be found in works of peers such as Rancière, Badiou, and Laclau, who on this point can be criticized for losing sight of the political-institutional side of emancipation.

35 Étienne Balibar, "The Infinite Contradiction," trans. Jean-Marc Poisson and Jacques Lezra, *Yale French Studies* 88 (January 1995): 157–8.

36 For an invaluable account of recent left-Heideggerian variants of this position that also includes a brief survey of other, earlier versions, see Marchart, *Post-Foundational Political Thought*.

37 Rancière takes an anomalous position on this question. Although he defines a single, transhistorical logic of "politics," to the extent that it

consists in challenging and displacing existing understandings of the political order, politics in his sense is always waged *against* "the political." See Rancière, *On the Shores of Politics*, 10–11, 96–8.

38 Balibar, "Three Concepts of Politics," 8.

39 Ibid., 11.

40 See Robin Celikates, "Die Demokratisierung der Demokratie: Étienne Balibar über die Dialektik von konstituierender und konstituierter Macht," in *Das Politische Denken: Zeitgenössiche Positionen*, ed. Ulrich Bröckling and Robert Feustel (Bielefeld, Germany: transcript, 2009), 59–76.

41 Balibar, "Ambiguous Universality," 160.

42 Claudia Aradau points out the distance of Balibar's use of this concept from Derrida's *conceptual* aporias: "Contrary to Derrida, Balibar's aporias are neither interminable resistances nor remainders implied by the very experience of the impossible." Instead they are *historical* and *practical* – "paradoxes of actuality," derived from specific historical conditions and with determinate, real-world consequences. See Claudia Aradau, "Only Aporias to Offer? Étienne Balibar's Politics and the Ambiguity of War," *New Formations* 58 (June 2006): 39.

43 Althusser's influential doctrine of economic determination in the last instance was widely accepted in Marxist circles in the 1970s, by Balibar as well as by such interlocutors as Poulantzas. Although by the 1990s Balibar had abandoned this position for the one I describe below, it should be noted that Althusser himself was already distancing himself from it in the late 1970s in favour of an "aleatory materialism" – and, contrary to claims still repeated by unfriendly critics, that Althusser's insistence that Marxism is a science never meant that it could be deductive or predictive.

44 Franck Fischbach, "Le déni du social, deux exemples contemporains: Abensour et Rancière," *Recherches sur la Philosophie et le Langage* 28 (2012): 29–46.

45 Balibar, "Preface," in *Politics and the Other Scene*, xiii.

46 Balibar, "Infinite Contradiction," 160.

47 For an early version of this analysis, see Étienne Balibar, "Foucault and Marx: The Question of Nominalism," in *Michel Foucault: Philosopher*, ed. Timothy Armstrong (New York: Routledge, 1991), 38–56.

48 Balibar, "Three Concepts of Politics," 20.

49 Étienne Balibar, "Violence et politique: quelques questions," in *Le Passage des frontiers: autour du travail de Jacques Derrida*, ed. Marie-Louise Mallet (Paris: Galilée, 1994).

50 Essays on this theme, starting with a revised version of the 1992 lecture and centring on his 1996 lectures at the University of California at Irvine,

have been collected in *Violence et civilité: Wellek Library Lectures et autres essais de philosophie politique* (Paris: Galilée, 2010). A sketch (the volume's concluding essay) is available in English as Étienne Balibar, "Violence and Civility: On the Limits of Political Anthropology," trans. Stephanie Bundy, *differences* 20, nos. 2–3 (2009): 9–35.

51 Étienne Balibar, "Stratégies de civilité," in *Violence et civilité*, 158.

52 Étienne Balibar, "*Gewalt*: violence et pouvoir dans la théorie marxiste," in *Violence et civilité*, 251–2.

53 See, e.g., Étienne Balibar, "Le moment messianique de Marx," in *Violence et civilité*, 243–63.

54 Balibar, "Violence et politique," 34–7.

55 Balibar, "Three Concepts of Politics," 21.

56 Ibid., 29.

57 A version of this question was put to Balibar at the New School for Social Research in 2007 with reference to John Rawls's idea of an "overlapping consensus." His considered response was that he did not object to calling the idea "liberal" in a broad sense, with the following caveat: "I see a difference in principle between the fact of setting conditions (which are basically moral) for the agreement of citizens on 'political values' isolated from 'non-political values' within a closed polity and the fact of looking for the 'civil' forms of conflictuality (or dissensus) within an open space, where the limit between the 'political' and the 'non-political' is not agreed on in advance." See Étienne Balibar, "Toward a Politics of the Universal," *Graduate Faculty Philosophy Journal* 29, no. 1 (2008): 24 n26.

58 Balibar, "Violence and Civility," 29; idem, "Lénine et Gandhi: une rencontre manquée?," in *Violence et civilité*, 305–21.

59 Balibar, "Three Concepts of Politics," 35.

60 Étienne Balibar, "La démocratie conflictuelle et le théorème de Machiavel," in *L'Europe, l'Amérique, la guerre: réflexions sur la médiation européenne* (Paris: La Découverte, 2003), 126–7. Balibar credits this "tribunal" interpretation of the historical role of the PCF to Georges Lavau, *À quoi sert le Parti communiste français?* (Paris: Fayard, 1981).

9 From a Critique of Totalitarian Domination to the Utopia of Insurgent Democracy: On the "Political Philosophy" of Miguel Abensour

MARTIN BREAUGH

In the late 1990s political philosophy made a definitive comeback in French ideas.[1] As we argued in the introduction, intellectual life in twentieth-century France was, for the most part, dominated by the social sciences and the Weberian fact/value distinction. As such it was not particularly receptive to political philosophy:[2] the study of political ideas was seen, at best, as a regional branch of philosophy; at worst, as ideology disguised as science.[3] By the *fin-de-siècle*, though, things radically changed for political philosophy, and even a cursory analysis of the intellectual context of the times reveals the factors that made a return of political philosophy possible. The crisis of Marxism, both theoretical and practical, as well as the exhaustion of structuralism[4] as the social sciences' paradigm of choice, opened a space for political philosophers to demonstrate the relevance of their approach and questions for a better understanding of contemporary life.[5]

The return of political philosophy in France, though, did not occur spontaneously; rather, it was a long-prepared comeback undertaken by young and ambitious thinkers, inspired by the events of May 1968 and immune to the trend-setting *doxa* emerging from the Left Bank of Paris. The work done in the "excellent and ephemeral"[6] journal *Libre* (1977–81) is a good illustration of this preparation. The editorial collective of the journal, composed notably of Claude Lefort, Cornelius Castoriadis, and Pierre Clastres, sought to restore a philosophical approach to the comprehension of political things. Articles on the Budapest revolt in 1956, on Leninism, on de Tocqueville's thought, on utopia, as well as on the events of May 68, were penned by a rising generation of political thinkers such as Pierre Manent, Marcel Gauchet, and Miguel Abensour.

Although the work of some of these thinkers is well known and discussed today, the pioneering work of others remains largely neglected in political theory. For example, to grasp the richness and diversity of the "return to political philosophy" in France, we ought to examine and understand the "political philosophy" of Miguel Abensour. As we will see, the term "political philosophy" must be bracketed constantly when speaking of Abensour's thought. Before clarifying why it is necessary to do so, a brief overview of his career might help situate his thought and the importance of his work.

From 1968 to 1973, Abensour taught at the prestigious Institut d'études politiques, and in 1973 he completed his *doctorat d'État* under the supervision first of Charles Eisenmann and then of Gilles Deleuze on the "Socialist-communist forms of utopia." That same year he was one of the first candidates to pass the new state examinations for political science (*agrégation*), which allowed him to become *Maître de conférence* (assistant professor) in political philosophy at the Université de Reims. In 1985 he succeeded Jean-François Lyotard as president of the Collège international de philosophie, and in 1990 he joined the Université de Paris VII-Denis Diderot, where he became emeritus professor in 2002. At the same time, Abensour developed an intensive and highly regarded career as a series editor for Éditions Payot (now Éditions Payot-Rivages), one of oldest and most important publishers in France. In 1974 he designed and created the "Critique de la politique" series, and has overseen its development ever since. In addition to publishing the works of the principal members of the Frankfurt School, Abensour has edited seminal works of political philosophy (Hegel, Fichte, La Boétie) as well as groundbreaking works by his generation of thinkers (Pierre Manent, Giorgio Agamben, Marc Richir). Of late, a new cohort of promising young French thinkers (Étienne Tassin, Nicolas Israël, Géraldine Mulhmann, Nicolas Poirier) has been published in the series.[7] As the French daily *Libération*'s influential book critic Robert Maggiori points out, had Abensour never published anything himself, he would still have an important "oeuvre" to his credit.[8]

The reason "political philosophy" must be put in brackets when speaking of Abensour's work is his extremely critical position towards the form taken by the return to political philosophy in France. Abensour opposes two type of "returns": on the one hand, a return to political philosophy seen as the restoration of a neglected academic discipline; on the other hand, a return of "political things" that "burst into the present"[9] and need to be interrogated anew. For Abensour the current return in France is taking the former route. With the creation of specialized journals and associations, the organization of colloquiums, and all sorts of customary academic activities, the French return is akin to a form of "normalization" of the discipline or even to its alignment on the American model. Indeed, as Mark Lilla points out, the return to political philosophy entails a return to liberalism[10] in its procedural, institutional, and historical incarnations. The newfound "legitimacy of the liberal age" is due in part to the introduction in France of the Anglo-American debates surrounding the work of John Rawls and Charles Taylor. However, even thinkers such as Marcel Gauchet who refuse the label "liberal" will agree that their political philosophy now embraces what Gauchet calls "normal politics."[11] In counterdistinction to this restoration, Abensour pleads for a "return to political things" that responds to a "need of humanity"[12] in the face of the political events that irrupt *hic et nunc*. For Abensour, political philosophy must be responsive to politics and thus cannot be reduced to an academic discipline or to the necessary history of political ideas.[13] In contemporary thought, Abensour associates two seminal thinkers to the "return of political things": Hannah Arendt and Claude Lefort.[14] For both Arendt and Lefort, the political novelty of the twentieth century, totalitarianism, obliges us to rethink the relationship to our "tradition of political thought," and opens to a phenomenology of action[15] for Arendt and to a phenomenology of democratic invention for Lefort. Abensour believes that Arendt and Lefort are exemplary thinkers inasmuch as they undertake a critique of domination that does not lead to a rejection of the political, but rather leads to a rediscovery of the forgotten, yet fundamental link between politics and emancipation.

This last point is of particular importance for Abensour. Indeed, we could say that it establishes the parameters of his work and approach to "political philosophy." As I have argued elsewhere,[16] Abensour's oeuvre is governed by two inseparable projects: a radical critique of all forms of domination and a determination to rethink the political as the realm of emancipation and freedom. For him, it is crucial that both projects be undertaken together to avoid the reduction of politics to a form of domination. Even more important, this approach aims at recognizing the beneficial role played by social division and conflict (both violent and non-violent) in the political realm. Societies are divided, argues Abensour, because of the simple fact of human plurality. In this sense Abensour assumes the full political consequences of Arendt's idea that "politics is based on the fact of human plurality":[17] if "politics arises *between men*"[18] because of the uniqueness of each, then societies are necessarily divided. In other words, social division is the "natural" outcome of plurality. As for conflict, Abensour regards it both as the consequence of plurality and, more important, as what enables an extension of freedom in the political realm. Conflict does not represent a menace or danger for a free political regime; it is rather the condition of possibility of such a regime. As I argue in this chapter, the idea of social division and of conflict as a motor of freedom permeates Abensour's work; it even offers his work its distinct flavour.

To distinguish his work clearly from the current restoration of political philosophy in France, Abensour calls his approach "critical political philosophy"[19] or, more precisely, "critico-utopian political philosophy."[20] Three key elements of his thought constitute his main contributions to contemporary political thought: 1) a conceptualization of totalitarianism as an attempt to destroy the possibility of politics; 2) a theory of "insurgent democracy"; and 3) a reading of utopia as emancipation. Although his work cannot be reduced to these three elements,[21] they nevertheless illustrate the fecundity and the novelty of his thought and approach.

Totalitarianism, Architecture, and the Social Bond

In an interview published in *Le Monde* in 2008, Abensour explains that two major "return of political things" shaped his generation's approach to politics: the Algerian war and the critique of Soviet totalitarianism.[22] While the former brought about a sustained critique of the authoritarian and oligarchic nature of the Fifth Republic,[23] the latter divided intellectuals in France. For some thinkers, the need to maintain a strong critique of capitalism trumped the need to denounce the atrocities of the Soviet regime. For others, the establishment of an anti-totalitarian movement based on a critique of totalitarian domination in the Soviet Union and in National Socialist Germany was the necessary precondition of a better understanding of democracy,[24] defined as the political regime of non-domination. For Abensour, as a prominent figure of the French anti-totalitarian movement, the development of a radical critique of totalitarianism represented "a need of humanity" in the twentieth century.

In *De la compacité: architecture et régimes totalitaires*,[25] Abensour develops a theory of totalitarianism understood as an attempt to destroy, through a sustained assault on the space existing between humans, the very condition of possibility of politics. Indeed, his hypothesis is that, under totalitarianism, architecture is mobilized to attack the "social bond" between individuals. Abensour makes this claim through an analysis of the work of the official architect of the National Socialist regime and close personal friend of the Führer, Albert Speer. Far from being a politically neutral exercise in aesthetics, architecture, to quote Adorno, is cast "in the same nature of the musical accompaniment with which the SS liked to drown out the screams of its victims."[26]

The starting point of Abensour's analysis is the relationship that a political regime establishes with time and space. Such an analysis is necessary insofar as such a relationship shapes the social bond. In the context of French political thought, the question of the social bond refers to the idea that political regimes partake in the creation of the ways by which citizens relate (or not) to one another. The link between architecture and totalitarianism thus can be examined through an investigation of the totalitarian institution of the social bond.

To determine the "nature" of the social bond under totalitarianism, however, one must first identify the political subject of such a regime. For Abensour, totalitarianism is the exact opposite of "the universe of citizenship" or of the "*res publica*,"[27] inasmuch as it is the realm of the "mass," a pseudo-political subject that is constituted neither in autonomy nor in agency or action, but as a submissive and even radically heteronymous entity with regards to the political movement and the order of the state.[28] Abensour points out that totalitarian regimes invent a specific manner of integrating the mass from a political point of view. Indeed, by denying the possibility of agency to the people that make up the mass, totalitarian regimes transform them into a "political" actor capable of being totally and unreservedly mobilized.

Architecture plays a pivotal role in mobilizing the mass by creating public spaces that encourage, reinforce, and sustain the reactions and feelings of the mass. Borrowing from Elias Canetti's *Crowds and Power*, Abensour sees the mass as a gathering of human beings that allows for the surmounting of the phobia of contact. More important, argues Abensour, this phobia "transforms itself into its opposite, the quest for contact, the fusion into an whole, [into] a dense body."[29] In other words, a "density" (*compacité*) is generated by the mass that actually abolishes the space that exists between humans. Such a phenomenon is desirable, because it creates a community that is blandly egalitarian and fusional. Elias Canetti writes: "in that density where there is scarcely any space between, and body presses against body, each man is as near the other as he is to himself; and an immense feeling of relief ensues. It is for the sake of this blessed moment, when no-one is greater or better than another, that people become a [mass]."[30]

It is precisely here that the junction between architecture and totalitarian regimes is found. Indeed, architecture partakes in the creation of density that suppresses the intervals between humans, and participates in the political project of total domination. "The colossal size of buildings, far from creating *public* space, produces massive and dense spaces in order to establish absolute cohesion,"[31] writes Abensour. The excessive nature of totalitarian architectural projects facilitates the assembly of the mass and allows for a fusion between all to occur. For example, Albert Speer's project "Der Grosse Platz" in Berlin (1937–40) illustrates how the creation of a gigantic "public" space makes the assembly of a few people seem incongruous, even absurd, and commands the presence of a mass. Speer himself was quite clear on the role of architecture in National Socialist Germany: for him, the regime's desire to subjugate individual will must be reflected in architecture.[32] Such massive spaces are indeed meant to mobilize the many, but only in a depoliticizing fashion. Thanks to a particular form of political aestheticization via rituals, music, and elaborate theatrical staging, "surrogate" political instances are bestowed on the mass.

Caught in the toils of density, humans are dispossessed of the interval that separates them from their fellow humans. This dispossession is precisely what characterizes the totalitarian institution of the social bond: by creating a form of unity through fusion, it suppresses division. By depriving people of the vital space necessary to establish relations and strong links with others, totalitarian regimes manage to harm the social bond and, ipso facto, the possibility of maintaining a political sphere. "The proper of totalitarian regimes," writes Abensour, "is not to do violence to a problematic human essence nor is it to push the boundaries of the human, it is to attack the human bond, to destroy the interhuman relationship and order." Thus, "as a refusal of plurality and denial of division," totalitarian regimes attempt to put an end to politics by destroying the social bond.[33]

Insurgent Democracy: Machiavelli, Marx, and the French Revolution

Among the protagonists of the anti-totalitarian movement, there was unanimous agreement that the political critique of total domination necessarily opened to a renewed understanding of democracy. For some, this meant an analysis of the potential dangers of democratic life;[34] for others, it meant the exploration of political practices and institutions promoting the coincidence of emancipation and democracy.[35] Miguel Abensour's analysis of democracy follows the second route as it seeks to critique a form of domination, state-centred liberal democracy, while conceptualizing politics as the realm of freedom and emancipation.

First published in 1997, Abensour's *Democracy Against the State: Marx and the Machiavellian Moment* appeared in France at a time when political liberalism was making a comeback and managed to provoke the serious ire of some of his former anti-totalitarian colleagues,[36] while bringing him closer to the positions of other radical democratic French thinkers such as Jacques Rancière. The idea of democracy contained in Abensour's work takes root, as we will see, in the thought of Machiavelli, is developed through a "heterodox reading" of Marx, and is refined by examining the democratic impulses that coalesced during the French Revolution. Indeed, the inclusion of a "Foreword" to the publication of the second French edition in 2004 as well as the publication of a new "Preface" to the Italian translation in 2008 afforded Abensour the opportunity to re-work his conception of democracy into that of "insurgent democracy."[37]

The reference to Machiavelli is central to understanding the genesis of insurgent democracy. Against the vulgar understanding of Machiavelli, whose books remain bedside reading for tyrants, as a thinker of hard-ball politics,[38] Abensour sees the Florentine secretary as a "political educator"[39] challenging us to break with our *idées reçues* about politics. One such received idea is that the political realm should be characterized by order, unity, and harmony. Machiavelli forcefully attacks this profoundly conservative idea. In *The Discourses*, Book I, Chapter 4, he argues that conflict and discord made Rome "free and powerful." Machiavelli even contends that "good laws" emerge from the tumults created by the division of desires, between those who desire to dominate (the Grandees) and those who desire not to be dominated (the Many).[40] According to Abensour, Machiavelli teaches us that "disunion becomes the condition of possibility of freedom as the negativity of the people can alone contain the desire of the Grandees."[41] The division that Machiavelli sees in the political realm is neither contingent nor temporary: it is inherent to the political field. To put things more strongly, one could say that division is what constitutes the being of the political itself, its ontological makeup. This is what Lefort, in his opus magnum on Machiavelli, calls "the originary division of the social."[42] For Abensour, Machiavelli's thought provides us a deeper understanding of the reasons political regimes of non-domination thrive on conflict and division.

It is within this context that Abensour turns to a rarely explored strain found in Marx's thought: the affirmation of a "true democracy" that brings with it the disappearance of the state. Indeed, in his early work, *The Critique of Hegel's Philosophy of Right* (1843), Marx writes, "in true democracy, the *political State would disappear*. This is correct inasmuch as *qua* political State, *qua* constitution it is no longer equivalent to the whole."[43] This enigmatic idea reappears in his 1871 work on the Paris Commune, *The Civil War in France*.[44] Abensour discovers here a "latent dimension in Marx's oeuvre, always susceptible to rise again and produce new fruit."[45] This dimension of "true democracy," following Abensour, can be understood in relation to a "Machiavellian moment," to use J.G.A. Pocock's expression – that is to say, a recognition of the autonomy of the political, a rehabilitation of *vita activa*, and a preference for a republican form of government.[46]

In Marx's thought, "true democracy" is characterized by four major claims. First, contrary to Hegel, Marx contends that sovereignty rests with the people struggling for liberty and not with the monarch; as such, "democracy is the consummate form of politics."[47] Second, the *demos*'s objectification in the political constitution is done via reduction. Marx means by this, that the constitutional objectification of the *demos* is reduced to a simple moment within the larger process of the expression of creativity. It thus allows the *demos* to renew with its "essence as a species-being."[48] Abensour writes that the "political mode of being leads, consequently, to the experience of the true universal existence, the essential experience of community, the unity of man with man."[49] It is only from the site of self-activity in the political realm that an irrigation of this creativity can occur in the other realms of human existence. Democracy is therefore the cornerstone of a truly human existence. Third, to offset the risks of alienation, "true democracy" must be understood as a never-ending experience of self-institution and self-determination; there can be no end term to the action of the many in the context of true democracy. Finally, as the previous claims imply, democracy holds an exceptional status in the political realm for Marx.

Although this conception of true democracy was eclipsed by Marx's discovery of political economy, it nevertheless was returned to, and even "enriched," by the experience of the Paris Commune of 1871. Through a political analysis of the "Communal Constitution," Marx argues that the Commune was instituted *against* the state and that its main political innovation was the establishment a non-state political form. Marx sees the apparently "modest" measures taken by the Commune, such as the recall of elected officials, the abolition of conscription, and the replacement of the standing army by the National Guard, which all citizens could join, as illustrations of what a political form can enact to preclude a fatal return to the state. For Abensour, Marx describes here the advent of social emancipation through a political mediation created in a movement against the state. Abensour writes: "the putting to play on a political stage of an agonistic relation that aims to forestall the State's return [and] to institute a new political form against this formalism … mobiliz[es] a critical knowledge and a *thumos* where the desire for liberty and hate of servitude are mixed indistinctly."[50]

If Abensour discovers with Machiavelli the salutary effects of division and conflict for politics, we can say that he takes from Marx the fundamental opposition between democracy and the state, as well as the relationship between emancipation and democracy. Indeed, as we will see, both thinkers inform Abensour's efforts to conceptualize "insurgent democracy," understood as a non-state political form that generates freedom through conflict and allows for social division to manifest itself in the public realm. As previously mentioned, this insight into the nature of democracy is also nourished by a novel examination of the democratic energies unleashed during the French Revolution.

Insurgent democracy must not be confused with "conflictual democracy." For the latter, political conflict is located within the confines of the state, and the end pursued by those engaged in "conflictual democracy" is the exercise of state power. But the location and ends of insurgent democracy are radically different. On the one hand, the conflict generated by insurgent democracy can be found only outside the state and state-legitimized instances of political negotiation (such as the legislature, the ballot box, all-candidates' debates, and so on). Insurgent democracy, in contrast, happens on the streets, in the squares, and just about anywhere people gather to struggle together against the state for more freedom, more equality, and more solidarity. As Abensour writes, insurgent democracy "does not shrink from rupture" inasmuch as "it is born out of the intuition that there is no true democracy without reactivating the anarchic impulse which first rises against the classic expression of *arche* – at once commencement and commandment – namely, the State."[51] On the other hand, the end of insurgent democracy is not to seize state power, but – just as the Commune of 1871 did – to invent another political form that brings with it the possibility of an emancipation of the Many from the political domination of the Few. It is not a question of finding a better "leader" or political party, but of creating the conditions of possibility of enacting a unique and inclusive way of engaging in the public realm.

In fact, insurgent democracy represents a "permanent" conflict with the state. As such, it is demanding, even *exhausting* for those who practise it *in actu*. This is so because the time of insurgent democracy is that of the "caesura between two state forms"[52] when an Old Regime is agonizing and the up-and-coming "new political masters" have yet to impose their *libido dominandi*. Insurgent democracy struggles thus on both statist fronts: against the declining rulers and against the rising new "rulers." Abensour finds the prototype of such struggles in the French Revolution, when the urban poor of Paris fought *contra* the remnants of the Old Regime and *contra* the emerging *libido dominandi* of the Jacobins after the proclamation of the First French Republic.[53] But this particular political configuration does not disappear with the end of the French Revolution. The time of insurgent democracy and its exhausting nature shed light on the events of the Arab Spring of 2011, as it does on the events of Budapest 1956, May 1968, and the "Colour" Revolutions of the early 2000s.[54]

Abensour also points out that the nature of insurgent democracy is to modify the political stakes: it is no longer a question of changing rulers or asserting the superiority of civil society over the state. In insurgent democracy we find the affirmation of a political community against the state. Such a community unveils the false pretence upon which the state asserts its monopoly of the political, and it allows for an extension of the realm of the possible in politics. In other words, by "dethroning the State," insurgent democracy "erects the political against the state and opens the too often concealed abyss between the political and the State."[55] To use the term "insurgent democracy" is therefore to recognize that democracy is "primarily an action, a modality of political agency"[56] that struggles for the creation of a state of non-domination. This specific type of action cannot be restricted to a specific moment in time, "but continues through time, always ready to spring up."[57]

With insurgent democracy, a new type of social bond appears. Indeed, a horizontal and non-contractual political bond is what allows for the political being-together of the Many under the conditions of non-domination. Here we can recognize what political anthropologist of antiquity Nicole Loraux calls, somewhat paradoxically, the "bond of division"[58] – that is to say, an interhuman relation born of the explicit recognition of the divided nature of political communities. As Abensour writes, one of "the underlying principle[s] of the insurrection … is the search for a political relationship, for a vital, intense, non-hierarchical political bond distinct from order."[59] At the time of the French Revolution, this type of bond was known by the Parisian *sans-culottes* as "fraternal disorder," and it represented "a non-restrictive and egalitarian political bond."[60] This must be contrasted with Abensour's understanding of totalitarianism as an attempt to destroy the social bond. That insurgent democracy attempts to deepen the social bond underscores the clear-cut, even radical, difference between totalitarianism and democracy.

For some, insurgent democracy might seem "above all a negativity anchored in the present of the insurrectionary movement"[61] or a pure political liquefaction that is unable to be institutionalized. But Abensour also explains the way by which insurgent democracy can find a "positive model of action" – that is to say, an institution. Once again, the experience of the French Revolution is decisive. Abensour considers that the still-born Constitution of 1793 is an example of an institution allowing for the expression of insurgent democracy. Indeed, this constitution provided for a guaranteed right to insurrection, thus paving the way for the preservation of insurgent democracy through time. For Abensour, insurgent democracy is selective in its choice of institutions, and its basic criteria for accepting an institution is that of non-domination. As long as an institutional framework allows for the promotion of non-domination, it is potentially compatible with insurgent democracy. By virtue of what it teaches us concerning the relationship between politics and conflict, democracy and action, and the possibility of another form of social bond, insurgent democracy represents a novel contribution to contemporary democratic theory.

Utopia and Emancipation

For mainstream democratic theorists, the idea of insurgent democracy easily could be dismissed as unrealistic, even "utopian." Instead of denying this claim, Abensour celebrates it.[62] Indeed, his political theory has always been concerned with a proper understanding of utopia, of its role in educating desire and its relationship to radical politics. For an Anglo-American audience, the centrality of utopia in Abensour's political thought is largely unknown,[63] if only because his many books on utopia have yet to be translated.

Refusing to associate utopia with totalitarianism, as many do today, Abensour develops a sustained critique of such an association and explores the relationship between emancipation/democracy and utopia.

By analysing the classification Abensour proposes of the different kinds of utopias born in the nineteenth and twentieth centuries – "utopian socialism," "neo-utopianism," and the "new utopian spirit" – we will understand why Abensour argues that the proper aim of the last category is to create a pathway between utopia and democracy. Finally, we can examine Abensour's contribution to utopian studies by exploring his reading and conceptualization of utopia. For him, utopias are neither imaginary worlds within which humans could live in perfect felicity nor blueprints or political programs that must be implemented here and now. Rather, they are to be understood as a way to educate desire, to "stimulate in its readers a *desire for a better life* and to motivate that desire toward action by conveying a sense that the world is not fixed once and for all."[64]

Against those who seek to prosecute the "master-dreamers"[65] responsible for creating and disseminating utopias understood as totalitarian enterprises, Abensour opposes a nuanced and complex reading of the utopian tradition that emphasizes the heterogeneity of utopian thought, and hence the difficulty of reducing utopia to a unique political regime. In fact, the problem with accusing utopias of being totalitarian is that such an accusation does not explain why totalitarian regimes have viciously attacked and repressed utopian experiences. For example, Abensour points out that "the arrival of Stalin in power brought with it the definitive suppression of any and all remnants of the utopian experience born in the wake of the Soviet Revolution."[66] In addition, for utopias to be totalitarian, they would have to share certain defining characteristics with totalitarian regimes, such as belief in the one-party system and desire to extend state power to all dimensions of human life. Yet there exists an important utopian tradition that resolutely opposes both the party system and the state (that of Joseph Déjacque[67] and William Morris[68]): by doing so, it seeks to revitalize social relations and encourage social experimentation through utopian practices and thought. Consequently, this tradition has nothing in common with totalitarianism. In point of fact, Abensour argues that "a society without utopia or deprived of utopia is very precisely a totalitarian society, inasmuch as it is captive to the illusion of accomplishment, of the return home or of the realized utopia."[69]

Instead of asking the simplistic question, "are utopias totalitarian?" Abensour invites us to explore the more subtle and complex question of the relationship that certain utopian traditions have with the desire for oneness – that is to say, the desire to overcome social division and conflict. After all, the fundamental analysis of totalitarianism undertaken by Lefort demonstrates how such regimes attempt to create an undivided society or, more exactly, a regime that produces manifestations of social alterity to better suppress it.[70] In an important article published in the early 1970s, Abensour explores this question through the establishment of a tripartite classification of socialist-communist utopian traditions of the past two centuries: "utopian socialism," "neo-utopianism," and the "new utopian spirit."[71] "Utopian socialism" corresponds to what nineteenth-century French socialist Pierre Leroux calls "the daybreak of socialism" and is made up of the three major "liberators": Henri de Saint-Simon, Charles Fourier, and Robert Owen.[72] The impulse behind this tradition is a will to happiness, seeking to constitute a new philosophy of life. Utopian socialism is also characterized by a call to overcome the limits of the possible and to emancipate ourselves from the prejudices that constrain thought and action. "Neo-utopianism," however, attempts to bring utopia into reality by proposing utopian models that are to be realized and that would institute a society without division or conflict (see, for example, Louis Blanc, Edward Bellamy, and Étienne Cabet). This tradition is motivated by a strong desire to create utopian societies *hic et nunc* through organizations founded upon utopian principles. But the price to pay for a desire to realize a utopian design is quite high: it entails "a loss of the original content, ... [since] what the utopia gains in social extension, it loses in utopian intensity."[73] For Abensour, neo-utopianism represents a regressive moment in the history of utopia. But this regression nevertheless has the great merit of opening a space for the emergence of the final and most important utopian tradition: the "new utopian spirit."

If neo-utopianism paves the way for the "new utopian spirit," it is because this spirit is born of a self-critique of the utopian movement, in reaction to the failures of neo-utopianism and to the radical critique of neo-utopianism by Marx and Engels.[74] The objective of the "new utopian spirit" is to identify the blind spots of utopian thinking that lead to the phantasmagorical desire to create a society that has overcome social division and conflict. This self-critique allows for a preservation of the emancipatory and liberating effects of utopia at its origins. The "new utopian spirit" was also generated by the major political events of the nineteenth century and made up of a constellation of thinkers. In the wake of the failure of the revolution of 1848 and thanks to the work undertaken in the social movement between 1848 and 1871, there was a renewed sense of the importance and problems of utopian thinking.

The "new utopian spirit," though, persists long after the Paris Commune of 1871, as Walter Benjamin, Ernest Bloch, and Emmanuel Levinas, among others, partook in it.

The work of the "new utopian spirit" can be described as that of a "rescue by way of transfer." The "new utopian spirit" puts utopia to the test of the most unfavourable and anti-utopian of ideas, notably that of "taking seriously the hypothesis of the repetition in history ... of catastrophe." For Abensour, "only a thought of utopia that does violence to itself, that includes in its own movement a critique of utopia, is strong enough to destroy the myths that undermine utopia."[75] In other words, the new utopian spirit seeks to purge utopia of its blind spots or myths to give life once again to its emancipatory energies. By proceeding in such a fashion, the new utopian spirit manages to open a "passage toward an unexplored elsewhere ... within which it struggles with its most contrary" ideas and principles.[76] By liberating utopia from its blind spots, the new utopian spirit provides for a better appreciation of the relationship between utopia and emancipation. This is an essential contribution to political theory because it uncovers the true *raison d'être* of utopian thinking: human emancipation. In fact, contends Abensour, there can be no utopia without a relationship to emancipation.

The nineteenth-century French philosopher Pierre Leroux argued that utopia represents the third wave of human emancipation that tries to organize the common world through association, not hierarchy. Abensour discovers in the work of Leroux a pathway that allows for an encounter between utopia and democracy.[77] Whereas the link between utopia and emancipation might be obvious, the link between utopia and democracy remains more obscure, if only because some utopian traditions seek to rid the world of politics. The last point is a precisely a utopian blind spot identified by Leroux, who attempted to conceptualize the social bond in a non-authoritarian fashion by postulating the existence of a mutual attraction between humans: "in the manner of democracy, attraction rests upon an experience of humanity, [of] the recognition of human beings by their fellow human beings."[78] As we can see with Leroux, utopian thought does not refuse politics or deny the importance of the political; it actually thinks through one of the most difficult political questions, the question of the social bond.

Although Abensour does not think that we can simply resume Leroux's project based on "mutual attraction" after the totalitarian attempt to destroy the political, he does believe that it nevertheless underscores a crucial aspect for our understanding of the relationship between utopia and democracy: the "human element." This is where the main protagonists of the new utopian spirit, such as Martin Buber or Emmanuel Levinas, will locate utopia – that is to say, in the interhuman relationship. Levinas' attempt to think utopia "otherwise"[79] – in the proximity of an encounter with the Other – does not abolish Otherness. On the contrary, the asymmetrical and infinite responsibility of the self for the Other, postulated by Levinas, preserves plurality and difference in the encounter with the Other. As for insurgent democracy, we have seen that it generates a particular type of social bond founded in division and conflict: "as paradoxical as this may seem," writes Abensour, "democracy is the form of society that institutes a human link across political struggles."[80] A social bond is thus established through the conflicting manifestation of division that occurs with the expression of human plurality. Does the totalitarian experience not demonstrate that conflict can be overcome only by suppressing plurality through the fusing of individuals into a dense mass?

The encounter between utopia and democracy occurs precisely at the confluence between plurality, conflict, and the interhuman relationship. Abensour writes: "on the level of non-coincidence, each of these two poles [utopia and democracy] designates a form of non-fusional community that is constituted, paradoxically, by and through a test of separation."[81] In a certain sense, one of the basic political problems that Abensour ceaselessly explores in his work on utopia and democracy is how both approach plurality, difference, and alterity through the recognition of the benefits of division and conflict. We could say that utopia and insurgent democracy thrive on plurality and difference, and seek to preserve and promote both.

The association of utopia with totalitarianism and the commonplace refusal of the idea that utopias seek emancipation also rest upon a longstanding misinterpretation of utopian thought. This misunderstanding can be traced back to two problematic, yet widely admitted, readings of Thomas More's *Utopia* (1516). Indeed, Abensour often asks if contemporary readers even know how to read utopias:[82] more than just a provocation aimed at "distracted readers,"[83] Abensour's interrogation seeks to open a hermeneutical space providing an understanding of the full complexity of utopian thought.

In his analysis of More's *Utopia*, Abensour radically critiques the two classical interpretations of the work. Both the "realist" reading of utopia, as a political blueprint that must be implemented,[84] and the "allegorical" reading of utopia as a pathway to God,[85] are seen as "tyrannical readings" that entail the rejection of central elements of More's work in order to be valid. The realist reading rejects the enigmatic nature of More's writing, whereas the allegorical reading overlooks the presence of the political question. For Abensour, a proper understanding of *Utopia* requires us to take seriously the question of how the work is written, the rhetorical strategies it employs, and its undeniable political dimensions. Abensour sees *Utopia* as a "treaty on the education of desire" that speaks to philosophers and non-philosophers alike. For the few who engage in philosophy, utopia helps prevent the hubris inherent in philosophical practice when it takes place under the illusion of possessing the "truth." Such an illusion would put an end to the quest for the Good and the Just and turn philosophic work into a dogmatic affirmation. For the many, however, utopia aims at sharpening the desire to participate in the quest for the Good and the Just. In both cases, utopia, understood as the "education of desire," allows careful readers to open themselves to what Abensour calls the "utopian disposition."[86] This mode of being implies a twofold relationship to existence. On the one hand, it calls for a cultivation of self-irony in order to prevent the development of a spirit of seriousness that could easily turn into dogmatism. On the other hand, it implies a rejection of the idea that the Good and the Just can be realized once and for all. For those who truly engage in this disposition, utopia is therefore a demanding test that develops itself within the boundaries of an irreducible, even absolute, "gap" between the quest for the Good and the Just and its necessarily contingent and incomplete manifestation in the world.

As the education of desire, utopia opens to a form of liberty that can only be a "difficult liberty" (Levinas). Utopia not only anticipates the risks of dogmatism by encouraging self-irony; it also allows for plurality to manifest itself by encouraging the Many to partake in the quest for the Good and the Just. Therefore utopia is a fundamental form of our relationship to liberty. At the same time, the utopian irony, which laughs at "the laws, the judge, and the gods,"[87] as well as at the self, serves as a reminder that the quest for a free political regime, a regime of non-domination, is a never-ending one and that we must accept to live within the "gap." Furthermore, utopia teaches us that liberty is realized by and through the relentless quest for liberty: liberty is thus vivifying, demanding, and exhausting – in a word, it is difficult. The importance bestowed here on the question of the gap affords yet another glimpse of the relationship between utopia and democracy in Abensour's thought. Indeed, both are conceptualized from the perspective of a division or a gap that prevents their full realization and, at the same time, preserves the impulse of liberty at the origins of their deployment.

From his early work on utopia to his later work on insurgent democracy, Miguel Abensour has persistently grappled with the enigmas of freedom and emncipation. At the same time, he has engaged in a relentless critique of political domination. If the guiding principle of his thought is the need for a political manifestation of human plurality, its condition of possibility is the public and even radical expression of division and conflict. Indeed, the gravediggers of political freedom, whether totalitarian "egocrats" or liberal oligarchs,[88] seek to impose oneness by neutralizing the democratic energies of the Many. Thus, the attempt on human plurality often takes the form of an assault on, to use Marx's term, "true democracy." This is why we can say that, although some contemporary thinkers offer hypothetical proposals for the future[89] and others offer, more modestly, a resignation to the current "normal" political order,[90] Abensour provides us something both more difficult and more exhilarating: an invitation to think and act in concert with others without sacrificing the quality of our liberty, an exhortation "to make political liberty synonymous with a living critique of domination."[91]

NOTES

1 For example, in 1999 the widely read *Magazine Littéraire*, a leading indicator of the state of ideas in France, published an issue entitled "The Renewal of Political Philosophy"; see *Magazine Littéraire*, no. 380 (October 1999).

2 For an excellent description of the intellectual context of twentieth-century France, see Manent, "Return of Political Philosophy."

3 Miguel Abensour, "Présentation," *Cahiers de philosophie politique* 1 (1983): 3.

4 Jon Elster, "Obscurantisme dur et obscurantisme mou dans les sciences humaines et sociales," *Diogène* 1–2, no. 229–230 (2010): 235.

5 Gilles Labelle and Daniel Tanguay, "Le retour de la philosophie politique en France," *Politique et Sociétés* 22, no. 3 (2003): 4.

6 Pierre Bouretz, "Pierre Clastres: *La société contre l'État*," in *Dictionnaire des œuvres politiques*, ed. François Chatelet, Olivier Duhamel, and Evelyne Pisier (Paris: Presses Universitaires de France, 1986), 151. Unless otherwise noted, I am translating throughout the chapter.

7 Jérôme Melançon, "Miguel Abensour, critique de la politique," *Politique et Sociétés* 28, no. 1 (2009): 229.

8 Robert Maggiori, "L'utopie de Miguel Abensour," *Libération* (11 June 2009).
9 Miguel Abensour, "De quel retour s'agit-il?" *Les cahiers de philosophie* 18 (1994): 6.
10 Lilla, "Legitimacy of the Liberal Age."
11 Marcel Gauchet, *La condition historique* (Paris: Stock, 2003), 160. For a scathing critique of this position, see Miguel Abensour, *Lettre d'un "révolt-iste" à Marcel Gauchet converti à la "politique normale"* (Paris: Sens & Tonka, 2005).
12 Feuerbach, quoted in Miguel Abensour, "Philosophie politique critique et émancipation?" *Politique et Sociétés*, 22, no. 3 (2003): 120.
13 See, for example, Miguel Abensour, *Hannah Arendt contre la philosophie politique?* For a condensed version of Abensour's argument, see idem, "Against the Sovereignty of Philosophy over Politics: Arendt's Reading of Plato's Cave Allegory," trans. Martin Breaugh, *Social Research* 74, no. 4 (2007): 955–82.
14 It is worth noting the absence of Castoriadis in this list of seminal thinkers. Although they did collaborate in the journals *Textures* and *Libre*, Abensour stopped reading Castoriadis in the early 1980s and did not return to his work before the late 2000s.
15 Tassin, *Trésor perdu*, 305.
16 See Martin Breaugh, "Critique de la domination, pensée de l'émancipation: sur la philosophie politique de Miguel Abensour," *Politique et Sociétés* 22, no. 3 (2003): 45–69, which offers a preliminary version of the ideas and arguments presented in this chapter.
17 Arendt, "Introduction into Politics," 93.
18 Ibid., 95.
19 Abensour, "Philosophie politique critique et émancipation?" 119–42.
20 Miguel Abensour, *Pour une philosophie politique critique* (Paris: Sens & Tonka, 2009).
21 For example, Abensour notably has developed a "counter-Hobbes" influenced by Pierre Clastres, as outlined in Chapter 3 of this volume, as well as a theory of heroism inspired by Saint-Just and Walter Benjamin.
22 Miguel Abensour, "Machiavel: le grand penseur du désordre, entretien avec Miguel Abensour," *Le Monde* (4 October 2008).
23 See, for example, Rancière, *Hatred of Democracy*.
24 See, for example, Pierre Rosanvallon, "Sur quelques chemins de traverse de la pensée du politique en France: un entretien avec Pierre Rosanvallon," *Raisons politiques* 1 (February 2001): 51.
25 Miguel Abensour, *De la compacité: architecture et régimes totalitaires* (Paris: Sens & Tonka, 1997).

26 Adorno, *Negative Dialectics*, 365.
27 Abensour, *De la compacité*, 22.
28 Ibid., 23.
29 Ibid., 37.
30 Elias Canetti, *Crowds and Power*, trans. Carol Stewart (New York: Farrar, Straus, and Giroux, 1984), 18. The original German title is *Masse und Macht*; the term *Masse* is, alas, incorrectly translated in English as "crowd." Translation modified.
31 Abensour, *De la compacité*, 54.
32 Ibid., 56.
33 A novel by Hans Fallada (1947) and a film by Florian Henckel von Donnersmarck (2006) offer vivid illustrations of the destruction of the social bond under the conditions of totalitarianism, the former in National Socialist Germany and the latter in communist East Germany. See Hans Fallada, *Every Man Dies Alone* (New York: Melville House Publishing, 2009); and *The Lives of Others*, dir. Florian Henckel von Donnersmarck (Sony Pictures, 2006).
34 See Marcel Gauchet, *La démocratie contre elle-même* (Paris: Gallimard-Tel, 2001); and Manent, *Tocqueville and the Nature of Democracy*.
35 See also Castoriadis, *Ce qui fait la Grèce 2*; and Pierre Rosanvallon, *Counter-Democracy: Politics in an Age of Distrust*, trans. Arthur Goldhammer (Cambridge: Cambridge University Press, 2008).
36 Marcel Gauchet violently attacks Abensour's work on democracy in *La condition historique*, 160.
37 Abensour, *Democracy Against the State*.
38 Pierre Manent, *Naissances de la politique moderne: Machiavel, Hobbes, Rousseau* (Paris: Payot, 1977), 15.
39 Abensour, "Machiavel."
40 Machiavelli, *Discourses on Livy*, book I, chap. 4.
41 Abensour, "Machiavel."
42 Lefort, *Machiavelli in the Making*.
43 Marx, *Critique of Hegel's Philosophy of Right*, 31.
44 Karl Marx, *The Civil War in France* (Moscow: Foreign Languages Publishing House, 1963).
45 Abensour, *Democracy Against the State*, 88.
46 Ibid., 6–7.
47 Ibid., 49.
48 Ibid., 54.
49 Ibid.
50 Ibid., 88.

51 Ibid., xl–xli.
52 Ibid., xli.
53 Ibid., xxiv.
54 I have offered a general theory and history of such struggles from the Roman Republic to the Paris Commune of 1871; see Martin Breaugh, *The Plebeian Experience: A Discontinuous History of Political Freedom*, trans. Lazer Lederhendler (New York: Columbia University Press, 2013).
55 Abensour, *Democracy Against the State*, xli.
56 Ibid., xxiii.
57 Ibid.
58 Nicole Loraux, *The Divided City: On Memory and Forgetting in Ancient Athens*, trans. Corinne Pache and Jeff Fort (New York: Zone Books, 2001).
59 Abensour, *Democracy Against the State*, xxiv.
60 Ibid., xxv.
61 Ibid.
62 Manuel Cervera-Marzal, *Miguel Abensour, critique de la domination, pensée de l'émancipation* (Paris: Sens & Tonka, 2013), 169.
63 For an analysis of the importance and impact of Abensour's work on the field of "utopian studies" in the Anglo-American world, see Christine Nadir, "Utopian Studies, Environmental Literature, and the Legacy of an Idea: Educating Desire in Miguel Abensour and Ursula K. Le Guin," *Utopian Studies* 21, no. 1 (2010): 24–56.
64 Tom Moyland, as quoted in ibid., emphasis added by Nadir.
65 Miguel Abensour, *Le procès des maîtres rêveurs* (Arles, France: Sulliver, 2000).
66 Ibid., 9.
67 Joseph Déjacque, *À bas les chefs* (Paris: Champ Libre, 1971).
68 William Morris, *News from Nowhere and Other Writings*, ed. Clive Wilmer (New York: Penguin Books, 1993). See also Miguel Abensour, "William Morris: The Politics of Romance," in *Revolutionary Romanticism*, ed. Max Blechman (San Francisco: City Lights Books, 1999), 125–61.
69 Miguel Abensour, *L'utopie de Thomas More à Walter Benjamin* (Paris: Sens & Tonka, 2000), 19–20.
70 Lefort, *Un homme en trop*. This book, of lasting influence in France and elsewhere, has yet to be translated in English.
71 Miguel Abensour, "L'histoire de l'utopie et le destin de sa critique I," *Textures* 6 (1973): 3–26; idem, "L'histoire de l'utopie et le destin de sa critique II," *Textures* 7 (1974): 55–81.
72 Abensour, "L'histoire de l'utopie et le destin de sa critique II," 55.
73 Ibid., 69.

74 Ibid., 67–70.
75 Miguel Abensour, "Le nouvel esprit utopique," *Cahiers Bernard Lazare*, nos. 128–130 (1991): 145.
76 Ibid., 151.
77 Abensour, *Procès des maîtres rêveurs*, 16.
78 Abensour, *Pour une philosophie politique critique*, 354.
79 See also Miguel Abensour, "To Think Utopia Otherwise," trans. Bettina Bergo, *Graduate Faculty Philosophy Journal* 20–21, nos. 1–2 (1998): 251–79.
80 Abensour, *Democracy Against the State*, 123.
81 Abensour, *Pour une philosophie politique critique*, 361.
82 Abensour, "Nouvel esprit utopique," fn. 3.
83 Horacio Gonzalez, "Le processus de libération des textes," in *Critique de la politique: Autour de Miguel Abensour*, ed. Anne Kupiec and Étienne Tassin (Paris: Sens & Tonka, 2006), 29.
84 Abensour, *L'utopie de Thomas More à Walter Benjamin*, 34–5.
85 Ibid., 39–41.
86 Miguel Abensour, "L'homme est un animal utopique: entretien avec Miguel Abensour," *Mouvements* 45–46 (May–August 2006): 86.
87 Miguel Abensour, *Rire des lois, du magistrat et des dieux: l'impulsion Saint-Just* (Lyon, France: Horlieu, 2005).
88 On the tension between liberalism and democracy, see, for example, Martin Breaugh and Francis Dupuis-Déri, eds., *La démocratie au-delà du libéralisme: perspectives critiques* (Montreal: Athéna Éditions, 2009).
89 Alain Badiou, *The Communist Hypothesis*, trans. David Macey and Steve Corcoran (London: Verso, 2010).
90 Gauchet, *Condition historique*, 160.
91 Abensour, *Democracy Against the State*, back cover; the blurb was written by Max Blechman.

Bibliography

Abensour, Miguel. "Against the Sovereignty of Philosophy over Politics: Arendt's Reading of Plato's Cave Allegory." Translated by Martin Breaugh. *Social Research* 74, no. 4 (2007): 955–82. doi:10.2307/40972036.

– "Le contre-Hobbes de Pierre Clastres." In *L'esprit des lois sauvages: Pierre Clastres ou une nouvelle anthropologie politique*, edited by Miguel Abensour, 115–44. Paris: Éditions du Seuil, 1987.

– *De la compacité: architecture et régimes totalitaire*. Paris: Sens & Tonka, 1997.

– "De quel retour s'agit-il?" *Les Cahiers de Philosophie* 18 (1994): 5–7.

– *Democracy Against the State: Marx and the Machiavellian Moment*. Translated by Max Blechman and Martin Breaugh. Cambridge, UK: Polity Press, 2011.

– ed. *L'esprit des lois sauvages: Pierre Clastres ou une nouvelle anthropologie politique*. Paris: Éditions du Seuil, 1987.

– *Hannah Arendt contre la philosophie politique?* Paris: Sens & Tonka, 2006.

– "L'histoire de l'utopie et le destin de sa critique I." *Textures* 6 (1973): 3–26.

– "L'histoire de l'utopie et le destin de sa critique II." *Textures* 7 (1974): 55–81.

– "L'homme est un animal utopique: entretien avec Miguel Abensour." *Mouvements* 45–46 (August 2006): 72–86.

– *Lettre d'un "Révoltiste" à Marcel Gauchet converti à la "politique normale."* Paris: Sens & Tonka, 2005.

– "Machiavel: le grand penseur du désordre, entretien avec Miguel Abensour." *Le Monde*, 4 October 2008.

– "Le nouvel esprit utopique." *Cahiers Bernard Lazare* no. 128–130 (1991): 132–63.

– "Philosophie politique critique et émancipation?" *Politique et Sociétés* 22, no. 3 (2003): 119–42. doi:10.7202/008853ar.

– *Pour une philosophie politique critique*. Paris: Sens & Tonka, 2009.

– "Présentation." *Cahiers de Philosophie Politique* 1 (1983): 1–8.

– *Le procès des maîtres rêveurs*. Arles, France: Sulliver, 2000.

– *Rire des lois, du magistrat et des dieux: l'impulsion Saint-Just*. Lyon, France: Horlieu, 2005.

– "To Think Utopia Otherwise:" Translated by Bettina Bergo. *Graduate Faculty Philosophy Journal* 20–21, no. 1–2 (1998): 251–79. doi:10.5840/gfpj199820/212/115.

– *L'utopie de Thomas More à Walter Benjamin*. Paris: Sens & Tonka, 2000.

– "William Morris: The Politics of Romance." In *Revolutionary Romanticism*, ed. Max Blechman, 125–61. San Francisco: City Lights Books, 1999.

Adams, Suzi. *Castoriadis's Ontology: Being and Creation*. New York: Fordham University Press, 2011.

Adorno, Theodor. *Negative Dialectics*. Translated by E.B. Ashton. New York: Routledge, 1973.

Althusser, Louis. *For Marx*. Translated by Ben Brewster. London: Verso, 2006.

– *The Future Lasts Forever: A Memoir*. Translated by Richard Veasey. New York: New Press, 1993.

– "Ideology and Ideological State Apparatuses." In *"Lenin and Philosophy" and Other Essays*. Translated by Ben Brewster, 127–86. London: New Left Books, 1971.

Althusser, Louis, and Étienne Balibar. *Reading Capital*. Translated by Ben Brewster. London: Verso, 1997.

Andreotti, Libero. "Play-Tactics of the Internationale Situationniste." *October* 91 (Winter 2000): 36–58.

Aradau, Claudia. "Only Aporias to Offer? Étienne Balibar's Politics and the Ambiguity of War." *New Formations* 58 (June 2006): 39–46.

Arendt, Hannah. "The Concept of History." In *Between Past and Future: Eight Exercises in Political Thought*, 41–90. New York: Penguin Books, 1993.

– *The Human Condition*. 2nd ed. Chicago: University of Chicago Press, 1998.

– "Introduction into Politics." In *The Promise of Politics*, edited by Jerome Kohn, 93–200. New York: Schocken Books, 2005.

– *Lectures on Kant's Political Philosophy*. Edited by Ronald Beiner. Chicago: University of Chicago Press, 1982.

– *The Life of the Mind*, vol. 1, *Thinking*. San Diego: Harcourt, 1978.

– *The Life of the Mind*, vol. 2, *Willing*. San Diego: Harcourt, 1978.

– *On Revolution*. New York: Viking Press, 1965.

– "On Violence." In *Crises of the Republic*, 103–98. New York: Harcourt Brace Jovanovich, 1972.

– "Thinking and Moral Considerations." In *Responsibility and Judgment*, edited by Jerome Kohn, 159–89. New York: Schocken Books, 2003.

– "Thoughts on Politics and Revolution: A Commentary." In *Crises of the Republic*, 199–233. New York: Harcourt Brace Jovanovich, 1972.

– "Totalitarian Imperialism: Reflections on the Hungarian Revolution." *Journal of Politics* 20, no. 1 (1958): 5–43.

– "The Tradition of Political Thought." In *The Promise of Politics*, edited by Jerome Kohn, 40–62. New York: Schocken Books, 2005.

– "Truth and Politics." In *Between Past and Future: Eight Exercises in Political Thought*, 227–64. New York: Penguin Books, 1993.

– "Understanding and Politics (The Difficulties of Understanding)." In *Essays in Understanding 1930–1954: Formation, Exile, and Totalitarianism*, edited by Jerome Kohn, 307–27. New York: Schocken Books, 2005.

– "What Is Freedom?" In *Between Past and Future: Eight Exercises in Political Thought*, 142–69. New York: Penguin Books, 1977.

– "'What Remains? The Language Remains': A Conversation with Günter Gaus." In *Essays in Understanding 1930–1954: Formation, Exile, and Totalitarianism*, edited by Jerome Kohn, 1–23. New York: Schocken Books, 1994.

Aristotle. *The Politics*. Translated by Carnes Lord. Chicago: University of Chicago Press, 1995.

Arnason, Johann. "Culture and Imaginary Significations." *Thesis Eleven* 22 (January 1989): 25–45.

Artous, Antoine. *Démocratie, citoyenneté, émancipation*. Paris: Syllepse, 2010.

Badiou, Alain. *The Communist Hypothesis*. Translated by David Macey and Steve Corcoran. London: Verso, 2010.

– *Ethics: An Essay on the Understanding of Evil*. Translated by Peter Hallward. London: Verso, 2001.

– *Metapolitics*. Translated by Jason Barker. London: Verso, 2005.

Balibar, Étienne. "Althusser and the Rue d'Ulm." Translated by David Fernbach. *New Left Review* 58 (August 2009): 91–107.

– "Ambiguous Universality." In *Politics and the Other Scene*. Translated by Chris Turner, 146–76. London: Verso, 2002.

– *Cinq études de materialisme historique*. Paris: F. Maspero, 1974.

– "De Charonne à Vitry." *Le Nouvel Observateur* (9–15 March 1981); reprinted in *Les frontières de la démocratie*, 19–34. Paris: Découverte, 1992.

– "La démocratie conflictuelle et le théorème de Machiavel." In *L'Europe, l'Amérique, la guerre: réflexions sur la médiation européenne*. Paris: La Découverte, 2003.

– *Equaliberty: Political Essays, 1989–2009*. Translated by James Ingram. Durham, NC: Duke University Press, 2014.

– "Foucault and Marx: The Question of Nominalism." In *Michel Foucault, Philosopher*, edited by T.J. Armstrong, 38–56. New York: Routledge, 1992.

– *Les frontières de la démocratie*. Paris: Découverte, 1992.

– "Gewalt: violence et pouvoir dans la théorie marxiste." In *Violence et civilité: Wellek Library lectures et autres essais de philosophie politique*. Paris: Galilée, 2010.

– "The Infinite Contradiction." Translated by Jean-Marc Poisson and Jacques Lezra. *Yale French Studies* no. 88 (January 1995): 142–64. doi:10.2307/2930105.
– "Is There a 'Neo-Racism'?" In *Race, Nation, Class: Ambiguous Identities*. Translated by Chris Turner, 17–28. London: Verso, 1991.
– "Un jacobin nommé Marx? Liberté, égalité, fraternité: à chacun de ces trois mots de la devise républicaine se rattache un moment de la pensée de Marx." *Magazine Littéraire* 258 (October 1988): 66–9.
– "Lénine et Gandhi: une rencontre manquée?" In *Violence et civilité: Wellek Library lectures et autres essais de philosophie politique*, 305–21. Paris: Galilée, 2010.
– *Masses, Classes, Ideas: Studies on Politics and Philosophy Before and After Marx*. Translated by James Swenson. New York: Routledge, 1994.
– "Le moment messianique de Marx." In *Violence et civilité: Wellek Library lectures et autres essais de philosophie politique*, 243–63. Paris: Galilée, 2010.
– *On the Dictatorship of the Proletariat*. Translated by Grahame Lock. London: New Left Books, 1977.
– "On the Dictatorship of the Proletariat." Contribution to the 22nd Congress of the French Communist Party, orig. pub. in *L'Humanité*, 22 October 1976. In *On the Dictatorship of the Proletariat*. Translated by Grahame Lock. London: New Left Books, 1977.
– *The Philosophy of Marx*. Translated by Chris Turner. London: Verso, 1995.
– "'Rights of Man' and 'Rights of the Citizen': The Modern Dialectic of Freedom and Equality?" In *Masses, Classes, Ideas: Studies on Politics and Philosophy Before and After Marx*. Translated by James Swenson, 39–59. New York: Routledge, 1994.
– *Spinoza and Politics*. Translated by Peter Snowdon. London: Verso, 1998.
– "Stratégies de civilité." In *Violence et civilité: Wellek Library lectures et autres essais de philosophie politique*. Paris: Galilée, 2010.
– "Sujets ou citoyens? (pour l'égalité)." *Les Temps Modernes* 452–4 (May 1984): 1726–53.
– "Three Concepts of Politics." In *Politics and the Other Scene*. Translated by Chris Turner, 1–39. London: Verso, 2002.
– "Toward a Politics of the Universal." *Graduate Faculty Philosophy Journal* 29, no. 1 (2008): 5–25. doi:10.5840/gfpj20082911.
– "Violence and Civility: On the Limits of Political Anthropology." Translated by Stephanie Bundy. *Differences* 20, no. 2–3 (2009): 9–35. doi:10.1215/10407391-2009-002.
– "Violence et politique: quelques questions." In *Le passage des frontières: autour du travail de Jacques Derrida*, edited by Marie-Louise Mallet, 203–10. Paris: Galilée, 1994.

Balibar, Étienne, and Immanuel Wallerstein. *Race, Nation, Class: Ambiguous Identities*. Translated by Chris Turner. London: Verso, 1991.

Beiner, Ronald. "Hannah Arendt on Judging." In *Lectures on Kant's Political Philosophy*, edited by Ronald Beiner, 89–156. Chicago: University of Chicago Press, 1982.

Benhabib, Seyla. *The Reluctant Modernism of Hannah Arendt*. Thousand Oaks, CA: Sage Publications, 1996.

Bennett, Jane. *Vibrant Matter: A Political Ecology of Things*. Durham, NC: Duke University Press, 2010.

Best, Steven, and Douglas Kellner. *The Postmodern Turn*. New York: Guilford Press, 1997.

Bosteels, Bruno. "Rancière's Leftism, Or, Politics and Its Discontents." In *Jacques Rancière: History, Politics, Aesthetics*, edited by Gabriel Rockhill and Philip Watts, 158–75. Durham, NC: Duke University Press, 2009.

Bouretz, Pierre. "Pierre Clastres: la société contre l'État." In *Dictionnaire des œuvres politiques*. Paris: Presses Universitaires de France, 1986.

Bracken, Len. *Guy Debord: Revolutionary*. Venice, CA: Feral House, 1997.

Breaugh, Martin. "Critique de la domination, pensée de l'émancipation: sur la philosophie politique de Miguel Abensour." *Politique et Sociétés* 22, no. 3 (2003): 45–69. doi:10.7202/008850ar.

– *The Plebeian Experience: A Discontinuous History of Political Freedom*. Translated by Lazer Lederhendler. New York: Columbia University Press, 2013.

Breaugh, Martin, and Francis Dupuis-Déri, eds. *La démocratie au-delà du libéralisme: perspectives critiques*. Montreal: Athéna Éditions, 2009.

Breckman, Warren. "Lefort and the Symbolic Dimension." In *Claude Lefort: Thinker of the Political*, edited by Martín Plot, 176–85. New York: Palgrave Macmillan, 2013.

Breckman, Warren, Peter Gordon, and Dirk Moses, eds. *The Modernist Imagination: Intellectual History and Critical Theory*. New York: Berghahn Books, 2009.

Buchstein, Hubertus. "Reviving Randomness for Political Rationality: Elements of a Theory of Aleatory Democracy." *Constellations* 17, no. 3 (2010): 435–54.

Caillois, Roger. *Man, Play, and Games*. Translated by Meyer Barash. New York: Free Press of Glencoe, 1961.

Canetti, Elias. *Crowds and Power*. Translated by Carol Stewart. New York: Farrar, Straus, and Giroux, 1984.

Carman, Taylor, and Mark Hansen, eds. *The Cambridge Companion to Merleau-Ponty*. Cambridge: Cambridge University Press, 2005.

Castoriadis, Cornelius. "Aeschylean Anthropogony and Sophoclean Self-Creation of *Anthrōpos*." In *Figures of the Thinkable*. Translated by Helen Arnold. Stanford, CA: Stanford University Press, 2007.

– *Ce qui fait la Grèce 1: d'Homère à Héraclite*. Paris: Seuil, 2004.
– *Ce qui fait la Grèce 2: la cité et les lois*. Paris: Seuil, 2008.
– *Ce qui fait la Grèce 3: Thucydide, la force et le droit*. Paris: Seuil, 2011.
– *Cornelius Castoriadis, Political and Social Writings*. Translated and edited by David Ames Curtis. 3 vols. Minneapolis: University of Minnesota Press, 1988.
– "The Crisis of Culture and the State." In *Philosophy, Politics, Autonomy: Essays in Political Philosophy*. Edited by David Ames Curtis, 219–42. Oxford: Oxford University Press, 1991.
– *Crossroads in the Labyrinth*. Translated by Kate Soper and Martin Ryle. Cambridge, MA: MIT Press, 1984.
– *Devant la guerre*. Paris: Fayard, 1981.
– *Domaines de l'homme*. Paris: Seuil, 1986.
– *Fait et à faire*. Paris: Seuil, 1997.
– *Fenêtre sur le chaos*. Paris: Seuil, 2007.
– *Figures of the Thinkable*. Translated by Helen Arnold. Stanford, CA: Stanford University Press, 2007.
– "The Greeks and Modern Political Imaginary." In *World in Fragments: Writings on Politics, Society, Psychoanalysis, and the Imagination*. Translated and edited by David Ames Curtis. Stanford, CA: Stanford University Press, 1997.
– "The Greek *Polis* and the Creation of Autonomy." In *Philosophy, Politics, Autonomy: Essays in Political Philosophy*. Edited by David Ames Curtis, 81–124. Oxford: Oxford University Press, 1991.
– *Histoire et création: textes philosophiques inédits 1945–1967*. Paris: Seuil, 2009.
– *The Imaginary Institution of Society*. Translated by Kathleen Blamey. Cambridge, MA: MIT Press, 1987.
– *L'institution imaginaire de la société*. Paris: Seuil, 1975.
– *Le monde morcelé*. Paris: Seuil, 1990.
– *La montée de l'insignifiance*. Paris: Seuil, 1996.
– *On Plato's Statesman*. Translated and edited by David Ames Curtis. Stanford, CA: Stanford University Press, 2002.
– "Power, Politics, Autonomy." In *Philosophy, Politics, Autonomy: Essays in Political Philosophy*. Edited by David Ames Curtis, 143–74. Oxford: Oxford University Press, 1991.
– "Reflections on Racism." In *World in Fragments: Writings on Politics, Society, Psychoanalysis, and the Imagination*. Translated and edited by David Ames Curtis, 19–31. Stanford, CA: Stanford University Press, 1997.
– *A Society Adrift: Interviews and Debates, 1974–1997*. Edited by Enrique Escobar, Myrto Gondicas, and Pascal Vernay. Translated by Helen Arnold. New York: Fordham University Press, 2010.

– *Sujet et vérité dans le monde social-historique: séminaires 1986–87*. Paris: Seuil, 2002.
– "A Thoroughgoing Shakeup of All Forms of Social Life." In *Postscript on Insignificancy*. Translated and edited by Anonymous. E-Book, 2011. Available online at http://www.notbored.org/PSRTI.pdf.
Castoriadis, Cornelius, and Daniel Cohn-Bendit. *De l'écologie à l'autonomie*. Paris: Seuil, 1981.
Castoriadis, Cornelius, and MAUSS. *Démocratie et relativisme*. Paris: Mille et une nuits, 2010.
Castoriadis, Cornelius, and Daniel Mermet. *Post-scriptum sur l'insignifiance*. Paris: Éditions de l'aube, 1998.
Celikates, Robin. "Die Demokratisierung der Demokratie: Étienne Balibar über die Dialektik von konstituierender und konstituierter Macht." In *Das Politische Denken. Zeitgenössiche Positionen*, edited by Ulrich Bröckling and Robert Feustel, 59–76. Bielefeld, Germany: transcript, 2009.
Cervera-Marzal, Manuel. *Miguel Abensour, critique de la domination, pensée de l'émancipation*. Paris: Sens & Tonka, 2013.
Chambers, Samuel. *The Lessons of Rancière*. Oxford: Oxford University Press, 2013.
Christofferson, Michael Scott. *French Intellectuals Against the Left: The Antitotalitarian Moment of the 1970s*. New York: Berghahn Books, 2004.
Clastres, Pierre. "Archeology of Violence: War in Primitive Societies." In *Archeology of Violence*. Translated by Jeanine Herman, 139–68. New York: Semiotext(e), 1994.
– "Entre silence et dialogue." *L'Arc*, numéro spécial consacré à Claude Lévi-Strauss (1968): 76–8.
– "Entretien avec Pierre Clastres (14 décembre 1974)." *L'Anti-Mythes* 9 (1975): 1.
– "Freedom, Misfortune, the Unnameable." In *Archeology of Violence*. Translated by Jeanine Herman, 93–104. New York: Semiotext(e), 1994.
– "Marxists and Their Anthropology." In *Archeology of Violence*. Translated by Jeanine Herman, 127–38. New York: Semiotext(e), 1994.
– "Power in Primitive Societies." In *Archeology of Violence*. Translated by Jeanine Herman, 87–92. New York: Semiotext(e), 1994.
– "The Return to Enlightenment." In *Archeology of Violence*. Translated by Jeanine Herman, 119–26. New York: Semiotext(e), 1994.
– "Savage Ethnography (On Yanoama)." In *Archeology of Violence*. Translated by Jeanine Herman, 29–42. New York: Semiotext(e), 1994.
– *Society Against the State: Essays in Political Anthropology*. Translated by Robert Hurley. New York: Zone Books, 1987.

– "Sorrows of the Savage Warrior." In *Archeology of Violence.* Translated by Jeanine Herman, 169–200. New York: Semiotext(e), 1994.

Cohen, Jean. "The Self-Institution of Society and Representative Government: Can the Circle Be Squared?" *Thesis Eleven* 80 (February 2005): 9–37.

Connolly, William. "A Critique of Pure Politics." *Philosophy and Social Criticism* 23, no. 5 (1997): 1–26.

Coole, Diana. *Merleau-Ponty and Modern Politics after Anti-humanism.* Lanham, MD: Rowman & Littlefield, 2007.

– "Philosophy as Political Engagement: Revisiting Merleau-Ponty and Reopening the Communist Question." *Contemporary Political Theory* 2, no. 3 (2003): 327–50.

Cooper, Barry. *Merleau-Ponty and Marxism: From Terror to Reform.* Toronto: University of Toronto Press, 1979.

Crozier, Michel. *The Bureaucratic Phenomenon.* Chicago: University of Chicago Press, 1964.

– "French Students: A Letter from Nanterre-La Folie." *National Affairs*, no. 13 (1968).

Dean, Jodi. "Politics without Politics." *Parallax* 15, no. 3 (2009): 20–36. doi:10.1080/13534640902982579.

Debord, Guy. "L'architecture et le jeu." In *Œuvres*, 189–91. Paris: Gallimard, 2006.

– *Correspondence: The Foundation of the Situationist International (June 1957–August 1960).* Translated by Stuart Kendall and John McHale. Los Angeles: Semiotext(e), 2009.

– "Howls for Sade." In *Complete Cinematic Works: Scripts, Stills, Documents.* Translated and edited by Ken Knabb, 1–12. Oakland, CA: AK Press, 2003.

– "Introduction to a Critique of Urban Geography." In *Situationist International Anthology.* Rev. ed. Translated and edited by Ken Knabb, 8–12. Berkeley, CA: Bureau of Public Secrets, 2006.

– "One More Try if You Want to Be Situationists (The SI in and against Decomposition)." In *Guy Debord and the Situationist International: Texts and Documents.* Edited by Tom McDonough. Translated by John Shepley, 51–9. Cambridge, MA: MIT Press, 2003.

– "Perspectives for Conscious Changes in Everyday Life." In *Situationist International Anthology.* Rev. ed. Translated and edited by Ken Knabb, 90–9. Berkeley, CA: Bureau of Public Secrets, 2006.

– "Report on the Construction of Situations and on the International Situationist Tendency's Conditions of Organization and Action." In *Situationist International Anthology.* Rev. ed. Translated and edited by Ken Knabb, 25–43. Berkeley, CA: Bureau of Public Secrets, 2006.

– "Report to the Seventh SI Conference in Paris." In *The Real Split in the International*. Translated by John McHale, 130–41. London: Pluto Press, 2003.
– *The Society of the Spectacle*. Translated by Donald Nicholson-Smith. New York: Zone Books, 1994.
– "The Society of the Spectacle." In *Complete Cinematic Works: Scripts, Stills, Documents*. Translated and edited by Ken Knabb, 43–110. Oakland, CA: AK Press, 2003.
– "The Theory of Dérive." In *Situationist International Anthology*. Rev. ed. Translated and edited by Ken Knabb, 62–6. Berkeley, CA: Bureau of Public Secrets, 2006.
– "Theses on Cultural Revolution." In *Situationist International Anthology*. Rev. ed. Translated and edited by Ken Knabb, 53–4. Berkeley, CA: Bureau of Public Secrets, 2006.
de Certeau, Michel. *The Practice of Everyday Life*. Translated by Steven Rendall. Berkeley: University of California Press, 1984.
Déjacque, Joseph. *À bas les chefs*. Paris: Champe Libre, 1971.
Dillon, M.C. *Merleau-Ponty's Ontology*. Evanston, IL: Northwestern University Press, 1992.
Disch, Lisa Jane. *Hannah Arendt and the Limits of Philosophy*. Ithaca, NY: Cornell University Press, 1994.
Elster, Jon. "Obscurantisme dur et obscurantisme mou dans les sciences humaines et sociales." *Diogène* 1–2, no. 229–30 (2010): 231–47.
Fallada, Hans. *Every Man Dies Alone*. New York: Melville House Publishing, 2009.
Fischbach, Franck. "Le déni du social, deux exemples contemporains: Abensour et Rancière." *Recherches sur la Philosophie et le Langage* 28 (2012): 29–46.
Flynn, Bernard. "The Development of the Political Philosophy of Merleau-Ponty." *Continental Philosophy Review* 40, no. 2 (2007): 125–38.
– *The Philosophy of Claude Lefort: Interpreting the Political*. Evanston, IL: Northwestern University Press, 2005.
Foucault, Michel. "Politics and the Study of Discourse." In *The Foucault Effect: Studies in Governmentality*, edited by Graham Burchell, Colin Gordon, and Peter Miller. Chicago: University of Chicago Press, 1991.
Galbraith, John Kenneth. *The Affluent Society*. 4th rev. ed. New York: New American Library, 1985.
Gauchet, Marcel. *La condition historique*. Paris: Stock, 2003.
– *La démocratie contre elle-même*. Paris: Gallimard-Tel, 2001.
– *The Disenchantment of the World: A Political History of Religion*. Translated by Oscar Borge. Princeton, NJ: Princeton University Press, 1997.

Gonzalez, Horacio. "Le processus de libération des textes." In *Critique de la politique: autour de Miguel Abensour*, edited by Anne Kupiec and Étienne Tassin. Paris: Sens & Tonka, 2006.

Habermas, Jürgen. *Between Facts and Norms: Contributions to a Discourse Theory of Law and Democracy*. Translated by William Regh. Cambridge, MA: MIT Press, 1996.

– *The Philosophical Discourse of Modernity: Twelve Lectures*. Translated by Frederick Lawrence. Cambridge, MA: MIT Press, 1987.

– *The Theory of Communicative Action*, vol. 1, *Reason and the Rationalization of Society*. Translated by Thomas McCarthy. Boston: Beacon Press, 1984.

Hallward, Peter. "Jacques Rancière and the Subversion of Mastery." *Paragraph* 28, no. 1 (2005): 26–45.

– "Staging Equality: Rancière's Theatrocracy and the Limits of Anarchic Equality." In *Jacques Rancière: History, Politics, Aesthetics*, edited by Gabriel Rockhill and Philip Watts, 140–57. Durham, NC: Duke University Press, 2009.

Harvey, David. *The Condition of Postmodernity: An Enquiry into the Origins of Cultural Change*. Oxford: Blackwell, 1989.

Hass, Lawrence. *Merleau-Ponty's Philosophy*. Bloomington: Indiana University Press, 2008.

Henckel von Donnersmarck, Florian. *The Lives of Others*. Film. Sony Pictures, 2006.

Hewlett, Nick. *Badiou, Balibar, Rancière: Rethinking Emancipation*. New York: Continuum Books, 2007.

Hobbes, Thomas. *Leviathan*. London: Penguin Books, 1968.

Holman, Christopher. "Dialectics and Distinction: Reconsidering Hannah Arendt's Critique of Marx." *Contemporary Political Theory* 10, no. 3 (2011): 332–53.

– *Politics as Radical Creation: Herbert Marcuse and Hannah Arendt on Political Performativity*. Toronto: University of Toronto Press, 2013.

Honig, Bonnie. *Political Theory and the Displacement of Politics*. Ithaca, NY: Cornell University Press, 1993.

– "Toward an Agonistic Feminism: Hannah Arendt and the Politics of Identity." In *Feminists Theorize the Political*, edited by Judith Butler and Joan Scott, 215–35. New York: Routledge, 1992.

Horowitz, Gad. "The Foucaultian Impasse: No Sex, No Self, No Revolution." *Political Theory* 5, no. 1 (1987): 61–80.

Howard, Dick. *The Marxian Legacy*. London: Macmillan, 1977.

– *The Primacy of the Political: A History of Political Thought from the Greek to the French & American Revolutions*. New York: Columbia University Press, 2010.

Huizinga, Johan. *Homo Ludens: A Study of the Play-Element in Culture*. Boston: Beacon Press, 1960.

Ingram, James. "The Politics of Claude Lefort's Political: Between Liberalism and Democracy." *Thesis Eleven* 87 (November 2006): 33–50.

– "What Is a 'Right to Have Rights'? Three Images of the Politics of Human Rights." *American Political Science Review* 102, no. 4 (2008): 401–16.

Jappe, Anselm. *Guy Debord*. Translated by Donald Nicholson-Smith. Berkeley: University of California Press, 1999.

Jay, Martin. *Downcast Eyes: The Denigration of Vision in Twentieth-Century French Thought*. Berkeley: University of California Press, 1993.

– *Marxism and Totality: The Adventures of a Concept from Lukács to Habermas*. Berkeley: University of California Press, 1984.

Kalyvas, Andreas. "The Institution of the Social: Lefort and Castoriadis." Paper delivered at *Claude Lefort: An Intellectual and Political Memorial*, New School for Social Research, New York, 30 October 2010.

Kantorowicz, Ernst. *The King's Two Bodies: A Study in Mediaeval Political Theology*. Princeton, NJ: Princeton University Press, 1997.

Kaufmann, Vincent. *Guy Debord: Revolution in the Service of Poetry*. Translated by Robert Bononno. Minneapolis: University of Minnesota Press, 2006.

Khayati, Mustapha. "Captive Words: Preface to a Situationist Dictionary." In *Situationist International Anthology*. Rev. ed. Translated and edited by Ken Knabb, 222–8. Berkeley, CA: Bureau of Public Secrets, 2006.

Klein, Naomi. *No Logo: Taking Aim at the Brand Bullies*. Toronto: Vintage Canada, 2000.

Knabb, Ken, ed. *Situationist International Anthology*. Rev. ed. Berkeley, CA: Bureau of Public Secrets, 2006.

Kropotkin, Peter. *Mutual Aid: A Factor in Evolution*. London: Allen Lane, 1972.

Kruks, Sonia. *The Political Philosophy of Merleau-Ponty*. Atlantic Highlands, NJ: Humanities Press, 1981.

Labelle, Gilles, and Daniel Tanguay. "Le retour de la philosophie politique en France." *Politique et Sociétés* 22, no. 3 (2003): 3–7.

Laclau, Ernesto. *On Populist Reason*. London: Verso, 2005.

Laclau, Ernesto, and Chantal Mouffe. *Hegemony and Socialist Strategy: Towards a Radical Democratic Politics*. London: Verso, 1985.

Lavau, Georges. *À quoi sert le Parti communiste français?* Paris: Fayard, 1981.

Lefebvre, Henri. *Critique of Everyday Life*, vol. 1. Translated by John Moore. London: Verso, 1991.

Lefort, Claude. "L'analyse marxiste et le fascisme." In *Le temps présent: écrits 1945–2005*, 31–6. Paris: Belin, 2007.

– *Democracy and Political Theory*. Translated by David Macey. Cambridge, UK: Polity Press, 1988.
– "Démocratie et avènement d'un 'lieu vide.'" In *Le temps présent: écrits 1945–2005*, 461–9. Paris: Belin, 2007.
– *Éléments d'une critique de la bureaucratie*. Paris: Gallimard, 1979.
– *Essais sur le politique*. Paris: Éditions du Seuil, 1986.
– *Les formes de l'histoire*. Paris: Gallimard, 1978.
– "Hannah Arendt and the Question of the Political." In *Democracy and Political Theory*. Translated by David Macey, 45–55. Cambridge, UK: Polity Press, 1988.
– *Un homme en trop: réflexions sur "L'archipel du goulag."* Paris: Éditions du Seuil, 1976.
– *L'invention démocratique: les limites de la domination totalitaire*. Paris: Fayard, 1981.
– "Libéralisme et démocratie." In *Le temps présent: écrits 1945–2005*, 745–59. Paris: Belin, 2007.
– "La liberté à l'ère du relativisme." In *Le temps présent: écrits 1945–2005*, 631–56. Paris: Belin, 2007.
– "La logique totalitaire." In *L'invention démocratique: les limites de la domination totalitaire*, 85–106. Paris: Fayard, 1981.
– *Machiavelli in the Making*. Translated by Michael Smith. Evanston, IL: Northwestern University Press, 2012.
– "Les pays coloniaux: analyse structurelle et stratégie révolutionnaire." In *Le temps présent: écrits 1945–2005*, 49–76. Paris: Belin, 2007.
– "The Permanence of the Theologico-Political?" In *Democracy and Political Theory*. Translated by David Macey, 213–55. Cambridge, UK: Polity Press, 1988.
– *The Political Forms of Modern Society: Bureaucracy, Democracy, Totalitarianism*, edited by John Thompson. Cambridge, MA: MIT Press, 1986.
– "Politics and Human Rights." In *The Political Forms of Modern Society: Bureaucracy, Democracy, Totalitarianism*, edited by John Thompson, 239–72. Cambridge, MA: MIT Press, 1986.
– "The Question of Democracy." In *Democracy and Political Theory*. Translated by David Macey, 9–20. Cambridge, UK: Polity Press, 1988.
– "Le relativisme déchaîne l'imbécillité." In *Le temps présent: écrits 1945–2005*, 683–8. Paris: Belin, 2007.
– *Le temps présent: écrits 1945–2005*. Paris: Belin, 2007.
– "Thinking with and against Hannah Arendt." *Social Research* 69, no. 2 (2002): 447–59.

Lenin, Vladimir. "What Is to Be Done?" In *Selected Works in Three Volumes*, vol. 1, 97–256. New York: International Publishers, 1967.

Lévêque, Pierre, and Pierre Vidal-Naquet. *Cleisthenes the Athenian: An Essay on the Representation of Space and Time in Greek Political Thought from the End of the Sixth Century to the Death of Plato*. Translated by David Ames Curtis. New York: Humanity Books, 1996.

Lévi-Strauss, Claude. *Tristes tropiques*. Translated by John Weightman and Doreen Weightman. New York: Atheneum, 1973.

Levin, David Michael. "Justice in the Flesh." In *Ontology and Alterity in Merleau-Ponty*, edited by Galen Johnson and Michael Smith, 35–44. Evanston, IL: Northwestern University Press, 1990.

Levinas, Emmanuel. *Totality and Infinity: An Essay on Exteriority*. Translated by Alphonso Lingus. Boston: Martinus Nijhoff, 1979.

Lilla, Mark. "The Legitimacy of the Liberal Age." In *New French Thought: Political Philosophy*, edited by Mark Lilla, 3–34. Princeton, NJ: Princeton University Press, 1994.

– ed. *New French Thought: Political Philosophy*. Princeton, NJ: Princeton University Press, 1994.

Little, Adrian, and Moya Lloyd, eds. *The Politics of Radical Democracy*. Edinburgh: Edinburgh University Press, 2009.

Loraux, Nicole. *The Divided City: On Memory and Forgetting in Ancient Athens*. Translated by Corinne Pache and Jeff Fort. New York: Zone Books, 2001.

Machiavelli, Niccolò. *Discourses on Livy*. Translated by Harvey Mansfield and Nathan Tarcov. Chicago: University of Chicago Press, 1996.

– *Discourses on the First Decade of Titus Livius*. Translated by Ninian Thomson. London: Kegan Paul, 1883.

– *The Prince*. Translated by Peter Bondanella. Oxford: Oxford University Press, 1984.

Maggiori, Robert. "L'utopie de Miguel Abensour." *Libération* (11 June 2009). Available online at http://www.liberation.fr/livres/2009/06/11/l-utopie-de-miguel-abensour_564086.

Manent, Pierre. *Naissances de la politique moderne: Machiavel, Hobbes, Rousseau*. Paris: Payot, 1977.

– "The Return of Political Philosophy." *First Things* no. 103 (May 2000): 15–22.

– *Tocqueville and the Nature of Democracy*. Translated by John Waggoner. Lanham, MD: Rowman & Littlefield, 1996.

– *A World beyond Politics? A Defense of the Nation State*. Translated by Marc LePain. Princeton, NJ: Princeton University Press, 2006.

Marchart, Oliver. *Post-foundational Political Thought: Political Difference in Nancy, Lefort, Badiou and Laclau*. Edinburgh: Edinburgh University Press, 2007.

Marcus, Greil. *Lipstick Traces: A Secret History of the Twentieth Century*. Cambridge, MA: Harvard University Press, 1989.

Marx, Karl. *Capital*, vol. 1. Translated by Ben Fowkes. New York: Penguin Books, 1981.
– *The Civil War in France*. Moscow: Foreign Languages Publishing House, 1963.
– *Critique of Hegel's "Philosophy of Right."* Translated by Annette Jolin and Joseph O'Malley. Cambridge: Cambridge University Press, 1972.
May, Todd. *The Political Thought of Jacques Rancière: Creating Equality*. University Park: Pennsylvania State University Press, 2008.
– "Rancière in South Carolina." In *Jacques Rancière: History, Politics, Aesthetics*, edited by Gabriel Rockhill and Philip Watts, 105–19. Durham, NV: Duke University Press, 2009.
McNeilly, F.S. *The Anatomy of Leviathan*. London: Macmillan, 1968.
Melançon, Jérôme. "Miguel Abensour, critique de la politique." *Politique et Sociétés* 28, no. 1 (2009): 229–47. doi:10.7202/001731ar.
Merleau-Ponty, Maurice. *Adventures of the Dialectic*. Translated by Joseph Bien. Evanston, IL: Northwestern University Press, 1973.
– "Everywhere and Nowhere." In *Signs*. Translated by Richard McCleary, 126–58. Evanston, IL: Northwestern University Press, 1964.
– "Eye and Mind." In *The Primacy of Perception, and Other Essays on Phenomenological Psychology, the Philosophy of Art, History, and Politics*. Translated by Carleton Dallery, 159–90. Evanston, IL: Northwestern University Press, 1964.
– *Humanism and Terror: An Essay on the Communist Problem*. Translated by John O'Neill. Boston: Beacon Press, 1969.
– *Institution and Passivity: Course Notes from the Collège de France (1954–1955)*. Translated by Leonard Lawlor and Heath Massey. Evanston, IL: Northwestern University Press, 2010.
– "Institution in Personal and Public History." In *In Praise of Philosophy and Other Essays*. Translated by John Wild and James Edie, 107–13. Evanston, IL: Northwestern University Press, 1963.
– "Marxism and Philosophy." In *Sense and Non-sense*. Translated by Hubert Dreyfus and Patricia Dreyfus, 125–38. Evanston, IL: Northwestern University Press, 1964.
– "Materials for a Theory of History." In *In Praise of Philosophy and Other Essays*. Translated by John Wild and James Edie, 95–106. Evanston, IL: Northwestern University Press, 1963.
– "A Note on Machiavelli." In *Signs*. Translated by Richard McCleary, 211–23. Evanston, IL: Northwestern University Press, 1964.
– *Phenomenology of Perception*. Translated by Colin Smith. New York: Routledge, 2002.

– "The Philosopher and His Shadow." In *Signs*. Translated by Richard McCleary, 159–81. Evanston, IL: Northwestern University Press, 1964.
– "Philosophy and Non-Philosophy since Hegel." *Telos* 29 (September 1976): 43–105. doi:10.3817/0976029043.
– "The Primacy of Perception and Its Philosophical Consequences." In *The Primacy of Perception, and Other Essays on Phenomenological Psychology, the Philosophy of Art, History, and Politics*. Translated by James M. Edie, 12–42. Evanston, IL: Northwestern University Press, 1964.
– *The Prose of the World*. Ed. Claude Lefort. Translated by John O'Neill. Evanston, IL: Northwestern University Press, 1973.
– "Reading Montaigne." In *Signs*. Translated by Richard McCleary, 198–210. Evanston, IL: Northwestern University Press, 1964.
– *Themes from the Lectures at the Collège de France, 1952–1960*. Translated by John O'Neill. Evanston, IL: Northwestern University Press, 1970.
– "An Unpublished Text by Maurice Merleau-Ponty: A Prospectus of His Work." In *The Primacy of Perception, and Other Essays on Phenomenological Psychology, the Philosophy of Art, History, and Politics*. Translated by Arleen Dallery, 3–11. Evanston, IL: Northwestern University Press, 1964.
– *The Visible and the Invisible*. Ed. Claude Lefort. Translated by Alphonso Lingus. Evanston, IL: Northwestern University Press, 1968.
– "Working Notes." In *The Visible and the Invisible*. Edited by Claude Lefort. Translated by Alphonso Lingus, 165–276. Evanston, IL: Northwestern University Press, 1968.
– *The World of Perception*. Translated by Oliver Davis. New York: Routledge, 2004.
Miller, James. *History and Human Existence: From Marx to Merleau-Ponty*. Berkeley: University of California Press, 1979.
Montesquieu, Charles. *Considerations on the Causes of the Grandeur and Decadence of the Romans*. Translated by Jehu Baker. New York: D. Appleton, 1894.
Morin, Edgar, Claude Lefort, and Cornelius Castoriadis. *Mai 68 la brèche: suivi de vingt ans après*. Paris: Complexe, 1988.
Morris, William. *News from Nowhere and Other Writings*, edited by Clive Wilmer. New York: Penguin Books, 1993.
Mouffe, Chantal. *The Democratic Paradox*. London: Verso, 2000.
Nadir, Christine. "Utopian Studies, Environmental Literature, and the Legacy of an Idea: Educating Desire in Miguel Abensour and Ursula K. Le Guin." *Utopian Studies* 21, no. 1 (2010): 24–56. doi:10.1353/utp.0.0014.
O'Neill, John. *Perception, Expression and History: The Social Phenomenology of Maurice Merleau-Ponty*. Evanston, IL: Northwestern University Press, 1970.
Panagia, Davide. "The Improper Event: On Jacques Rancière's Mannerism." *Citizenship Studies* 13, no. 3 (2009): 297–308. doi:10.1080/13621020902850700.

Parekh, Bhikhu. *Hannah Arendt and the Search for a New Political Philosophy*. London: Macmillan, 1981.
Passerin d'Entrèves, Maurizio. *The Political Philosophy of Hannah Arendt*. London: Routledge, 1994.
Pettit, Philip. "Representation, Responsive and Indicative." *Constellations* 17, no. 3 (2010): 426–34.
Pitkin, Hanna. *The Attack of the Blob: Hannah Arendt's Concept of the Social*. Chicago: University of Chicago Press, 1998.
Plant, Sadie. *The Most Radical Gesture: The Situationist International in a Post-modern Age*. London: Routledge, 1992.
Plot, Martín, ed. *Claude Lefort: Thinker of the Political*. New York: Palgrave Macmillan, 2013.
– "Our Element: Flesh and Democracy in Merleau-Ponty." *Continental Philosophy Review* 45, no. 2 (2012): 235–59.
Poirier, Nicolas. *L'ontologie politique de Castoriadis: création et institution*. Paris: Payot, 2011.
Poster, Mark. *Existential Marxism in Postwar France: From Sartre to Althusser*. Princeton, NJ: Princeton University Press, 1975.
Power, Nina. "Which Equality? Badiou and Rancière in Light of Ludwig Feuerbach." *Parallax* 15, no. 3 (2009): 63–80. doi:10.1080/13534640902982744.
Rancière, Jacques. "Afterword/The Method of Equality: An Answer to Some Questions." In *Jacques Rancière: History, Politics, Aesthetics*, edited by Gabriel Rockhill and Philip Watts, 273–88. Durham, NC: Duke University Press, 2009.
– *Althusser's Lesson*. Translated by Emiliano Battista. New York: Continuum, 2011.
– "Democracy, Dissensus and the Aesthetics of Class Struggle: An Exchange with Jacques Rancière." *Historical Materialism* 13, no. 4 (2005): 285–301.
– *Disagreement: Politics and Philosophy*. Translated by Julie Rose. Minneapolis: University of Minnesota Press, 1999.
– *The Emancipated Spectator*. Translated by Gregory Elliott. London: Verso, 2009.
– "A Few Remarks on the Method of Jacques Rancière." *Parallax* 15, no. 3 (2009): 114–23. doi:10.1080/13534640902982983.
– *Hatred of Democracy*. Translated by Steve Corcoran. London: Verso, 2006.
– *The Ignorant Schoolmaster: Five Lessons in Intellectual Emancipation*. Translated by Kristin Ross. Stanford, CA: Stanford University Press, 1991.
– *On the Shores of Politics*. Translated by Liz Heron. London: Verso, 1995.
– *The Philosopher and His Poor*. Translated by John Drury, Corinne Oster, and Andrew Parker. Durham, NC: Duke University Press, 2003.
– "Politics, Identification and Subjectivization." In *The Identity in Question*, edited by John Rajchman, 63–70. New York: Routledge, 1995.

– *Short Voyages to the Land of the People*. Translated by James Swenson. Stanford, CA: Stanford University Press, 2003.
– "Ten Theses on Politics." Translated by Rachel Bowlby and Davide Panagia. *Theory & Event* 5, no. 3 (2001). doi:10.1353/tae.2001.0028.
Rancière, Jacques, and Davide Panagia. "Dissenting Words: A Conversation with Jacques Rancière." *Diacritics* 30, no. 2 (2000): 113–26. doi:10.2307/1566474.
Raspaud, Jean-Jacques, and Jean-Pierre Voyer. *L'Internationale Situationniste: chronologie, bibliographie, protagonistes*. Paris: Champ Libre, 1972.
Rawls, John. *Political Liberalism*. New York: Columbia University Press, 1995.
Raynaud, Philippe. *L'extrême gauche plurielle*. Paris: Perrin, 2010.
Reid, Don. "Étienne Balibar: Algeria, Althusser, and *Altereuropéenisation*." *South Central Review* 25, no. 3 (2008): 68–85. doi:10.1353/scr.0.0021.
Reynolds, Jack. *Merleau-Ponty and Derrida: Intertwining Embodiment and Alterity*. Athens: Ohio University Press, 2004.
Rockhill, Gabriel. "The Politics of Aesthetics: Political History and the Hermeneutics of Art." In *Jacques Rancière: History, Politics, Aesthetics*, edited by Gabriel Rockhill and Philip Watts, 195–215. Durham, NC: Duke University Press, 2009.
Rockhill, Gabriel, and Philip Watts, eds. *Jacques Rancière: History, Politics, Aesthetics*. Durham, NC: Duke University Press, 2009.
Rosanvallon, Pierre. *Counter-Democracy: Politics in an Age of Distrust*. Translated by Arthur Goldhammer. Cambridge: Cambridge University Press, 2008.
– "Sur quelques chemins de traverse de la pensée du politique en France: un entretien avec Pierre Rosanvallon." *Raisons Politiques* 1 (February 2001): 49–62.
Rousseau, Jean-Jacques. "Of the Social Contract." In *Of the Social Contract and Other Political Writings*, 5–133. New York: Penguin Books, 2012.
Sahlins, Marshall. *Stone Age Economics*. Chicago: Aldine-Anderton, 1972.
Santos, Boaventura de Sousa, ed. *Democratizing Democracy: Beyond the Liberal Democratic Canon*. London: Verso, 2005.
Sartre, Jean Paul. *Being and Nothingness: An Essay on Phenomenological Ontology*. Translated by Hazel Barnes. New York: Washington Square Press, 1966.
– "Merleau-Ponty Vivant." In *The Debate between Sartre and Merleau-Ponty*, edited by Jon Stewart, 565–625. Evanston, IL: Northwestern University Press, 1998.
Schaap, Andrew. *Political Reconciliation*. New York: Routledge, 2005.
– "Political Theory and the Agony of Politics." *Political Studies Review* 5, no. 1 (2007): 56–76.
Schmidt, James. *Maurice Merleau-Ponty: Between Phenomenology and Structuralism*. New York: St. Martin's Press, 1985.

Shepard, Benjamin. "If I Can't Dance: Play, Creativity, and Social Movements." PhD Dissertation, City University of New York, 2006.

– "Play, Creativity, and the New Community Organizing." *Journal of Progressive Human Services* 16, no. 2 (2005): 47–69.

Shepard, Benjamin, L.M. Bogad, and Stephen Duncombe. "Performing vs. the Insurmountable: Theatrics, Activism, and Social Movements." *Liminalities: A Journal of Performance Studies* 4, no. 3 (2008): 1–30.

Sim, Stuart. *Post-Marxism: An Intellectual History*. London: Routledge, 2000.

Sitton, John. "Hannah Arendt's Argument for Council Democracy." In *Hannah Arendt: Critical Essays*, edited by Lewis Hinchman and Sandra Hinchman, 307–35. Albany: State University of New York Press, 1994.

Situationist International. "All the King's Men." In *Situationist International Anthology*. Rev. ed. Translated and edited by Ken Knabb, 149–53. Berkeley, CA: Bureau of Public Secrets, 2006.

– "The Avant-Garde of Presence." In *Situationist International Anthology*. Rev. ed. Translated and edited by Ken Knabb, 142–5. Berkeley, CA: Bureau of Public Secrets, 2006.

– "Détournement as Negation and Prelude." In *Situationist International Anthology*. Rev. ed. Translated and edited by Ken Knabb, 67–8. Berkeley, CA: Bureau of Public Secrets, 2006.

– "Ideologies, Classes, and the Domination of Nature." In *Situationist International Anthology*. Rev. ed. Translated and edited by Ken Knabb, 131–42. Berkeley, CA: Bureau of Public Secrets, 2006.

– "Minimum Definition of Revolutionary Organizations." In *Situationist International Anthology*. Rev. ed. Translated and edited by Ken Knabb, 285–6. Berkeley, CA: Bureau of Public Secrets, 2006.

– "Preliminary Problems in Constructing a Situation." In *Situationist International Anthology*. Rev. ed. Translated and edited by Ken Knabb, 49–51. Berkeley, CA: Bureau of Public Secrets, 2006.

– "Provisional Statutes of the SI." In *Situationist International Anthology*. Rev. ed. Translated and edited by Ken Knabb, 461–3. Berkeley, CA: Bureau of Public Secrets, 2006.

– "Questionnaire." In *Situationist International Anthology*. Rev. ed. Translated and edited by Ken Knabb, 178–83. Berkeley, CA: Bureau of Public Secrets, 2006.

– "Response to a Questionnaire from the Centre for Socio-Experimental Art." In *Situationist International Anthology*. Rev. ed. Translated and edited by Ken Knabb, 183–8. Berkeley, CA: Bureau of Public Secrets, 2006.

Smith, Karl. "The Constitution of Modernity: A Critique of Castoriadis." *European Journal of Social Theory* 12, no. 4 (2009): 505–21.

Solzhenitsyn, Alexandr. *The Gulag Archipelago, 1918–1956: An Experiment in Literary Investigation*. Translated by Thomas Whitney. New York: Harper & Row, 1974.

Spinoza, Baruch. "Political Treatise." In *Spinoza: Complete Works*. Edited by Michael Morgan. Translated by Samuel Shirley. Indianapolis, IN: Hackett Publishing, 2002.

Stewart, Jon. "Philosophy and Political Engagement: Letters from the Quarrel between Sartre and Merleau-Ponty." In *The Debate between Sartre and Merleau-Ponty*, edited by Jon Stewart, 327–54. Evanston, IL: Northwestern University Press, 1998.

Tassin, Étienne. *Le trésor perdu: Hannah Arendt et l'intelligence de l'action politique*. Paris: Payot, 1999.

Tønder, Lars, and Lasse Thomassen, eds. *Radical Democracy: Politics between Abundance and Lack*. Manchester, UK: Manchester University Press, 2005.

Torgerson, Douglas. "Farewell to the Green Movement? Political Action and the Green Public Sphere." *Environmental Politics* 9, no. 4 (2000): 1–19.

Tully, James. *Strange Multiplicity: Constitutionalism in an Age of Diversity*. Cambridge: Cambridge University Press, 1995.

Urbinati, Nadia, and Mark Warren. "The Concept of Representation in Contemporary Democratic Theory." *Annual Review of Political Science* 11 (2008): 387–412.

Valero, Helena, and Ettore Biocca. *Yanoama: The Narrative of a White Girl Kidnapped by Amazonian Indians*. New York: Dutton, 1970.

Vaneigem, Raoul. "Notice to the Civilized Concerning Generalized Self-Management." In *Situationist International Anthology*. Rev. ed. Translated and edited by Ken Knabb, 363–71. Berkeley, CA: Bureau of Public Secrets, 2006.

– *The Revolution of Everyday Life*. Translated by Donald Nicholson-Smith. London: Rebel Press, 2006.

Vatter, Miguel. "Machiavelli After Marx: The Self-Overcoming of Marxism in the Late Althusser." *Theory & Event* 7, no. 4 (2004). doi: 10.1353/tae.2005.0060.

Vidal-Naquet, Pierre. "Castoriadis et la Grèce ancienne." In Cornelius Castoriadis, *Ce qui fait la Grèce 1: d'Homère à Héraclite*. Paris: Seuil, 2004.

Ward, Tom. "The Situationists Reconsidered." In *Cultures in Contention*, edited by Douglas Khan and Diane Neumaier, 144–65. Seattle: Real Comet Press, 1985.

Weber, Max. *The Protestant Ethic and the "Spirit" of Capitalism and Other Writings*. Translated by Peter Baehr and Gordon Wells. New York: Penguin, 2002.

Weil, Éric. "La philosophie politique." *Encyclopaedia Universalis*. Paris: 1970.

Wolin, Sheldon. "Fugitive Democracy." *Constellations* 1, no. 1 (1994): 11–25.

Zerilli, Linda. "Castoriadis, Arendt, and the Problem of the New." *Constellations* 9, no. 4 (2002): 540–53.

Žižek, Slavoj. "Against Human Rights." *New Left Review* 34 (August 2005): 115–31.

– *The Ticklish Subject: The Absent Centre of Political Ontology*. London: Verso, 1999.

Contributors

Miguel Abensour is Professor Emeritus in Political Philosophy at the Université Paris Diderot. His books include *L'Utopie de Thomas More à Walter Benjamin* (2000), *Hannah Arendt contre la philosophie politique?* (2006), *Pour une philosophie politique critique* (2009), and *L'homme est un animal politique* (2010). The English translation of his book *La démocratie contre l'État: Marx et le moment machiavélien* (1997) was published by Polity Press in 2011.

Carlo Invernizzi Accetti is currently a Research Fellow at the Université Libre de Bruxelles and a lecturer at the Institut d'études politiques de Paris. He obtained a PhD in Political Theory from Columbia University in 2012. He has a book forthcoming from Columbia University Press entitled *Relativism in Democracy: Religious Discourse and Democratic Theory in Post-Secular Societies.* He has also published articles in several international journals, including *The Political Quarterly, Constellations, Raisons Politiques,* and *Critica Liberale.*

Martin Breaugh is Associate Professor of Political Theory at York University. He is the author of *The Plebeian Experience: A Discontinuous History of Political Freedom* (Columbia University Press, 2013), and editor of *La démocratie au-delà du libéralisme* (with Francis Dupuis-Déri, Éditions Athéna, 2009) and *Les usages des anciens dans la pensée politique contemporaine* (with Yves Couture, PUL, 2010).

Christopher Holman is an Assistant Professor in the Public Policy and Global Affairs Program at Nanyang Technological University. His first book, *Politics as Radical Creation: Herbert Marcuse and Hannah Arendt* *on Political Perfomativity,* was published in 2013 by the University of Toronto Press. He has also published a variety of scholarly articles in journals such as *Contemporary Political Theory, New Political Science, New German Critique, Critical Horizons, Radical Philosophy Review, Rethinking Marxism,* and *Telos.*

James D. Ingram is an Associate Professor in the Department of Political Science at McMaster University. He is the author of *Radical Cosmopolitics: The Ethics and Politics of Democratic Universalism* (Columbia University Press, 2013), as well as articles on contemporary French and German political theory, democracy, utopianism, and the politics of human rights. He has also worked extensively as a translator from French and German.

Rachel Magnusson teaches in the Political Ecology stream of the School of Environmental Studies at the University of Victoria. Her own research explores the tensions between democracy and education. Her PhD dissertation, entitled "Thinking Politics and Education alongside Jacques Rancière," uses the writings of Rancière to explore the limitations of our political thinking about education and the potential of thinking through equality.

Paul Mazzocchi is an Instructor at York University. His PhD dissertation, entitled "The Flesh of History: Intersubjectivity and Experience in Merleau-Ponty and Benjamin," explores the intersection between ontology, history, and politics in the writings of Maurice Merleau-Ponty and Walter Benjamin. He has published articles in *Critical Horizons* and *Critical Studies in History.*

Devin Penner is an Assistant Professor in the Department of Political Studies at Trent University. He has a PhD from the Department of Political Science at York University, with a dissertation on Guy Debord and Situationist International entitled "Rethinking the Spectacle: Radical Political Agency in the Information Society." He has a forthcoming bibliographic article on "the spectacle" in *Oxford Bibliographies in Political Science,* and has published articles in a variety of journals, including *Science & Society* and the *Review of Radical Political Economics.*

Brian C.J. Singer is a Professor of Sociology at Glendon College, York University, and is associated with the Graduate Program in Social and

Political Thought. He is the author of two books, *Montesquieu and the Discovery of the Social* (Palgrave Macmillan, 2013) and *Society, Theory and the French Revolution: Studies in the Revolutionary Imaginary* (Macmillan/St. Martin's Press, 1986), as well as many articles. Among the latter are "The Early Castoriadis: Socialism, Barbarism and the Bureaucratic Thread" and "The Later Castoriadis: Institution under Interrogation," *Canadian Journal of Political and Social Theory* (1979–80); "Thinking the 'Social' with Claude Lefort," *Thesis Eleven* (2006); and "Democracy Beyond the Political: Reconsidering the Social," in *Claude Lefort: Thinker of the Political*, ed. Martin Plot (Basingstoke, UK: Palgrave Macmillan, 2013).

www.ingramcontent.com/pod-product-compliance
Lightning Source LLC
LaVergne TN
LVHW040151080826
844660LV00014B/919/J